A STUDY GUIDE FOR THE TELEVISED COURSE

HUMANITIES
THROUGH THE ARTS

THIRD EDITION

Chancellor, Coast Community College District	ALFRED R. FERNANDEZ, Ph.D.
President, Coastline Community College	WILLIAM M. VEGA, Ed.D.
Director, Alternative Learning Systems	LESLIE N. PURDY, Ed.D.
Publications Editor	MICHAEL S. WERTHMAN
Assistant Publications Editor	MARJI JAMES
Writer of the Study Guide	RICHARD T. SEARLES
Third Edition Revisions	VALERIE LYNCH LEE

A STUDY GUIDE FOR THE TELEVISED COURSE

HUMANITIES THROUGH THE ARTS

THIRD EDITION

Coast Community College District

McGraw-Hill, Inc.
New York   St. Louis   San Francisco   Auckland   Bogotá
Caracas   Lisbon   London   Madrid   Mexico   Milan
Montreal   New Delhi   Paris   San Juan   Singapore
Sydney   Tokyo   Toronto

ACKNOWLEDGMENTS

Page 35: Erwin Panofsky, *Style and Medium in the Motion Pictures*. Bulletin of the Department of Art and Archaeology, Princeton University, 1934. Reprinted by permission of Dr. Gerda Panofsky. Prefatory remarks from *Modern Culture and the Arts* by James Hall and Barry Ulanov. Reprinted by permission of McGraw-Hill Book Co.

Page 61: Ingmar Bergman, *Four Screen Plays of Ingmar Bergman*, "Film Has Nothing to Do with Literature." Copyright © 1960 by Ingmar Bergman. Reprinted by permission of Simon & Schuster, a Division of Gulf & Western Corporation. Prefatory remarks from *Modern Culture and the Arts* by James Hall and Barry Ulanov. Reprinted by permission of McGraw-Hill Book Co.

Page 99: Bernard Shaw, *The Problem Play—A Symposium*. Reprinted by permission of The Society of Authors on behalf of the Bernard Shaw Estate. Prefatory remarks from *Modern Culture and the Arts* by James Hall and Barry Ulanov. Reprinted by permission of McGraw-Hill Book Co.

Page 114: F. David Martin and Lee A. Jacobus, *The Humanities through the Arts*, third edition, "A Brief Glossary of Styles and Genres—with Suggestions for Listening." Reprinted by permission of the authors and McGraw-Hill, Inc.

Page 155: John Tasker Howard, *This Modern Music*, "What is Modern Music—and Why Have People Never Liked It, at First?" Reprinted by permission of McIntosh and Otis, Inc.

Page 197: C. Day Lewis, *How a Poem Is Made*. Reprinted by permission of A D Peters & Co Ltd. Prefatory remarks from *Modern Culture and the Arts* by James Hall and Barry Ulanov. Reprinted by permission of McGraw-Hill Book Co.

Page 200: "Ars Poetica" from *New and Collected Poems* 1917-1976 by Archibald MacLeish. Copyright © 1976 by Archibald MacLeish. Reprinted by permission of Houghton Mifflin Company.

Page 269: "Notes on Sculpture" from *Henry Moore on Sculpture*, edited by Philip James. Copyright © 1966, 1971 by Philip James & Henry Moore. Reprinted by permission of The Viking Press. Prefatory remarks from *Modern Culture and the Arts* by James Hall and Barry Ulanov. Reprinted by permission of McGraw-Hill Book Co.

Page 309: Gio Ponti, *In Praise of Architecture*, "The Architect, the Artist," translated by Guiseppina and Mario Salvadore. Reprinted by permission of Vitale E. Ghianda.

A Study Guide for the Televised Course: HUMANITIES THROUGH THE ARTS

3 4 5 6 7 8 9 0   DOC DOC   9 5 4 3 2 1

IS BN 0-07-040726-6

The editor was Peter Labella;
the production supervisor was Friederich W. Schulte.
R. R. Donnelley & Sons Company was printer and binder.

CONTENTS

A FEW WORDS FOR THE STUDENT

Confronted as we are on every hand by enormous scientific and technological advances, by rapid social change, and by the philosophical and ethical issues raised by these realities, we are forced to a continual questioning of who we are as individuals and of who and what we shall be as a society. In this process of searching for identity, we are—of necessity—always defining and redefining our personal values and goals.

Science and technology provide us *objective* information in the form of "facts," but it is to the humanities that we must turn for the *subjective* insights that help us develop the intellectual ability and the critical wisdom to understand, examine, and use the values that give shape to our personal identity and undergird our goals. The humanities emphasize subjectivity; they extol the importance of the human being and the necessity for individual human expressiveness. However, not all of the humanities contribute in the same way to awareness of self and society. For example, it is the *arts* that reveal values to us, while other humanistic disciplines *reflect* upon these values and *clarify* them.

This telecourse, *Humanities through the Arts,* has been created to develop in students a keen awareness of values, self, and society and to enhance students' participation in and enjoyment of the arts. Specifically, by the end of this course, you should attain:

- an understanding of the historical influences of political, cultural, and scientific values upon art.
- some knowledge of the basic elements and tools an artist uses to create a work of art.
- an awareness of the different ways of "seeing" and interpreting a work of art.
- an appreciation of the processes of criticism and evaluation.

The course begins with a few introductory notes about the quest for self and the importance of the arts to this quest. In this course, the focus is on seven art forms: film, drama, music, literature, painting, sculpture, and architecture. Each form is studied in a cluster of four lessons and television programs and each form is examined individually in terms of four perspectives. First, the course surveys the art from a historical standpoint, emphasizing those periods and events that reflect changes in how people perceive themselves and their world. Next, the course considers the elements basic to each art form, looking at both those that are common to more than one art and those that are unique to a particular art. From a third perspective, the course explores the form employed by the artist and attempts to interpret the meaning revealed in specific works of art. In a fourth approach to each art form, the course uses evaluative criteria to help you participate better with a work of art, and presents the opinions of some nationally recognized authorities, chosen for their knowledge and familiarity with the seven art forms.

The course concludes with some notes on the interrelationships among the seven art forms and some comments on the continuing quest for self.

COURSE COMPONENTS

Humanities through the Arts is a multimedia course created for college-level students and suitable for college-level credit. It consists of thirty half-hour television programs produced by KOCE-TV (Channel 50), with Coastline Community College, Coast Community College District; a main textbook, *The Humanities through the Arts*, fourth edition, written by F. David Martin and Lee A. Jacobus, published by McGraw-Hill, Inc.; and this study guide, written by Richard T. Searles and revised by Valerie Lynch Lee for Coast Community College District and published by McGraw-Hill.

Host for the television program is Maya Angelou, producer-director, writer, actress, dancer, and choreographer.

The multimedia aspect of this telecourse affords you the opportunity to explore many enjoyable experiences in a convenient and comfortable setting, and the four-perspective approach to the arts upon which the course focuses invites you to a deeper, more satisfying study than is ordinarily possible with conventional means of study.

You need not have had previous experience with a telecourse to complete this course successfully. It is necessary, however, that you—as a student—use this study guide as it is designed to be used because it is specifically written to give you direction, assistance, and a means of checking on your progress as you proceed from assignment to assignment.

The individual lessons in this study guide have the following components:

Overview. A brief discussion of the main points of the lesson and a summary of the television programs.

Learning Objectives. Statements of what you should learn from reading the textbook assignment, completing the activities in the study guide, and viewing the television program.

Assignments.   Detailed instructions on activities and reading assignments to be completed before and after viewing each television program.

Aids for Study.   Activities and questions designed to help focus your thinking about the various subjects covered in the lesson.

Review Quiz.   A brief objective quiz that allows you to test your understanding of the material in the lesson. Answers to the review quizzes (along with pertinent textbook, study guide, and television program references) are printed at the back of this study guide.

Additional Activities.   Suggestions for further study and experimentation with the arts. (Your instructor may also use these as assignments for extra credit.)

This study guide also contains selected readings, which are assigned in addition to the textbook material. These readings accompany specific lessons for six of the seven units of this telecourse: film, drama, music, literature, sculpture, and architecture.

HOW TO TAKE A TELECOURSE

If you are new to college courses in general, and telecourse in particular, you may benefit from suggestions about how to study and how to complete *Humanities through the Arts* successfully. These suggestions were compiled from students who have satisfactorily completed telecourses:

- *Do* buy both the textbook and the study guide for *Humanities through the Arts* or arrange to share copies with a friend. Do *not* try to get through this course without these books.

- *Do* watch each of the television programs. In order to pass the examinations, you will need to read and study the textbook and to view the television programs. If you have a videocassette recorder, tape the programs for later review.

- *Do* keep up with your work for this course every week. Even if you do not have any class sessions on campus or any assignments to turn in, you should read the textbook and do the assignments in the study guide, as well as watch the television programs. Set aside viewing, reading, and study time each week and stick to your schedule.

- *Do* get in touch with the faculty member who is in charge of *Humanities through the Arts* at your college or university. The instructor can answer any questions you have about the material covered in the course. Your faculty member can also help you catch up if you are behind, advise you about additional assignments, discuss the type of test questions you can expect, and tell you where you might be able to watch programs you have missed or wish to review.

- *Do* complete the study activities and review quizzes provided in this guide. These will help you master the learning objectives and prepare for formal examinations.

- If you miss a program or fall behind in your study schedule, don't give up. Many television stations repeat broadcasts of the programs later in the week or on weekends. Your college might have videocassette copies of programs available in the campus library or media center. And do call on your course faculty member or manager to help if you have problems of any kind. This person is assigned specifically to help you succeed in *Humanities through the Arts.*

INTRODUCTION

THE QUEST FOR SELF

OVERVIEW

We begin with a consideration of the humanities. The humanities are
those studies that are directly concerned with humankind, rather than
with the world or universe in which humans dwell. Unlike the sciences,
which, by definition, must be objective, the humanities are subjective,
concerned with human values.

In the view of Martin and Jacobus (authors of the textbook for this
course), the values studied in the humanities are revealed through the
arts. This course's basic purpose is to familiarize us with how values are
revealed in seven different art forms: film, drama, music, literature,
painting, sculpture, and architecture. In our study of each art form, we
will consider four distinct perspectives. One perspective is historical—an
examination of how the art form has grown and changed over time.
Another perspective focuses on the elements of a specific art, while the
third perspective seeks to make us aware of the different forms of an art
and of the meanings of those forms. The final perspective is critical; that
is, it encourages us to develop our critical and analytical skills in
responding to art. Thus, in the coming weeks, we will learn not only how

artists reveal values through their works, we will also become more sensitive to those aspects of life and art that reflect those values.

It would be difficult indeed to separate our sense of values from our feelings and emotions. Our own feelings and reactions—our own participation in the arts we study in these lessons—are an essential ingredient of our learning experience. The first chapter of the textbook presents a challenge to our tastes, responses, and perceptions of art. We are shown two pictures that usually evoke strong, if unpleasant, reactions. We learn that these paintings are meant to reveal unpleasant values to us. In fact, the artists deliberately use many elements to lead our minds toward the meanings they wish to reveal. This careful organization of the elements within a work is termed "artistic form." We will study other examples of artistic form in this chapter and discover, perhaps to our surprise, that additional reflection upon a painting or poem may actually bring out deeper subjective responses from us.

In the second chapter, the textbook proposes a description of "a work of art" by listing four primary characteristics: artistic form, content, subject matter, and participation. This last characteristic, participation, is deemed no less important than the skill of the artist in the first three. We look at a contemporary photograph and a decades-old painting, which, at first glance, have almost identical subject matter. Yet our participation with each quickly shows that one has a unity, a depth, and an interpretation of the subject that stands the test of time, whereas the other merely records an event.

Art demands our participation. We must yield to its demand for undivided and continued attention, seeking what is within the work itself. The insight we may gain from the artist's interpretation of his or her subject matter may then become a part of us. For example, it may provide a clearer value for ourselves when we encounter the same object or event in our less tightly organized and designed world. Or we may find our senses more acutely tuned to the many elements that make up an art as well as make up life.

Although some of us may welcome this opportunity for participation and a frank acceptance of the subjective aspects of our thinking and feeling, many of us may feel somewhat threatened. Perhaps we fear that our feeling may be "wrong." Perhaps we fail to sense something someone else perceives. To many of us, it may seem easier just to gather facts and organize them rather than to seek insights and respond to an artist's meaning. But, after all, it is our emotional responses—joy, sadness, pleasure, love, delight, pain, excitement—that provide our lives with texture and enrichment. Whether our responses and insights are "right" or "wrong" is of less importance than whether they grow or atrophy.

LEARNING OBJECTIVES

ON COMPLETING YOUR STUDY OF THIS LESSON, YOU SHOULD BE ABLE TO:

1. Select the appropriate definition of artistic form.
2. State a relationship between the arts and values.
3. State a relationship between concrete images and abstract ideas.
4. Appreciate the importance of one's participation in a work of art.
5. List four essential characteristics of a work of art and suggest some relationships between them.

ASSIGNMENTS

BEFORE VIEWING THE PROGRAM:

Read the "Overview" and familiarize yourself with the "Learning Objectives" for this lesson.

Consult a dictionary for a standard definition of these terms (the scope of these definitions will be refined by the text):

    art
    fine arts
    humanities
    perception (Note that dictionary definitions refer to the act of
        perceiving through the physical senses, as well as to insight or
        appreciation.)

Look over the "Aids for Study" for this lesson.

VIEW THE PROGRAM "Introduction: The Quest for Self."

AFTER VIEWING THE PROGRAM:

In the textbook, *Humanities through the Arts:*
- Read Chapter 1, "The Humanities: An Introduction" (pages 1–15) and Chapter 2, "What Is a Work of Art?" (pages 17–46).

Review what you have learned, using the "Aids for Study" again.

Evaluate your learning with the "Review Quiz," then check your answers with the "Answer Key" at the back of this study guide.

In accordance with your own interests or your instructor's assignment, complete selected "Additional Activities."

AIDS FOR STUDY

1. According to the textbook, what are the elements that may be arranged in an artistic form? In Chapter 1, particular emphasis is placed on the visual art form of painting. Can you think of additional elements that might be important to such other art forms as music or drama?

2. What is the overall form of Blume's *Eternal City?* What is the overall form of Cummings' "1(a"? Try to describe the outstanding characteristics of each in one or two sentences.

3. Briefly describe the humanities. Then describe the arts. If you wish, bring your own understandings into your description, as well as the generalizations given in the textbook. In the opinion of the authors of the textbook, what differentiates the arts from the other humanities? Does your answer include the role of each in the study of human values?

4. In your study of Okara's "Piano and Drums" (textbook pages 13–14), what is the relationship of concrete and abstract ideas? Which leads to the understanding of the other? Give an example of one concrete idea and one related abstract idea in this poem. Do you see a similar abstract/concrete relationship in Picasso's *Guernica?* (Remember, of course, that you may not be

able to express in words either the "concrete" or "abstract" idea to your satisfaction. After all, if the artist could have *stated* his or her purposes succinctly in words, what would have been the need for expression in sculpture, painting, or music? We can seek to *approximate* an artist's meanings in words so that we can communicate our thoughts to another and aid ourselves in appreciating art and participating in the art experience more fully.)

5. Comment upon the textbook's description of participation as "undivided and sustained attention." Do you agree that such participation cannot be forced by oneself? Why does Goya's painting bring forth such participation, whereas the Adams photograph does not? Assume for a moment that neither the photograph nor the painting immediately invites you to "sustained attention." Having read Chapter 2, which would you study more closely for elements that you have overlooked? Why?

6. Review in your mind the four elements that distinguish art. Explain these descriptions (consulting the textbook again, if necessary):
    artistic form: a strong degree of perceptible unity
    content: meaning fused with artistic form
    subject matter: the values that are interpreted in a work of art, what the art "is about"
    participation: the experience that leads to our insight into the form, content, and subject matter of a work of art and gives us greater sensitivity in our future encounters with the same values

REVIEW QUIZ

Select the one best answer.

1. Which of the following is the best definition of artistic form?
    a. the general outline or shape of an object
    b. the meaning that the artist expresses in his or her art
    c. the interrelationship of all elements, such as lines, textures, and shapes in the work of art
    d. the distortions of normal objects or events that the artist creates

2. In E. E. Cummings' poem "1(a," the artistic form is perceived as the
    a. overall design made by the letters, the words themselves, and the images created by the words.
    b. manner in which the words are obscured.
    c. vertical, rather than horizontal, arrangement of letters.
    d. idea of loneliness.

3. The authors of the textbook believe that the arts provide a means for
    a. studying values.
    b. revealing values.
    c. revealing beauty.
    d. interpreting beauty.

4. Analysis of a work of art such as a painting
    a. tends to destroy the enjoyment one feels when just looking at it.
    b. is important only to one who wishes to become an artist.
    c. should be done only after one fully perceives the work.
    d. may intensify our enjoyment of the work, as we come to see things that were missed earlier.

5. In the poems "1(a" and "Piano and Drums"
    a. abstract ideas, such as loneliness or childhood, are used to clarify concrete images.
    b. concrete images, such as a falling leaf or musical instruments, are used to clarify abstract ideas.
    c. only abstract ideas are described and commented upon.
    d. concrete objects and events are described to help the reader appreciate their beauty.

6. Participation in a work of art might be described as
    a. attempting to create a similar poem, painting, or other work of art.
    b. identifying the parts of the work that others feel are most significant.
    c. giving sustained and undivided attention to the work.
    d. seeking a single clue to the meaning of the poem, painting, or other work of art.

7. The textbook authors consider Goya's *May 3, 1808* to be a work of art, as opposed to Adams' *Execution in Saigon*, partly because
    a. the Adams work is a photograph.
    b. the elements of the Goya painting attract sustained attention, whereas the elements in the photograph do not.
    c. painting is usually considered art.
    d. the painting is more realistic than the photograph.

8. Four characteristics of art described in the textbook are
    a. artistic form, color, content, and subject matter.
    b. artistic form, content, simplicity, and participation.
    c. artistic form, content, subject matter, and participation.
    d. artistic form, content, distortion, and participation.

9. In the sense used in the text, *content* refers to the
    a. meaning of a work of art.
    b. human value that the artist wishes to interpret.
    c. response of the viewer.
    d. shape or use of elements such as texture and line.

10. Based on the definition given in this lesson, the subject matter of Goya's *May 3, 1808* is
    a. the total effect of colors, lines, shapes, and tones employed by the artist.
    b. the viewer's response to the painting.
    c. human barbarity in an execution.
    d. the brutality and wastefulness of violence.

ADDITIONAL ACTIVITIES

1. Select one work of art discussed in this lesson—perhaps *Echo of a Scream* or *Eternal City*—that became more meaningful to you after you had read the discussion in the textbook and had participated in the related perception keys. Describe only what you sensed in the work at first viewing. Then list the additional elements that you noticed during and after the discussion in the textbook. Were these elements primarily related to artistic form? To content? To subject matter? Or can you separate one from the other?

2. Describe the relationship between artistic form, content, and subject matter. Is it possible for one to exist without the other? Develop a diagram that shows how one of these characteristics affects the other in artistic works.

3. Select a work from among those reproduced in the textbook. Does the work inspire your participation? Attempt in a few sentences to describe the subject matter of the work. How is this subject matter interpreted? Comment on the artistic form and content of the example.

FILM

TWENTIETH-CENTURY LEGACY

The question of whether or not film is a true form of art, deserving of the same consideration given such older forms as painting and literature, is still rather widely debated among those who study and enjoy the arts. Some people claim that the motion picture, born in the twentieth century, is the *only* true art form produced in this century. Yet others insist that film is not an art form at all; not only is it too new, they contend, it is also merely a business form of mass entertainment that depends heavily on both technology and large financial investments (and large financial returns). In this course, the position is taken that film is a contemporary art form. And, although it is true that its development has been compressed into the relatively short span of less than 100 years, film is—from our perspective—a *mature* art form.

Our host for the television program begins and ends the lesson by posing the question: Is film an art form? We are also asked to consider whether film is a "harmless form of mass entertainment" or an engine of massive social influence. After the lesson is completed, it is up to each of us individually to decide whether we agree with the judgments expressed.

Because film developed so recently, its history is current history. In this lesson, we see some examples of technological developments that led to the reality of "images in motion," the audience that eagerly accepted this new form of entertainment, and the forms of entertainment that were recorded in the earliest days. You will probably find it easy to identify with this age of new inventions and with those appeals of action, humor, and adventure that were current in the earliest films, as well as those you see today.

An art unique to film, not borrowed from the stage, developed early in the history of filmmaking. This was the technique of "cutting" back and forth between two parallel lines of action to establish a relationship between the two. Earliest films followed a single line of action from beginning to end in the belief that audiences could attend to only one line of action at a time. In the visual presentation of this lesson, we will see excerpts from *The Great Train Robbery*, (considered the first "modern" film) in which this seemingly simple technique of cutting away or editing is used, setting the film apart from those produced earlier.

An artist named D. W. Griffith is introduced, and highlights of his history, preserved on film, will reveal some innovations he perfected in order to exploit the potential of this medium. We suggest you take careful note of three techniques he used in his films: picture composition to achieve an illusion of depth, editing, and the close-up. As a climax to the discussion of Griffith's contributions, you will view scenes from *Birth of a Nation*—a silent movie, to be sure, but one that "thundered across the motion picture screen" nevertheless, for it was the first full-length motion picture ever produced.

We see only fragmentary moments from this three-hour epic, but in these few moments some important considerations are raised. Maya Angelou asks about the social influence and moral responsibility of the filmmaker. These questions didn't originate with *Birth of a Nation*, of course, as the little vignette called *The Kiss* amply illustrates. But because it inadvertently contributed with telling effect to a negative stereotype of blacks, Griffith's *Birth of a Nation* demonstrates clearly what a powerful force the motion picture can be in promoting or combating social injustice. In excerpts from *Something to Sing About* and *The Pawnbroker*, we see two examples of the positive influence that film is capable of exerting.

In direct contrast to the American preoccupation with "stars," both the Martin and Jacobus textbook and the television program emphasize the role of the director in the development of a film. You may recognize the names of some personalities mentioned, and you should come to a greater appreciation of the director's role.

LEARNING OBJECTIVES

AFTER COMPLETING YOUR STUDY OF THIS LESSON, YOU SHOULD BE ABLE TO:

1. Demonstrate an understanding of film as a unique art form by listing three techniques used by D. W. Griffith in producing his motion pictures.
2. Name at least two significant directors in addition to Griffith and explain their contributions to film.
3. Contrast the subject matter and techniques of the earliest motion pictures with later ones.
4. List two reasons film is accused of being a business rather than an art.
5. Understand social and economic conditions prevailing in America that influenced the development of film in the 1900s.
6. Appreciate the impact upon social belief and custom that is possible through film
   a. as demonstrated by identification of a social environment both reflected and promoted by *Birth of a Nation*.
   b. as demonstrated by awareness of the social environment that provides the context for a film.

ASSIGNMENTS

BEFORE VIEWING THE PROGRAM:

Read the "Overview" and the "Learning Objectives" for this lesson.

In the textbook, Chapter 2, "What Is a Work of Art?":
• Review pages 26–28 ("Content").

Familiarize yourself with the following terms:

auteur: author, or one primarily responsible for the work's form, content, and arrangement of elements
close-up: pictured from a distance much closer than normal viewing
composition: arrangement of elements in a picture
context: the interrelated conditions providing the environment for an occurrence
narrative: a story, meaningful retelling of a series of events
parallel action: presentation of two related events in such a sequence that the audience understands they are happening simultaneously
protagonist: the central character of a story
sound synchronization: the technique that makes a recorded sound occur at the precise time the visual event appears on the screen.

Look over the "Aids for Study" for this lesson.

VIEW THE TELEVISION PROGRAM *"Twentieth-Century Legacy."*

AFTER VIEWING THE PROGRAM:

In the textbook, Chapter 11, "The Film":
  • Read pages 347–349 (introductory material, "Griffith and Einstein," and "Directing and Editing"); pages 359–362 ("Sound"); and pages 364–366 ("Content").

Review what you have learned, using the "Aids for Study" again.

Evaluate your learning with the "Review Quiz," then check your answers with the "Answer Key" at the back of this study guide.

In accordance with your own interests or your instructor's assignment, complete selected "Additional Activities."

1. In the opinion of some, film should be classified as what kind of activity, rather than art? What may contribute to this opinion, particularly in the methods of financing films and in the nature of their appeal?

2. What were the earliest subjects to be filmed and viewed as entertainment for others?

3. What was the title of the first motion picture to portray two simultaneous events by shifting the scene from one to the other?

4. Why did motion pictures appeal to a wider audience than other performing arts at the turn of the century?

5. Describe some techniques used by D. W. Griffith. How did these techniques help to clarify film's position as a unique art, separate from stage or documentary recording?

6. What examples are given in the television program to illustrate the effect of a film may have on social standards and values? Why may film have a stronger impact than another form, such a painting, for example?

7. List some significant directors whose names you recognize. You may wish to add names of one or more films they have directed. You can probably find the names of several directors familiar to you by scanning the assigned text reading.

8. Read the Perception Key "Camera Vision" (textbook page 356), and perform one or more of the exercises (other than number 2). Comment on your personal finding: Should the motion of images be predominant in film? Is this usually the case today?

REVIEW QUIZ

Select the one best answer or write the answers in the spaces provided.

1. D. W. Griffith's contribution to the art of the film is best described as
   a. creating new techniques of filming and presentation.
   b. perfecting a technology that gave the appearance of motion to a series of still pictures.
   c. adapting many techniques to create effects unique to films.
   d. adding the dimension of sound to previously silent films.

2. Which of the following film techniques focuses the viewer's attention on a small detail?
   a. the close-up
   b. parallel action
   c. a view of depth
   d. the sound

3. List two significant film directors other than D. W. Griffith.

   Bergman
   Coppola

4. The earliest motion picture films most often showed scenes that
   a. portrayed magic tricks and illusions.
   b. were influenced by Griffith.
   c. were duplicates of situations that could have been observed elsewhere.
   d. were duplicates of the dramatic stage.

5. Before synchronized sound was introduced into film
   a. films were viewed in silent theaters.
   b. recorded music was played during viewing.
   c. a script was read aloud during viewing.
   d. special music was played during the viewing.

6. The textbook states that sound in film is
   a. the basic element in modern fine filming.
   b. a distraction from visual impact.
   c. a supplemental element of the film art.
   d. not necessary in modern films.

7. Give two reasons for the opinion held by some that films are a business rather than an art:

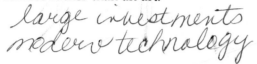

large investments
modern technology

8. The film *Birth of a Nation* evidently encouraged attitudes promoting
   a. war.
   b. racism.
   c. slavery.
   d. terrorism.

9. The influence of *Birth of a Nation* evidently is thought to have occurred because
   a. the filmmaker's own values were unconsciously reflected in the production.
   b. the filmmaker deliberately slanted his material.
   c. the "message" of the film was misinterpreted.
   d. the film was later edited to stress a particular view.

10. A knowledge of history may be essential to understanding the
    a. literary basis of a film.
    b. director's technique and purpose.
    c. film's contribution to art.
    d. social context within which the film was created.

ADDITIONAL ACTIVITIES

1. Attend a current, well-rated motion picture. Identify and list
    some of the elements that were discussed in this lesson. Were
    there any portions of this picture in which the visual effect so
    predominated that no sound was (or would have been)
    necessary?

2. From your own motion-picture viewing experience, recall and
    describe one film in which the narrative was presented with
    little action. Does this example tend to make you agree or
    disagree with the statement that "this almost invariably
    results in a film of little importance"?

3. Do you attend motion pictures to "see art" or to be "entertained"?
    Is there a difference? After your experiences in this lesson,
    would you call film an art? Is there a difference between what
    one experiences in perceiving art and being entertained? Support
    your answers with examples. As you discuss or write your ideas,
    you may wish to consult one or more of the books on films listed
    in the bibliography of your textbook.

4. Compare some outstanding scenes from *Birth of a Nation* (as seen
    in the television program) with scenes commonly shown in two or
    three films you have seen recently.

FILM

THE DYNAMIC ILLUSION

In this lesson, we consider the elements composing the art of film. Specifically, we explore how those elements are combined and employed to create illusions—illusions that, in many instances, can be almost real to the viewers of a film. If you have ever seen the original Cinerama film, *This Is Cinerama*, or been to Disneyland or Disneyworld and seen the film presented in the Circle-Vision 360 theater, you are well aware of how these elements can create most realistic physical feelings and sensations. In *This Is Cinerama*, for instance, images projected from three cameras onto a large, curved screen give audiences the sensation that they are riding a roller coaster and taking the first, steep plunge over the top. Many who have viewed the film presented in the Circle-Vision 360 theater have experienced distinct vertigo as, in one segment of the film, they "ride" a fire engine as it careens up and down the steep streets of San Francisco.

Such instances are extreme examples of the capacity of films to create illusions for viewers. Most films strive to create more subtle, less physical illusions for their viewers. In most films, directors manipulate the elements to create effects that will give viewers a sense of intimacy or identity with a character, animal, or even an inanimate object. The elements of film can be combined in such a way so as to produce responses in viewers unequaled by any other art form.

This lesson focuses on the visual aspects of film as an art form. Specific aspects considered in the television program include photography, lighting, and editing. The various effects that can be created with different photographic, lighting, and editing techniques are demonstrated with scenes from a number of different films, including *Rain*, *The Pawnbroker*, *Citizen Kane*, *Psycho*, *Wuthering Heights*, and *Potemkin*. The television program also stresses the fact that film is a collective art form—the end result of the efforts of writers, actors, set and costume designers, camera and editing personnel, and a number of others, all guided by the particular perceptions and goals of the director.

The textbook explores in detail some of the specific techniques directors are likely to use to create desired illusions. For instance, certain directors feel it important to compose each frame of a film as carefully as if it were a painting. The art of film, however, is the art of motion, and certain forms of this motion are most effective in involving the viewers in the film. Among the more common forms of motion employed by directors are the various angles from which a camera will record a scene: from the side, front, or rear; from a very high or a very low position; or even from a position that human eyes would not normally view a scene. The camera, rather than the scene itself, can be the object that provides the motion in a film. The camera can move through a sweeping panorama, directing and focusing our attention on an entire landscape, or it can be mounted on a moving vehicle to carry us through or to a scene. The zoom lens technique is yet another means of creating motion that can rapidly focus our attention on a specific object within a larger scene.

As the preceding lesson explained, many of the visual elements of film were developed in the early years of film making, well before synchronized sound was introduced. In this lesson, you may find it interesting to consider sound as one of the key elements of film rather than as a purely historical development. Later lessons, particularly those on drama and painting, will provide additional insights to use in analyzing such elements of film as characterization and frame composition.

The first lesson of this course considered whether the close study of our responses to, and participation in, an art form enhanced or hindered our enjoyment of that form. The material in this lesson should enable us to enjoy films more fully, for it provides us with an understanding of the tools and techniques directors use to transform their visions into films.

LEARNING OBJECTIVES

ON COMPLETING YOUR STUDY OF THIS LESSON, YOU SHOULD BE ABLE TO:

1. Describe how photography, lighting, and editing contribute to the illusions presented by film.
2. Determine whether or not frame composition is crucial to artistic success of a film.
3. Describe various aspects of a subject's or object's motion.
4. Identify various types of camera motion.
5. Appreciate how each type of motion may elicit responses from the participant.
6. Consider the point at which technique may interfere with the overall effect of film.
7. Analyze the viewer response to visual and sound elements of a film.

ASSIGNMENTS

BEFORE VIEWING THE PROGRAM:

Read the "Overview" and familiarize yourself with the "Learning Objectives" for this lesson.

Consult a dictionary for definitions of the following terms:

    composition (art)
    frame (film term)
    pan (film term)

Look over the "Aids for Study" for this lesson

Experiment with the Perception Key "Camera Vision" on textbook page 356.

VIEW THE TELEVISION PROGRAM *"The Dynamic Illusion."*

AFTER VIEWING THE PROGRAM:

In the textbook, Chapter 11, "The Film":
  • Read pages 351–358 ("The Moving Image" and "Camera Point of View").
  • Review pages 359–362 ("Sound").

Review what you have learned, using the "Aids for Study" again.

Evaluate what you have learned by taking the "Review Quiz," then check your answers with the "Answer Key" at the back of this study guide.

In accordance with your own interests or your instructor's assignment, complete selected "Additional Activities."

AIDS FOR STUDY

1. How does the film—a succession of individual pictures—achieve the illusion of motion? Perhaps you have seen turn-of-the-century "moving picture" machines in which the effect of motion was created by the flipping of a series of still photographs when the viewer turned a crank. Can you think of any settings in which the illusion of motion is not perfect (for example, wagon wheels in some westerns appear to turn backwards as the wagon picks up speed)?

2. Why do the textbook authors feel individual frame composition is not essential to a film's success? In what type of situation could frame composition be most important? Can you recall at least one film you have seen in which the composition of a scene was especially striking?

3, One technique for directing a viewer's attention in a nonmoving scene is that of changing focus. Why should it be "used in moderation" as suggested by the text? Does this technique mimic or parallel our own ability to focus first on one object, then on another?

4. In what ways can a subject move before the camera? What is the "catapult" effect described in the textbook? Would you be able to duplicate this with the camera-vision mask you constructed for the perception key experiment before viewing the program? Can you think of scenes in films you have viewed in which especially dramatic effects have been achieved by the subject's moving directly toward or away from the screen?

5. In your experiment with the camera-vision mask, what was the effect of closing one eye? Does the "frame" of the enclosing rectangle direct your attention to what you see?

6. One camera technique implied but not mentioned in the textbook is the panorama shot, in which the camera is turned or moved to follow the moving subject (less frequently, the camera "pans" a setting that has no movement, allowing the viewer to "take in" a scene by segments). Can you duplicate this effect with the mask you used in the experiment? Can you move your head more rapidly in such movements than the camera would be able to move?

7. What is a zoom lens? What is the effect of viewing a scene as if from a great distance, then "zooming" in for a much closer view? What kind of movement is implied here?

8. What kinds of effects may be achieved when the camera actually travels with the movement? Can this effect be duplicated with the camera-vision mask? What other examples of the moving camera have you seen?

9. At what point can technique actually interfere with participation in a film?

10. Can you add further examples to those given in the text in which sound contributed to the visual effects of a scene? What would happen if the sounds were to become most important to our attention?

REVIEW QUIZ

Select the one best answer.

1. Film editing can be used to
    a. establish the relationship between characters.
    b. compress time.
    c. heighten the impact of a scene.
    d. do all of the above.

2. Motion in a film
    a. is an illusion created by a series of still pictures shown in rapid succession.
    b. is continuous and smooth, just as we view movement in other settings.
    c. results only from the movement of a subject.
    d. results only from the movement of a camera.

3. The authors of the textbook think that, for the artistic success of a film,
    a. frame composition is less important than motion.
    b. motion is more important than frame composition.
    c. composition and motion are equally important.
    d. neither composition nor motion is important.

4. Composition may be especially important in a scene
    a. with much movement of the subjects.
    b. in which the camera is actually moving.
    c. in which there is little movement.
    d. in which both subject and camera are moving.

5. A panorama shot is one in which the
    a. camera turns to follow the movement of a subject.
    b. camera travels at the same speed as the subject.
    c. camera travels but the subject does not.
    d. scene changes from a view of a wide area to a close-up view.

6. In experimenting with the camera-vision mask, the most "filmlike" view is experienced by
   a. viewing through both eyes.
   b. viewing through a single eye.
   c. viewing while turning the head rapidly.
   d. all of the above.

7. One effect of the limited field of vision provided by the film screen is that it
   a. makes the viewer imagine what happens outside the area shown.
   b. focuses the attention of the viewer.
   c. distracts from the action on the screen.
   d. requires careful composition of every frame.

8. If a zoom lens effect is used, an illusion of motion is created as if the
   a. subject had started moving faster.
   b. viewer had moved toward or away from the subject.
   c. subject had moved across the screen.
   d. camera had turned to follow the action.

9. A film cited by the textbook authors as an example of a film in which technique was the most interesting and memorable as part of the "cinematic experience" was
   a. *The Misfits.*
   b. *2001: A Space Odyssey.*
   c. *Cries and Whispers.*
   d. *Lawrence of Arabia.*

10. Sound effects in a film
    a. have become one of the most important elements of film.
    b. may intensify our experience of film.
    c. may take the place of motion in certain instances.
    d. usually distract from important movement.

ADDITIONAL ACTIVITIES

1. Do certain types of motion cause consistent reactions from the viewer? Read over the textbook comments concerning the locomotive traveling directly toward the camera. What is your usual reaction to such a scene? From your own experiences in viewing a film, select and discuss three or four other examples of subject motion or camera motion that cause you to have a fairly consistent response, although it may be less dramatic than the one caused by the locomotive scene.

2. Have you ever viewed a presentation in which the primary focus of attention was sound, such as music, with the visual component a secondary aspect? Disney's *Fantasia* was created in response to the sound (symphonic music), and portions of this film might be considered primarily an auditory experience, with abstract visuals contributing to the participant's enjoyment. Discuss whether or not such an art form could be developed, in your opinion, in which the visual element would have a secondary, supporting role.

3. Analyze the motion in a film or television program, preferably without listening to sound at all. Try to identify specific uses of movement, particularly camera movement, that seem to call for viewer response.

FILM

NOT JUST THE GREAT ESCAPE

In participating with *any* of the arts, we have the capacity to react in two very opposite ways to any given work that is presented to us. We can either respond in such a way that we learn more about the work and thus learn more about ourselves and our world, or we can identify with the work in such a way that we are fantasizing, seeing ourselves as the "hero," indulging in a sort of hero worship, from which we learn nothing.

Although all of the arts are capable of evoking both of these reactions, no art is so powerful as film in evoking the self-indulgent "escape" reaction. Textbook authors Martin and Jacobus note, for example, that two Paul Newman films, *The Hustler* and *The Sting*, had wide popular appeal, especially with young people who saw themselves in Newman's roles and lost themselves so completely to the "escape" appeal that they probably never considered—much less understood or appreciated—the structure of these films or whatever messages they might have meant to communicate to their viewers.

The purpose of this lesson is to explore form and meaning in film in the hope that we will experience not necessarily mere escape but a more rewarding participation from which we can learn. The problem is that filmic meaning often defies translation into language (as does music) because—for all its elements—the substance of any film remains a series of *visual* sequences.

Another difficulty in attempting to probe the form and meaning of film is pointed out in the article by German-American art historian Erwin Panofsky. He emphasized that the motion picture "has no aesthetic existence independent of its performance, and . . . its characters have no aesthetic existence outside the actors." In this way, film is like architecture and painting but very unlike a play that can be read or presented in hundreds of performances, each with its own interpretation. However, Panofsky also stressed the importance of understanding form and meaning in modern film because, in his opinion, film is one of the few visual arts that is still "entirely alive" and because film has more impact than *any other single* force on the opinions, taste, dress, behavior, and language of "at least 60 percent of the world's population."

Because of the special difficulties in interpreting form and meaning in film and because of the importance of this art form to modern life, you are asked to read Panofsky's article, "Style and Medium in the Motion Pictures," which is reprinted at the end of this lesson.

As we learned in Lesson 3, action and motion are the essence of illusion in film, and the elements of lighting, photography, directing, editing, and sound all contribute to the creation of illusion. Some of these same elements are also important to the form and meaning of the film. For example, the editor's work gives meaning by showing—not telling—us what is happening. Photography cannot be separated from form in the film; structural qualities develop from juxtaposition of different kinds of images. Certain sequences presented in context give meaning to the film. Selectivity and technique—or what the director chooses to show us—clearly affect form and meaning in the film. The interrelationship of these elements in the creation of a film is explored by Martin and Jacobus in their discusson of Francis Ford Coppola's *The Godfather*.

As noted in Lesson 3, sound revolutionized the motion picture, but Panofsky wrote that it did so only as an element supplemental to the strength of the art. Panofsky described sound as "coexpressible" to the basic substance of the film, which is still the visual image. Nonetheless, sound effects play an important part in the movies today. For example, sound effects (the sounds of a high-speed car chase) are profoundly important to meaning in the movie *The French Connection* and profoundly important in a different way to Stanley Kubrick's *2001: A Space Odyssey*, where the music of Strauss was fused with careful cutting and editing of film.

Narrative line and plot also give structure and meaning to film. (As Panofsky quoted Aristotle, the film should have "a beginning, a middle, and an end.") Narrative can be directed either toward outward action or toward psychological action; it can fit a formula, or it can follow a very tenuous line.

In his essay, Panofsky suggested that two other qualities must be reckoned with in understanding the form and meaning of film. He described these qualities as the dynamization of space and the spatialization of time, which mean—briefly—that while the viewers remain still in their seats, the film maker can, through camera, cutting, and editing, put them in "permanent motion," taking them backward or forward in time anywhere in the world—a feat no other art can accomplish.

In the television program for this lesson, we will examine form and meaning of some specific films, and in Lesson 5, we will consider ways in which we can employ what we have learned about elements, form, and meaning to help us participate in the film with greater discernment and enjoyment.

LEARNING OBJECTIVES

ON COMPLETING YOUR STUDY OF THIS LESSON, YOU SHOULD BE ABLE TO:

1. Describe the "escape" reaction as a response to the motion picture and identify a possible contrasting reaction.

2. Understand why film exerts such powerful influence over potential responses.

3. Discuss two problems that make it difficult to explore form and meaning in the motion picture.

4. Name at least six qualities or elements that give structure and meaning to the motion picture and briefly explain their contribution to meaning.

5. Explain film's unique capability to portray space and time relationships, according to Erwin Panofsky.

6. Give examples of the sound-visual "principle of coexpressibility" stated by Panofsky.

7. State an essential difference between a stage drama and a film.

ASSIGNMENTS

BEFORE VIEWING THE PROGRAM:

Read the "Overview" and familiarize yourself with the "Learning Objectives" for this lesson.

Consult previous lessons for discussion of the concepts of

cutting
motion
sound on film

Consult a dictionary for acquaintance with these terms:

dynamics
medium
style

Look over the "Aids for Study" for this lesson.

In the textbook, Chapter 11, "The Film":
• Read pages 349–351 ("The Participative Experience and Film"), pages 358–359 ("Selectivity in Film"), pages 362–364 ("The Question of Structure" and "Editing"), and pages 366–373 ("Francis Ford Coppola's *The Godfather*," "Experimentation," and "Summary").

Review all textbook assignments for earlier lessons on film.

In the study guide:
• Read pages 35–51, "Style and Medium in the Motion Pictures" by Erwin Panofsky.

VIEW THE TELEVISION PROGRAM *"Film: Not Just the Great Escape."*

AFTER VIEWING THE PROGRAM:

Review what you have learned, using the "Aids for Study" again.

Evaluate your learning with the "Review Quiz," then check your answers with the "Answer Key" at the back of this study guide.

In accordance with your own interests or your instructor's assignment, complete selected "Additional Activities."

AIDS FOR STUDY

1. What do the textbook authors mean when they state that two opposite reactions are possible in participating with a film? Why do they characterize one of these as "a kind of self-indulgence that depends on self-justifying fantasies"? Try to recall an instance in which you may have responded in this way to a motion picture. How is it suggested that such a response can be avoided?

2. What does Panofsky say about the importance and the influence of film as an art in "Style and Medium in the Motion Pictures"?

3. Panofsky, Martin, and Jacobus all comment that the form and meaning of a film may be somewhat harder to study than they are in other arts. Why is this so?

4. Narrative line or plot is important to the meaning of a film. Discuss the possible uses of narrative line in film and try to give examples.

5. In speaking of the "dynamization of space," Panofsky contrasts the film screen with the stage. How is space made a dynamic, moving element? How can time be made to appear to pass at different rates through the technique of moving through space?

6. Panofsky's judgment against depending on the spoken word is strongly stated, and a similar evaluation also appears in the text. What can film use in place of words to reveal emotional content?

7. What does Panofsky mean by the "principle of coexpressibility"? In what way does he compare the silent films to the ballet? To the stage play? In Panofsky's view, how does the use of the close-up support his contention that the use of sound and dialogue in film is limited? What types of scenes and settings does he feel are appropriate to the stage and the screen? How do these scenes differ?

8. What was the "hitherto unknown language" of the silent film mentioned by Panofsky? What are the "fixed attitudes and attributes" he mentioned? Panofsky provided several examples of standardized plots and events that were still prevalent at the time he wrote. Are similar standardized, recognized type characters and stock situations recognizable today?

9. What is the significance of the fact that a film play is permanently recorded and unchangeable? Panofsky's statement implies that the film itself and its characters exist only in that one film. How does this contrast with a drama written for stage? Is this characteristic of film related to the writer's earlier statement that unlike a stage drama, a screen scenario does not usually make good reading?

10. In the final paragraph of his essay, Panofsky drew another contrast between films and other arts. Other arts begin with "neutral" media. With what do films begin?

Select the one best answer.

1. Panofsky stated that films began as "folk art" because
   a. films were popular entertainment.
   b. the first efforts were by amateurs.
   c. the earliest films depicted stage plays.
   d. the earliest films lacked motion.

2. Of the following qualities or elements, the one that is regarded as the basic substance of film is
   a. plot.
   b. sound.
   c. visual images.
   d. the acting.

3. The contrast between drama on the stage and in film is most evident
   a. because time can appear to pass more quickly on the screen.
   b. in what Panofsky calls the "dynamization of space."
   c. in the increased attention to dialogue given in films.
   d. because films are considered "commercial."

4. According to Panofsky, any attempt in a film to convey thought and feeling primarily by words will
   a. tend to embarrass or bore the audience.
   b. convey the writer's and director's meaning more precisely.
   c. be more successful than in a stage drama production.
   d. tend to hold the audience's attention.

5. The term "principle of coexpressibility" is used to explain that
   a. a good drama written for stage will be suitable for film.
   b. more than one event may be shown at nearly the same time on the screen.
   c. an action can be viewed from more than one location.
   d. any sound cannot convey more than what is seen on the screen.

6. A "new language" learned by the viewers of the silent films was
   a. standardized music that revealed the emotions.
   b. printed titles that capsulized the dialogue.
   c. standardized appearance and behavior of type characters.
   d. a spoken explanation by a "movie house" employee.

7. Which of the following is true of a film?
   a. Like a stage play, it may be changed, with each viewing.
   b. Unlike a play written for stage, it is unchanging once it is performed.
   c. The characters in the play are not dependent upon the attributes of the actors.
   d. A good scenario for a film should be as readable as the script for a stage play.

8. By "commercial art" is meant any art
   a. produced on a large scale.
   b. produced to please the artist.
   c. produced to please a buying public.
   d. that has been successfully sold.

9. One reason it is difficult to study form and meaning in the motion picture is
   a. film is too much like other art forms.
   b. viewers tend to identify too closely with realistic films.
   c. most film is of the "escape" variety.
   d. filmic meaning can be hard to translate into words.

10. Film art, unlike many other arts,
    a. begins with physical reality as its medium.
    b. begins with a neutral medium.
    c. should develop carefully stylized settings.
    d. is not dependent on any medium.

ADDITIONAL ACTIVITIES

1. If possible, obtain a motion picture scenario or script for reading. Assuming you would enjoy the film if it were seen, do you find it enjoyable reading? What elements do you find in the script of a stage drama that make it more appealing? Discuss whether or not film scenarios may become more popular reading in the future, as some plays have.

2. Find reviews of films that have been produced a second time, such as *Stagecoach* or *Dark Victory*. Do these reviews seem to indicate that such an undertaking results in essentially "a new play"? Do these reviews support or refute Panofsky's statement on the uniqueness of each film? If you have seen, or can arrange to see, two separate filmings of what was basically the same scenario, discuss your own impressions about them.

Few essays—or books, for that matter—written about the film say as much about the nature of the medium and its stylistic possibilities as this piece by art historian Erwin Panofsky (1892–1968). Originally developed from an address in support of the creation of the Museum of Modern Art Film Library, . . . its understanding of the problems and achievements of film is timeless, however; the essay needs no bringing up to date to make current what it says about the recording of movement, the dynamization of space and the spacialization of time, the place of speech in the film, the communicability of film and its translation into and out of commercial and noncommercial values. Panofsky's great experience and understanding as a historian of the visual arts allow him to make large-scale comparisons between the development of the film and, for example, the mosaic and line engraving and to make them convincingly. He sees the films of the first years of this century as establishing "the subject matter and methods of the moving picture as we know it." The central problem remains the one with which film has always been confronted: "to manipulate and shoot unstylized reality in such a way that the result has style. This is a proposition no less difficult than any proposition in the older arts."

STYLE AND MEDIUM
IN THE MOTION PICTURES

Erwin Panofsky

Film art is the only art the development of which men now living have witnessed from the very beginnings; and this development is all the more interesting as it took place under conditions contrary to precedent. It was not an artistic urge that gave rise to discovery and gradual perfection of a new technique; it was a technical invention that gave rise to the discovery and gradual perfection of a new art.

From this we understand two fundamental facts. First, that the primordial basis of the enjoyment of moving pictures was not an objective interest in a specific subject matter, much less an aesthetic interest in the formal presenation of subject matter, but the sheer delight in the fact that things seemed to move, no matter what things they were. Second, that films—first exhibited in "kinetoscopes," viz., cinematographic peep shows, but projectable to a screen since as early as 1894—are, originally, a product of genuine folk art (whereas, as a rule, folk art derives from what is known as "higher art"). At the very beginning of things we find the simple recording of movements: galloping horses, railroad trains, fire engines, sporting events, street scenes. And when it had come to the making of narrative films these were produced by photographers who were anything but "producers" or "directors," performed by people who were anything but actors, and enjoyed by people who would have been much offended had anyone called them "art lovers."

The casts of these archaic films were usually collected in a "café" where unemployed supers or ordinary citizens possessed of a suitable exterior were wont to assemble at a given hour. An enterprising photographer would walk in, hire four or five convenient characters and make the picture while carefully instructing them what to do: "Now, you pretend to hit this lady over the head"; and (to the lady): "And you pretend to fall down in a heap." Productions like these were shown, together with those purely factual recordings of "movement for movement's sake," in a few small and dingy cinemas mostly frequented by the "lower classes" and a sprinkling of youngsters in quest of adventure (about 1905, I happen to remember, there was only one obscure and faintly disreputable *kino* in the whole city of Berlin, bearing, for some unfathomable reason, the English name of "The Meeting Room"). Small wonder that the "better classes," when they slowly began to venture into these early picture theaters, did so, not by way of seeking normal and possibly serious entertainment, but with that characteristic sensation of self-conscious condescension with which we may plunge, in gay company, into the folkloristic depths of Coney Island or a European kermis; even a few years ago it was the regulation attitude of the socially or intellectually prominent that one could confess to enjoying such austerely educational films as *The Sex Life of the Starfish* or films with "beautiful scenery," but never to a serious liking for narratives.

Today there is no denying that narrative films are not only "art"— not often good art, to be sure, but this applies to other media as well—but also, besides architecture, cartooning and "commercial design," the only visual art entirely alive. The "movies" have re-established that dynamic contact between art production and art consumption which, for reasons too complex to be considered here, is sorely attenuated, if not entirely interrupted, in many other fields of artistic endeavor. Whether we like it or not, it is the movies that mold, more than any other single force, the opinions, the taste, the language, the dress, the behavior, and even the physical appearance of a public comprising more than 60 percent of the population of the earth. If all the serious lyrical poets, composers, painters and sculptors were forced by law to stop their activities, a rather small fraction of the general public would become aware of the fact and a still smaller fraction would seriously regret it. If the same thing were to happen with the movies, the social consequences would be catastrophic.

In the beginning, then, there were the straight recordings of movement no matter what moved, viz., the prehistoric ancestors of our "documentaries"; and, soon after, the early narratives, viz., the prehistoric ancestors of our "feature films." The craving for a narrative element could be satisfied only by borrowing from older arts, and one should expect that the natural thing would have been to borrow from the theater, a theater play being apparently the *genus proximum* to a narrative film in that it consists of a narrative enacted by persons that move. But in reality the imitation of stage performances was a comparatively late and thoroughly frustrated development. What happened at the start was a very different thing. Instead of imitating a theatrical performance already endowed with a certain amount of motion, the earliest films added movement to works of art originally stationary, so that the dazzling technical invention might achieve a triumph of its own without intruding upon the sphere of higher culture. The living language, which is always right, has endorsed this sensible choice when it still speaks of a "moving picture" or, simply, a "picture," instead of accepting the pretentious and fundamentally erroneous "screen play."

The stationary works enlivened in the earliest movies were indeed pictures: bad nineteenth-century paintings and postcards (or waxworks à la Madame Tussaud's), supplemented by the comic strips—a most important root of cinematic art—and the subject matter of popular songs, pulp magazines and dime novels; and the films descending from this ancestry appealed directly and very intensely to a folk art mentality. They gratified—often simultaneously—first, a primitive sense of justice and decorum when virtue and industry were rewarded while vice and laziness were punished; second, plain sentimentality when "the thin trickle of a fictive love interest" took its course "through somewhat serpentine channels," or when Father, dear Father, returned from the saloon to find his child dying of diphtheria; third, a primordial instinct for bloodshed and cruelty when Andreas Hofer faced the firing squad, or when (in a film of 1893–1894) the head of Mary Queen of Scots actually came off; fourth, a taste for mild pornography (I remember with great pleasure a French film of ca. 1900 wherein a seemingly but not really well-rounded lady as well as a seemingly but not really slender one were shown changing to bathing suits—an honest, straightforward *porcheria* much less objectionable than the now extinct Betty Boop films and, I am sorry to say, some of the more recent Walt Disney productions); and, finally, that crude sense of humor, graphically described as "slapstick," which feeds upon the sadistic and the pornographic instinct, either singly or in combination.

Not until as late as ca. 1905 was a film adaptation of *Faust* ventured upon (cast still "unknown," characteristically enough), and not until 1911 did Sarah Bernhardt lend her prestige to an unbelievably funny film tragedy, *Queen Elizabeth of England*. These films represent the first conscious attempt at transplanting the movies from the folk art level to that of "real art"; but they also bear witness to the fact that this commendable goal could not be reached in so simple a manner. It was soon realized that the imitation of a theater performance with a set stage, fixed entries and exits, and distinctly literary ambitions is the one thing the film must avoid.

The legitimate paths of evolution were opened, not by running away from the folk art character of the primitive film but by developing it within the limits of its own possibilities. Those primordial archetypes of film productions on the folk art level—success or retribution, sentiment, sensation, pornography, and crude humor—could blossom forth into genuine history, tragedy and romance, crime and adventure, and comedy, as soon as it was realized that they could be transfigured—not by an artificial injection of literary values but by the exploitation of the unique and specific possibilities of the new medium. Significantly, the beginnings of this legitimate development antedate the attempts at endowing the film with higher values of a foreign order (the crucial period being the years from 1902 to ca. 1905), and the decisive steps were taken by people who were laymen or outsiders from the viewpoint of the serious stage.

These unique and specific possibilities can be defined as *dynamization of space* and, accordingly, *spacialization of time*. This statement is self-evident to the point of triviality, but it belongs to those kinds of truths which, just because of their triviality, are easily forgotten or neglected.

In a theater, space is static; that is, the space represented on the stage, as well as the spatial relation of the beholder to the spectacle, is unalterably fixed. The spectator cannot leave his seat, and the setting of the stage cannot change during one act (except for such incidentals as rising moons or gathering clouds and such illegitimate reborrowings from the film as turning wings or gliding backdrops). But, in return for this restriction, the theater has the advantage that time, the medium of emotion and thought conveyable by speech, is free and independent of anything that may happen in visible space. Hamlet may deliver his famous monologue lying on a couch in the middle distance, doing nothing and only dimly discernible to the spectator and listener, and yet by his mere words enthrall him with a feeling of intense emotional action.

With the movies the situation is reversed. Here, too, the spectator occupies a fixed seat, but only physically, not as the subject of an aesthetic experience. Aesthetically, he is in permanent motion as his eye identifies itself with the lens of the camera, which permanently shifts in distance and direction. And as movable as the spectator is, as movable is, for the same reason, the space presented to him. Not only bodies move in space, but space itself does, approaching, receding, turning, dissolving and recrystallizing as it appears through the controlled locomotion and focusing of the camera and through the cutting and editing of the various shots—not to mention such special effects as visions, transformations, disappearances, slow-motion and fast-motion shots, reversals and trick films. This opens up a world of possibilities of which the stage can never dream. Quite apart from such photographic tricks as the participation of disembodied spirits in the action of the "Topper" series, or the more effective wonders wrought by Roland Young in *The Man Who Could Work Miracles*, there is, on the purely factual level, an untold wealth of themes as inaccessible to the "legitimate" stage as a fog or a snowstorm is to the sculptor; all sorts of violent elemental phenomena and, conversely, events too microscopic to be visible under normal conditions (such as the life-saving injection with the serum flown in at the very last moment, or the fatal bite of the yellow-fever mosquito); full-scale battle scenes; all kinds of operations, not only in the surgical sense but also in the sense of any actual construction, destruction or experimentation, as in *Louis Pasteur* or *Madame Curie*; a really grand party, moving through many rooms of a mansion or a palace. Features like these, even the mere shifting of the scene from one place to another by means of a car perilously negotiating heavy traffic or a motorboat steered through a nocturnal harbor, will not only always retain their primitive cinematic appeal but also remain enormously effective as a means of stirring the emotions and creating suspense. In addition, the movies have the power, entirely denied to the theater, to convey psychological experiences by directly projecting their content to the screen, substituting, as it were, the eye of the beholder for the consciousness of the character (as when the imaginings and hallucinations of the drunkard in the otherwise overrated *Lost Weekend* appear as stark realities instead of being described by mere words). But any attempt to convey thought and feelings exclusively, or even primarily, by speech leaves us with a feeling of embarrassment, boredom, or both.

What I mean by thoughts and feelings "conveyed exclusively, or even primarily, by speech" is simply this: Contrary to naïve expectation, the invention of the sound track in 1928 has been unable to change the basic fact that a moving picture, even when it has learned to talk, remains a picture that moves and does not convert itself into a piece of writing that is enacted. Its substance remains a series of visual sequences held together by an uninterrupted flow of movement in space (except, of course, for such checks and pauses as have the same compositional value as a rest in music), and not a sustained study in human character and destiny transmitted by effective, let alone "beautiful," diction. I cannot remember a more misleading statement about the movies than Mr. Eric Russell Bentley's in the spring number of the *Kenyon Review*, 1945: "The potentialities of the talking screen differ from those of the silent screen in adding the dimension of dialogue—which could be poetry." I would suggest: "The potentialities of the talking screen differ from those of the silent screen in integrating visible movement with dialogue which, therefore, had better not be poetry."

All of us, if we are old enough to remember the period prior to 1928, recall the old-time pianist who, with his eyes glued on the screen, would accompany the events with music adapted to their mood and rhythm; and we also recall the weird and spectral feeling overtaking us when this pianist left his post for a few minutes and the film was allowed to run by itself, the darkness haunted by the monotonous rattle of the machinery. Even the silent film, then, was never mute. The visible spectacle always required, and received, an audible accompaniment which, from the very beginning, distinguished the film from simple pantomime and rather classed it—*Mutatis mutandis*—with the ballet. The advent of the talkie meant not so much an "addition" as a transformation: the transformation of musical sound into articulate speech and, therefore, of quasi pantomime into an entirely new species of spectacle which differs from the ballet, and agrees with the stage play, in that its acoustic component consists of intelligible words, but differs from the stage play and agrees with the ballet in that this acoustic component is not detachable from the visual. In a film, that which we hear remains, for good or worse, inextricably fused with that which we see; the sound, articulate or not, cannot express any more than is expressed, at the same time, by visible movement; and in a good film it does not even attempt to do so. To put it briefly, the play—or, as it is very properly called, the "script"—of a moving picture is subject to what might be termed the *principle of coexpressibility*.

Empirical proof of this principle is furnished by the fact that, wherever the dialogical or monological element gains temporary prominence, there appears, with the inevitability of a natural low, the "close-up." What does the close-up achieve? In showing us, in magnification, either the face of the speaker or the face of the listeners or both in alternation, the camera transforms the human physiognomy into a huge field of action where—given the qualification of the performers— every subtle movement of the features, almost imperceptible from a natural distance, becomes an expressive event in visible space and thereby completely integrates itself with the expressive content of the spoken word; whereas, on the stage, the spoken word makes a stronger rather than a weaker impression if we are not permitted to count the hairs in Romeo's mustache.

This does not mean that the scenario is a negligible factor in the making of a moving picture. It only means that its artistic intention differs in kind from that of a stage play, and much more from that of a novel or a piece of poetry. As the success of a Gothic jamb figure depends not only upon its quality as a piece of sculpture but also, or even more so, upon its integrability with the architecture of the portal, so does the success of a movie script—not unlike that of an opera libretto—depend, not only upon its quality as a piece of literature but also, or even more so, upon its integrability with the events on the screen.

As a result—another empirical proof of the coexpressibility principle—good movie scripts are unlikely to make good reading and have seldom been published in book form; whereas, conversely, good stage plays have to be severely altered, cut, and, on the other hand, enriched by interpolations to make good movie scripts. In Shaw's *Pygmalion*, for instance, the actual process of Eliza's phonetic education and, still more important, her final triumph at the grand party, are wisely omitted; we see—or, rather, hear—some samples of her gradual linguistic improvement and finally encounter her, upon her return from the reception, victorious and splendidly arrayed but deeply hurt for want of recognition and sympathy. In the film adaptation, precisely these two scenes are not only supplied but also strongly emphasized; we witness the fascinating activities in the laboratory with its array of spinning disks and mirrors, organ pipes and dancing flames, and we participate in the ambassadorial party, with many moments of impending catastrophe and a little counterintrigue thrown in for suspense. Unquestionably these two scenes, entirely absent from the play, and indeed unachievable upon the stage, were the highlights of the film; whereas the Shavian dialogue, however severely cut, turned out to fall a little flat in certain moments. And wherever, as in so many other films, a poetic emotion, a musical outburst, or a literary conceit (even, I am grieved to say, some of the wisecracks of Groucho Marx) entirely lose contact with visible movement, they strike the sensitive spectator as, literally, out of place. It is certainly terrible when a soft-boiled he-man, after the suicide of his mistress, casts a twelve-foot glance upon her photograph and says something less-than-coexpressible to the effect that he will never forget her. But when he recites, instead, a piece of poetry as sublimely more-than-coexpressible as Romeo's monologue at the bier of Juliet, it is still worse. Reinhardt's *Midsummer Night's Dream* is probably the most unfortunate major film ever produced; and Olivier's *Henry V* owes its comparative success, apart from the all but providential adaptability of this particular play, to so many *tours de force* that it will, God willing, remain an exception rather than set a pattern. It combines "judicious pruning" with the interpolation of pageantry, nonverbal comedy and melodrama; it uses a device perhaps best designated as "oblique close-up" (Mr. Olivier's beautiful face inwardly listening to but not pronouncing the great soliloquy); and, most notably, it shifts between three levels of archaelogical reality: a reconstruction of Elizabethan London, a reconstruction of the events of 1415 as laid down in Shakespeare's play, and the reconstruction of a performance of this play on Shakespeare's own stage. All this is perfectly legitimate; but, even so, the highest praise of the film will always come from those who, like the critic of the *New Yorker*, are not quite in sympathy with either the movies *au naturel* or Shakespeare *au naturel*.

As the writings of Conan Doyle potentially contain all modern mystery stories (except for the tough specimens of the Dashiell Hammett school), so do the films produced between 1900 and 1910 preestablish the subject matter and methods of the moving picture as we know it. This period produced the incunabula of the Western and the crime film (Edwin S. Porter's amazing *Great Train Robbery* of 1903) from which developed the modern gangster, adventure, and mystery pictures (the latter, if well done, is still one of the most honest and genuine forms of film entertainment, space being doubly charged with time as the beholder asks himself not only "What is going to happen?" but also "What has happened before?"). The same period saw the emergence of the fantastically imaginative film (*Méliès*) which was to lead to the expressionist and surrealist experiments (*The Cabinet of Dr. Caligari, Sand d'un Poéte*, etc.), on the one hand, and to the more superficial and spectacular fairly tales à la Arabian Nights, on the other. Comedy, later to triumph in Charlie Chaplin, the still insufficiently appreciated Buster Keaton, the Marx Brothers and the pre-Hollywood creations of René Clair, reached a respectable level in Max Linder and others. In historical and melodramatic films the foundations were laid for movie iconography and movie symbolism, and in the early work of D. W. Griffith we find, not only remarkable attempts at psychological analysis (*Edgar Allan Poe*) and social criticism (*A Corner in Wheat*) but also such basic technical innovations as the long shot, the flashback and the close-up. And modest trick films and cartoons paved the way to Felix the Cat, Popeye the Sailor, and Felix's prodigious offspring, Mickey Mouse.

Within their self-imposed limitations, the earlier Disney films, and certain sequences in the later ones, represent, as it were, a chemically pure distillation of cinematic possibilities. They retain the most important folkloristic elements—sadism, pornography, the humor engendered by both, and moral justice—almost without dilution and often fuse these elements into a variation on the primitive and inexhaustible David-and-Goliath motif, the triumph of the seemingly weak over the seemingly strong; and their fantastic independence of the natural laws gives them the power to integrate space with time to such perfection that the spatial and temporal experiences of sight and hearing come to be almost interconvertible. A series of soap bubbles, successively punctured, emits a series of sounds exactly corresponding in pitch and volume to the size of the bubbles; the three uvulae of Willie the Whale—small, large and medium—vibrate in consonance with tenor, bass and baritone notes; and the very concept of stationary existence is completely abolished. No object in creation, whether it be a house, a piano, a tree or an alarm clock, lacks the faculties of organic, in fact anthropomorphic, movement, facial expression and phonetic articulation. Incidentally, even in normal, "realistic" films the inanimate object, provided that it is dynamizable, can play the role of a leading character as do the ancient railroad engines in Buster Keaton's *General and Niagara Falls*. How the earlier Russian films exploited the possibility of heroizing all sorts of machinery lives in everybody's memory; and it is perhaps more than an accident that the two films which will go down in history as the great comical and the great serious masterpiece of the silent period bear the names and immortalize the personalities of two big ships: Keaton's *Navigator* (1924) and Eisenstein's *Potemkin* (1925).

The evolution from the jerky beginnings to this grand climax offers the fascinating spectacle of a new artistic medium gradually becoming conscious of its legitimate, that is, exclusive, possibilities and limitations—a spectacle not unlike the development of the mosaic, which started out with transposing illusionistic genre pictures into a more durable material and culminated in the hieratic supernaturalism of Ravenna; or the development of line engraving, which started out as a cheap and handy substitute for book illumination and culminated in the purely "graphic" style of Dürer.

Just so the silent movies developed a definite style of their own, adapted to the specific conditions of the medium. A hitherto unknown language was forced upon a public not yet capable of reading it, and the more proficient the public became the more refinement could develop in the language. For a Saxon peasant of around 800 it was not easy to understand the meaning of a picture showing a man as he pours water over the head of another man, and even later many people found it difficult to grasp the significance of two ladies standing behind the throne of an emperor. For the public of around 1910 it was no less difficult to understand the meaning of the speechless action in a moving picture, and the producers employed means of clarification similar to those we find in medieval art. One of these was printed tiles or letters, striking equivalents of the medieval *tituli* and scrolls (at a still earlier date there even used to be explainers who would say, *viva voce*, "Now he thinks his wife is dead but she isn't" or "I don't wish to offend the ladies in the audience but I doubt that any of them would have done that much for her child"). Another, less obtrusive method of explanation was the introduction of a fixed iconography which from the outset informed the spectator about the basic facts and characters, much as the two ladies behind the emperor, when carrying a sword and a cross respectively, were uniquely determined as Fortitude and Faith. There arose, identifiable by standardized appearance, behavior and attributes, the well-remembered types of the Vamp and the Straight Girl (perhaps the most convincing modern equivalents of the medieval personifications of the Vices and Virtues), the Family Man, and the Villain, the latter marked by a black mustache and walking stick. Nocturnal scenes were printed on blue or green film. A checkered tablecloth meant, once for all, a "poor but honest" milieu; a happy marriage, soon to be endangered by the shadows from the past, was symbolized by the young wife's pouring the breakfast coffee for her husband; the first kiss was invariably announced by the lady's gently playing with her partner's necktie and was invariably accompanied by her kicking out with her left foot. The conduct of the characters was predetermined accordingly. The poor but honest laborer who, after leaving his little house with the checkered tablecloth, came upon an abandoned baby could not but take it to his home and bring it up as best he could; the Family Man could not but yield, however temporarily, to the temptations of the Vamp. As a result these early melodramas had a highly gratifying and soothing quality in that events took shape, without the complications of individual psychology, according to a pure Aristotelian logic so badly missed in real life.

Devices like these became gradually less necessary as the public grew accustomed to interpret the action by itself and were virtually abolished by the invention of the talking film. But even now there survive—quite legitimately, I think—the remnants of a "fixed attitude and attribute" principle and, more basic, a primitive or folkloristic concept of plot construction. Even today we take it for granted that the diphtheria of a baby tends to occur when the parents are out and, having occurred, solves all their matrimonial problems. Even today we demand of a decent mystery film that the butler, though he may be anything from an agent of the British Secret Service to the real father of the daughter of the house, must not turn out to be the murderer. Even today we love to see Pasteur, Zola, or Ehrlich win out against stupidity and wickedness, with their respective wives trusting and trusting all the time. Even today we much prefer a happy finale to a gloomy one and insist, at the very least, on the observance of the Aristotelian rule that the story have a beginning, a middle, and an ending—a rule the abrogation of which has done so much to estrange the general public from the more elevated spheres of modern writing. Primitive symbolism, too, survives in such amusing details as the last sequence of *Casablanca* where the delightfully crooked and right-minded *préfet de police* casts an empty bottle of Vichy water into the wastepaper basket; and in such telling symbols of the supernatural as Sir Cedric Hardwicke's death in the guise of a "gentlemen in a dustcoat trying" (*On Borrowed Time*) or Claude Rains' Hermes Psychopompos in the striped trousers of an airline manager (*Here Comes Mister Jordan*).

The most conspicuous advances were made in directing, lighting, camera work, cutting and acting proper. But while in most of these fields the evolution proceeded continuously—though, of course, not without detours, breakdowns and archaic relapses—the development of acting suffered a sudden interruption by the invention of the talking film; so that the style of acting in the silents can already be evaluated in retrospect, as a lost art not unlike the painting technique of Jan van Eyck or, to take up our previous simile, the burin technique of Dürer. It was soon realized that acting in a silent film neither meant a pantomimic exaggeration of stage acting (as was generally and erroneously assumed by professional stage actors who more and more frequently condescended to perform in the movies), nor could dispense with stylization altogether; a man photographed while walking down a gangway in ordinary, everyday-life fashion looked like anything but a man walking down a gangway when the result appeared on the screen. If the picture was to look both natural and meaningful the acting had to be done in a manner equally different from the style of the stage and the reality of ordinary life; speech had to be made dispensable by establishing an organic relation between the acting and the technical procedure of cinephotography—much as in Dürer's prints, color had been made dispensable by establishing an organic relation between the design and the technical procedure of line engraving.

This was precisely what the great actors of the silent period accomplished, and it is a significant fact that the best of them did not come from the stage, whose crystallized tradition prevented Duse's only film, *Cenere*, from being more than a priceless record of Duse. They came instead from the circus or the variety, as was the case of Chaplin, Keaton and Will Rogers; from nothing in particular, as was the case of Theda Bara, of her greater European parallel, the Danish actress Asta Nielsen, and of Garbo; or from everything under the sun, as was the case of Douglas Fairbanks. The style of these "old masters" was indeed comparable to the style of line engraving in that it was, and had to be, exaggerated in comparison with stage acting (just as the sharply incised and vigorously curved *tailles* of the burin are exaggerated in comparison with pencil strokes or brushwork), but richer, subtler and infinitely more precise. The advent of the talkies, reducing if not abolishing this difference between screen acting and stage acting, thus confronted the actors and actresses of the silent screen with a serious problem. Buster Keaton yielded to temptation and fell. Chaplin first tried to stand his ground and to remain an exquisite archaist but finally gave in, with only moderate success (*The Great Dictator*). Only the glorious Harpo has thus far successfully refused to utter a single articulate sound; and only Greta Garbo succeeded, in a measure, in transforming her style in principle. But even in her case, one cannot help feeling that her first talking picture, *Anna Christie*, where she could ensconce herself, most of the time, in mute or monosyllabic sullenness, was better than her later performances; and in the second, talking version of *Anna Karenina*, the weakest moment is certainly when she delivers a big Ibsenian speech to her husband, and the strongest when she silently moves along the platform of the railroad station while her despair takes shape in the consonance of her movement (and expression) with the movement of the nocturnal space around her, filled with the real noises of the trains and the imaginary sound of the "little men with the iron hammers" that drives her, relentlessly and almost without her realizing it, under the wheels.

Small wonder that there is sometimes felt a kind of nostalgia for the silent period and that devices have been worked out to combine the virtues of sound and speech with those of silent acting, such as the "oblique close-up" already mentioned in connection with *Henry V*; the dance behind glass doors in *Sous les Toits de Paris*; or, in the *Histoire d'un Tricheur*, Sacha Guitry's recital of the events of his youth while the events themselves are "silently" enacted on the screen. However, this nostalgic feeling is no argument against the talkies as such. Their evolution has shown that, in art, every gain entails a certain loss on the other side of the ledger; but that the gain remains a gain, provided that the basic nature of the medium is realized and respected. One can imagine that, when the caveman of Altamira began to paint their buffaloes in natural colors instead of merely incising the contours, the more conservative cave men foretold the end of paleolithic art. But paleolithic art went on, and so will the movies. New technical inventions always tend to dwarf the values already attained, especially in a medium that owes its very existence to technical experimentation. The earliest talkies were infinitely inferior to the then mature silents, and most of the present technicolor films are still inferior to the now mature talkies in black and white. But even if Aldous Huxley's nightmare should be added to those of sight and hearing, even then we may say with the Apostle, as we have said when first confronted with the sound track and the technical film, "We are troubled on every side, yet not distressed; we are perplexed, but not in despair."

From the law of time-charged space and space-bound time, there follows the fact that the screenplay, in contrast to the theater play, *has no aesthetic existence independent of its performance, and that its characters have no aesthetic existence outside the actors.*

The playwright writes in the fond hope that his work will be an imperishable jewel in the treasure house of civilization and will be presented in hundreds of performances that are but transient variations on a "work" that is constant. The scriptwriter, on the other hand, writes for one producer, one director and one cast. Their work achieves the same degree of permanence as does his; and should the same or a similar scenario ever be filmed by a different director and a different cast there will result an altogether different "play."

Othello or Nora are definite, substantial figures created by the playwright. They can be played well or badly, and they can be "interpreted" in one way or another; but they most definitely exist, no matter who plays them or even whether they are played at all. The character in a film, however, lives and dies with the actor. It is not the entity "Othello" interpreted by Robeson or the entity "Nora" interpreted by Duse; it is the entity "Greta Garbo" incarnate in a figure called Anna Christie or the entity "Robert Montgomery" incarnate in a murderer who, for all we know or care to know, may forever remain anonymous but will never cease to haunt our memories. Even when the names of the characters happen to be Henry VIII or Anna Karenina, the king who ruled England from 1509 to 1547 and the woman created by Tolstoy, they do not exist outside the being of Garbo and Laughton. They are but empty and incorporeal outlines like the shadows in Homer's Hades, assuming the character of reality only when filled with the lifeblood of an actor. Conversely, if a movie role is badly played there remains literally nothing of it, no matter how interesting the character's psychology or how elaborate the words.

What applies to the actor applies, *mutatis mutandis*, to most of the other artists, or artisans, who contribute to the making of a film: the director, the sound man, the enormously important cameraman, even the make-up man. A stage production is rehearsed until everything is ready, and then it is repeatedly performed in three consecutive hours. At each performance everybody has to be on hand and does his work; and afterward he goes home and to bed. The work of the stage actor may thus be likened to that of a musician, and that of the stage director to that of a conductor. Like these, they have a certain repertoire which they have studied and present in a number of complete but transitory performances, be it *Hamlet* today and *Ghosts* tomorrow, or *Life with Father per saecula saeculorum*. The activities of the film actor and the film director, however, are comparable, respectively, to those of the plastic artist and the architect, rather than to those of the musician and the conductor. Stage work is continuous but transitory; film work is discontinuous but permanent. Individual sequences are done piecemeal and out of order according to the most efficient use of sets and personnel. Each bit is done over and over again until it stands; and when the whole had been cut and composed everyone is through with it forever. Needless to say that this very procedure cannot but emphasize the curious consubstantiality that exists between the person of the movie actor and his role. Coming into existence piece by piece, regardless of the natural sequence of events, the "character" can grow into a unified whole only if the actor manages to be, not merely to play, Henry VIII or Anna Karenina throughout the entire wearisome period of shooting. I have it on the best of authorities that

Laughton was really difficult to live with in the particular six or eight weeks during which he was doing—or rather being—Captain Bligh.

It might be said that a film, called into being by a co-operative effort in which all contributions have the same degree of permanence, is the nearest modern equivalent of a medieval cathedral; the role of the producer corresponding, more or less, to that of the bishop or archbishop; that of the director to that of the architect in chief; that of the scenario writers to that of the scholastic advisers establishing the iconographical program; and that of the actors, cameramen, cutters, sound men, make-up men and the divers technicians to that of those whose work provided the physical entity of the finished product, from the sculptors, glass painters, bronze casters, carpenters and skilled masons down to the quarry men and woodsmen. And if you speak to any one of these collaborators he will tell you, with perfect *bona fides*, that his is really the most important job—which is quite true to the extent that it it indispensable.

This comparison may seem sacrilegious, not only because there are, proportionally, fewer good films than there are good cathedrals but also because the movies are commercial. However, if commercial art be defined as all art not primarily produced in order to gratify the creative urge of its maker but primarily intended to meet the requirements of a patron or a buying public, it must be said that noncommercial art is the exception rather than the rule, and a fairly recent and not always felicitous exception at that. While it is true that commercial art is always in danger of ending up as a prostitute, it is equally true that noncommercial art is always in danger of ending up as an old maid. Noncommercial art has given us Seurat's "Grande Jatte" and Shakespeare's sonnets, but also much that is esoteric to the point of incommunicability. Conversely, commercial art has given us much that is vulgar or snobbish (two aspects of the same thing) to the point of loathsomeness, but also Dürer's prints and Shakespeare's plays. For, we must not forget that Dürer's prints were partly made on commission and partly intended to be sold in the open market; and that Shakespeare's plays—in contrast to the earlier masques and intermezzi which were produced at court by aristocratic amateurs and could afford to be so incomprehensible that even those who described them in printed monographs occasionally failed to grasp their intended significance—were meant to appeal, and did appeal, not only to the select few but also to everyone who was prepared to pay a shilling for admission.

It is for this requirement of communicability that makes commercial art more vital than noncommercial, and therefore potentially much more effective for better or for worse. The commercial producer can both educate and pervert the general public, and can allow the general public—or rather his idea of the general public—both to educate and to pervert himself. As is demonstrated by a number of excellent films that proved to be great box office successes, the public does not refuse to accept good products if it gets them. That it does not get them very often is caused not so much by commercialism as such as by too little discernment and, paradoxical though it may seem, too much timidity in its application. Hollywood believes that it must produce "what the public wants" while the public would take whatever Hollywood produces. If Hollywood were to decide for itself what it wants it would get away with it—even if it should decide to "depart from evil and do good." For, to revert to whence we started, in modern life the movies are what most other forms of art have ceased to be, not an adornment but a necessity.

That this should be so is understandable, not only from a sociological but also from an art-historical point of view. The processes of all the earlier representational arts conform, in a higher or lesser degree, to an idealistic conception of the world. These arts operate from top to bottom, so to speak, and not from bottom to top; they start with an idea to be projected into shapeless matter and not with the objects that constitute the physical world. The painter works on a blank wall or canvas which he organizes into a likeness of things and persons according to his idea (however much this idea may have been nourished by reality); he does not work with the things and persons themselves even if he works "from the model." The same is true of the sculptor with his shapeless mass of clay or his untooled block of stone or wood; of the writer with his sheet of paper or his dictaphone; and even of the stage designer with his empty and sorely limited section of space. It is the movies, and only the movies, that do justice to that materialistic interpretation of the universe which, whether we like it or not, pervades contemporary civilization. Excepting the very special case of the animated cartoon, the movies organize material things and persons, not a neutral medium, into a composition that receives its style, and may even become fantastic or pretervoluntarily symbolic, not so much by an interpretation in the artist's mind as by the actual manipulation of physical objects and recording machinery. The medium of the movies is physical reality as such: the physical reality of eighteenth-century Versailles—no matter whether it be the original or a Hollywood facsimile indistinguishable therefore for all aesthetic intents and purposes—or of a suburban home in Westchester; the physical reality of the Rue de Lappe in Paris or of the Gobi Desert, of Paul Ehrlich's apartment in Frankfurt or of the streets of

New York in the rain; the physical reality of engines and animals, of Edward G. Robinson and Jimmy Cagney. All these objects and persons must be organized into a work of art. They can be arranged in all sorts of ways ("arrangement" comprising, of course, such things as make-up, lighting and camera work); but there is no running away from them. From this point of view it becomes evident that at attempt at subjecting the world to artistic prestylization, as in the expressionist settings of *The Cabinet of Dr. Caligari* (1919), could be no more than an exciting experiment that could exert but little influence upon the general course of events. To prestylize reality prior to tackling it amounts to dodging the problem. The problem is to manipulate and shoot unstylized reality in such a way that the result has style. This is a proposition no less legitimate and no less difficult than any proposition in the older arts.

I cannot help feeling that the final sequence of the new Marx Brothers film *Night in Casablanca*—where Harpo unaccountably usurps the pilot's seat of a big airplane, causes incalculable havoc by flicking one tiny little control after another, and waxes the more insane with joy the greater the disproportion between the smallness of his effort and the magnitude of the disaster—is a magnificent and terrifying symbol of man's behavior in the atomic age. No doubt the Marx Brothers would vigorously reject this interpretation; but so would Dürer have done had anyone told him that his *Apocalypse* forshadowed the cataclysm of the Reformation.

FILM

SEEING ALL THERE IS

OVERVIEW

Criticism is a natural experience for anyone participating with a work of art. Each of us responds to what we see or hear; at the very least, we may think "I like this," or "I don't like that." Such judgments are commonplace in our lives, yet judgment (or evaluation) is really a basic and important dimension of formal criticism. We are challenged by this course to increase and refine our critical skills, for skillful criticism can deepen our participation with art and enhance our delight in it. Moreover, recent decades have brought immense changes in art, and our critical skills must grow and change, too, if we are to continue enjoying new and different expressions of art.

Criticism is related to, but quite different from, participative enjoyment. Criticism sharpens our perception and reveals what we might otherwise miss in perceiving a work of art; it makes complexities and subtleties more available to us. For example, viewing a film twice—once just for participative enjoyment alone and once for critical participation—can be interesting and exciting. We may not see all there is to see for the first time.

In this lesson, we are introduced to three approaches to criticism that are essential to understanding any work of art: descriptive criticism, or focusing on form; interpretative criticism, focusing on content; and evaluative criticism, focusing on the relative merits. The textbook for this course classifies historical criticism as an enrichment and supplement for these three, although some authors consider historical criticism a distinctly separate approach. These approaches will be studied in detail in later lessons, but it is important to be aware of them at this point.

The reading assignment for this lesson reviews some areas of film content that might be overlooked by the casual viewer. Study of elements and form in an earlier lesson may also suggest some additional aspects of film that you have not previously considered or enjoyed. You are also assigned to read an interesting statement about filmmaking written by noted film director Ingmar Bergman. Bergman provides a fascinating personal description of the early development of a film idea. For him, a film begins as a complex of nonverbal feelings and emotions, which he must later interpret into a written script and a motion picture. He takes some pains to describe those elements that cannot be adequately noted in a script. If we view a Bergman film in the future (and perhaps those of other directors as well), we should be sensitive to these components that, to him, are most difficult to express in a written script, yet are most important to his artistic creation.

Literature, according to Bergman, appeals to the intellect first and is assimilated by conscious acts before making an impact on the emotion and the imagination, whereas film does just the opposite, affecting the emotions directly, not the intellect. Perhaps Bergman's comments can help us become more adept at identifying what is unique to a film or a literary work—what could not be as well represented by any other form of art. Such awareness should contribute to our enjoyment of the work.

The textbook and other written portions of this lesson emphasize increasing your critical skills. However, there are important functions that the formal critic can provide; thus, the television portion of the lesson will provide further critical views of the film.

LEARNING OBJECTIVES

ON COMPLETING YOUR STUDY OF THIS LESSON, YOU SHOULD BE ABLE TO:

1. Appreciate the importance of change and growth in one's critical skills.
2. Identify three types of criticism.
3. List several aspects of film content that may be described in addition to the narrative story or dialogue.
4. Perform a simple critical description for one film.
5. Identify a significant difference between the arts of film and literature.
6. State one way in which increased critical skills may add to enjoyment of art.

ASSIGNMENTS

BEFORE VIEWING THE PROGRAM:

Read the "Overview" and familiarize yourself with the "Learning Objectives" for this lesson.

Consult a dictionary, an encyclopedia, or the textbook to acquaint yourself with these terms:

context
criticism
participation
stills

Look over the "Aids for Study" for this lesson.

In the textbook, Chapter 3, "Being a Critic of the Arts":
• Read pages 47–59 ("You Are Already an Art Critic," "Participation and the Critic," and "Kinds of Criticism").

In the textbook, Chapter 11, "The Film":
- Review pages 351–358 ("The Moving Image" and "Camera Point of View"), pages 364–366 ("Content") and pages 371–372 ("Experimentation").

In the study guide:
- Read "Film Has Nothing to Do with Literature" by Ingmar Bergman, pages 61–64.

During the week you devote to this lesson, view one well-rated film at a theater or on television. If this is difficult, devote some time to recalling two or three good films you have seen in recent months.

VIEW THE TELEVISION PROGRAM *Film: Seeing All There Is.*

AFTER VIEWING THE PROGRAM:

Perform the Perception Key "Kinds of Criticism," textbook page 50.

Review the critical comments of the guests on the television program. Use some of their comments with the perception key.

Review what you have learned, using the "Aids for Study" again.

Evaluate your learning with the "Review Quiz," then check your answers with the "Answer Key" at the back of this study guide.

In accordance with your own interests or your instructor's assignment, complete selected "Additional Activities."

AIDS FOR STUDY

1. Describe your growth in tastes and preferences among the arts during the past three to five years, particularly with reference to films. Have your preferences changed during this time? Does this show growth in your awareness of the art or in your own critical skills? You may wish to evaluate your answers with the comments in the textbook.

2. Define in your own words the three aspects or types of criticism identified in the textbook. Consider whether you agree that historical criticism is a supplementary or secondary type of criticism.

3. What are the possible contents of a film that could not be readily conveyed by a narrative script, according to Bergman? Can you add still other contents from your reading?

4. The importance of a gesture in the film *Claire's Knee* is described in the textbook. Can you think of a film you have viewed in which a gesture, setting, or scene acquired special meaning through repetition?

5. What are the elements that Bergman considers basic to a film? Which of them can be more easily wrtitten into a script? Which are difficult or impossible to put into a script?

6. Why is the appeal of a film more like that of music than of literature? Or, from your personal experience with films, music, poetry, and fiction, do you agree with Bergman's criticism of this aspect of film?

7. As a result of your reading and the television presentation, what aspects of form and content in film may be more evident to you in the future?

Select the one best answer or write the words in the spaces provided.

1. Critics of the arts include anyone
   a. who makes his or her living by art criticism.
   b. who participates in, or reacts to, a work of art.
   c. whose criticisms are published.
   d. who does not like a particular piece of art.

2. According to the textbook, one sign of good criticism is
   a. one's tastes change and enlarge over the years.
   b. one's preferences remain consistent over the years.
   c. one avoids making judgments about the worth of any work.
   d. one's judgment is respected by others.

3. List the three types of criticism distinguished in the textbook.

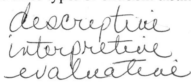
descriptive
interpretive
evaluative

4. According to the textbook, historical criticism is
   a. a distinct aspect of criticism.
   b. not a valid aspect of criticism.
   c. the most important aspect of criticism.
   d. a supplemental aspect of criticism.

5. The content or meaning of the film *Claire's Knee* that could not
   have been adequately expressed in language was
   a. a certain gesture.
   b. the dialogue.
   c. the setting.
   d. the narrative.

6. List at least three of the "embryonic elements" that Bergman says inspire him to develop a script for a film.

   rhythm   tensions   tones
   mood   sequences   scents
   atmosphere

7. Bergman says "film has nothing to do with literature," because film
   a. is irrational and literature is rational.
   b. requires sound and literature may be read silently.
   c. appeals directly to the emotions, whereas literature reaches emotion through the intellect.
   d. and literature appeal to different senses.

8. We can determine the meaning of a particular gesture or event in a film only
   a. within the context of the film.
   b. by reading the script.
   c. by comparing it with its meaning in settings other than the film.
   d. by listening to the narrative.

9. In discussing frame composition and motion, the textbook states that
   a. frame composition is usually more important than motion.
   b. motion is usually more important than frame composition.
   c. both motion and the composition of a single frame are equally important.
   d. neither motion nor composition is especially important to a successful film.

10. A type of criticism that involves describing only form and content still requires development of critical skills because
    a. some aspects of form and content may be easily overlooked.
    b. new forms and content are constantly introduced in most art forms.
    c. one must know the history of the period to describe form and content.
    d. one should be able to evaluate the worth of the form and content.

ADDITIONAL ACTIVITIES

1. Describe one motion picture you have seen. If possible, it should
    be the motion picture you viewed during the week devoted to
    this lesson. Be certain to include elements other than the
    narrative and setting such as emotion, mood, motion, and gesture.

2. Discuss how you can view a film directed by Ingmar Bergman
    differently as a result of this lesson.

3. Perhaps you have found yourself in a difference of opinion with
    the critics or the general public. Can you think of a film that,
    although popular or highly acclaimed, you would not want to
    see a second time? Is there a film that (as far as you know) was
    not popular with the public or critics but that you would like to
    see again? Suggest some reasons your opinion differs from others.

4. This lesson has served as an introduction to criticism as well as a
    conclusion of the unit on the film. List some forms or types of arts
    (in any field) that you would like to enjoy more at this point.
    Has this lesson suggested some ways you might facilitate your
    enjoyment of them?

It is clear from his films that Ingmar Bergman (1918–   ) pursues ideas with a relentlessness and determination unmatched among film directors. His pursuit is manifest in the films themselves, not in the construction of scripts or the literary interpretation of the novels or plays that may inspire them. Nonetheless, there is no mistaking the great influence upon Bergman of Strindberg, several of whose plays the director produced when he was head of the Swedish National Theatre in Stockholm. Nor can one miss the large literary traditions, medieval and modern, Swedish, European, and American, that feed the hungry speculations of such Bergman films as The Seventh Seal, The Virgin Spring, Wild Strawberries, Winter Light, The Silence, Persona, *and* The Passion of Anna. *There is something paradoxical, then, about the assertions in this statement, something not quite complete. The assertions are necessary; they add much to our understanding of Bergman without destroying the air of mystification that pervades all Bergman films.*

FILM HAS NOTHING TO DO WITH LITERATURE

Ingmar Bergman

A film for me begins with something very vague—a chance remark or a bit of conversation, a hazy but agreeable event unrelated to any particular situation. It can be a few bars of music, a shaft of light across the street. Sometimes in my work at the theatre I have envisioned actors made up for yet unplayed roles.

These are split-second impressions that disappear as quickly as they come, yet leave behind a mood—like pleasant dreams. It is a mental state, not an actual story, but one abounding in fertile associations and images. Most of all, it is a brightly colored thread sticking out of the dark sack of the unconscious. If I begin to wind up this thread, and do it carefully, a complete film will emerge.

This primitive nucleus strives to achieve definite form, moving in a way that may be lazy and half asleep at first. Its stirring is accompanied by vibrations and rhythms which are very special and unique to each film. The picture sequences then assume a pattern in accordance with these rhythms, obeying laws born out of and conditioned by my original stimulus.

If that embryonic substance seems to have enough strength to be made into a film, I decide to materialize it. Then comes something very complicated and difficult: the transformation of rhythms, moods, atmosphere, tensions, sequences, tones and scents into words and sentences, into an understandable screenplay.

This is an almost impossible task.

The only thing that can be satisfactorily transferred from that original complex of rhythms and moods is the dialogue, and even dialogue is a sensitive substance which may offer resistance. Written dialogue is like a musical score, almost incomprehensible to the average person. Its interpretation demands a technical knack plus a certain kind of imagination and feeling—qualities which are so often lacking, even among actors. One can write dialogue, but how it should be delivered, its rhythm and tempo, what is to take place between lines—all this must be omitted for practical reasons. Such a detailed script would be unreadable. I try to squeeze instructions as to location, characterization and atmosphere into my screenplays in understandable terms, but the success of this depends on my writing ability and the perceptiveness of the reader, which are not always predictable.

Now we come to essentials, by which I mean montage, rhythm and the relation of one picture to another—the vital third dimension without which the film is merely a dead product from a factory. Here I cannot clearly give a key, as in a musical score, nor a specific idea of the tempo which determines the relationship of the elements involved. It is quite impossible for me to indicate the way in which the film "breathes" and pulsates.

I have often wished for a kind of notation which would enable me to put on paper all the shades and tones of my vision, to record distinctly the inner structure of a film. For when I stand in the artistically devastating atmosphere of the studio, my hands and head full of all the trivial and irritating details that go with motion-picture production, it often takes a tremendous effort to remember how I originally saw and thought out this or that sequence, or what was the relation between the scene of four weeks ago and that of today. If I could express myself clearly, in explicit symbols, then this problem would be almost eliminated and I could work with absolute confidence that whenever I liked I could prove the relationship between the part and the whole and put my finger on the rhythm, the continuity of the film.

Thus the script is a very imperfect *technical* basis for a film. And there is another important point in this connection which I should like to mention. Film has nothing to do with literature; the character and substance of the two art forms are usually in conflict. This probably has something to do with the receptive process of the mind. The written word is read and assimilated by a conscious act of the will in alliance with the intellect; little by little it affects the imagination and the emotions. The process is different with a motion picture. When we experience a film, we consciously prime ourselves for illusion. Putting aside will and intellect, we make way for it in our imagination. The sequence of pictures plays directly on our feelings.

Music works in the same fashion; I would say that there is no art form that has so much in common with film as music. Both affect our emotions directly, not via the intellect. And film is mainly rhythm; it is inhalation and exhalation in continuous sequence. Ever since childhood, music has been my great source of recreation and stimulation, and I often experience a film or play musically.

It is mainly because of this difference between film and literature that we should avoid making films out of books. The irrational dimension of a literary work, the germ of its existence, is often untranslatable into visual terms—and it, in turn, destroys the special, irrational dimension of the film. If, despite this, we wish to translate something literary into film terms, we must make an infinite number of complicated adjustments which often bear little or not fruit in proportion to the effort expended.

I myself have never had any ambition to be an author. I do not want to write novels, short stories, essays, biographies, or even plays for the theatre. I only want to make films—films about conditions, tensions, pictures, rhythms and characters which are in one way or another important to me. The motion picture, with its complicated process of birth, is my method of saying what I want to my fellow men. I am a filmmaker, not an author.

People ask what are my intentions with my films—my aims. It is a difficult and dangerous question, and I usually give an evasive answer: I try to tell the truth about the human condition, the truth as I see it. This answer seems to satisfy everyone, but it is not quite correct. I prefer to describe what I would like my aim to be.

There is an old story of how the cathedral of Chartres was struck by lightning and burned to the ground. Then thousands of people came from all points of the compass, like a giant procession of ants, and together they began to rebuild the cathedral on its old site. They worked until the building was completed—master builders, artists, laborers, clowns, noblemen, priests, burghers. But they all remained anonymous, and no one knows to this day who built the cathedral of Chartres.

Regardless of my own beliefs and my own doubts, which are unimportant in this connection, it is my opinion that art lost its basic creative drive the moment it was separated from worship. It severed an umbilical cord and now lives its own sterile life, generating and degenerating itself. In former days the artist remained unknown and his work was to the glory of God. He lived and died without being more or less important than other artisans; "eternal values," "immortality," and "masterpiece" were terms not applicable in his case. The ability to create was a gift. In such a world flourished invulnerable assurance and natural humility.

Today the individual has become the highest form and the greatest bane of artistic creation. The smallest wound or pain of the ego is examined under a microscope as if it were of eternal importance. The artist considers his isolation, his subjectivity, his individualism almost holy. Thus we finally gather in one large pen, where we stand and bleat about our loneliness without listening to each other and without realizing that we are smothering each other to death. The individualists stare into each other's eyes and yet deny the existence of each other. We walk in circles, so limited by our own anxieties that we can no longer distinguish between true and false, between the gangster's whim and the purest ideal.

Thus if I am asked what I would like the general purpose of my films to be, I would reply that I want to be one of the artists in the cathedral on the great plain. I want to make a dragon's head, an angel, a devil—or perhaps a saint—out of stone. It does not matter which; it is the sense of satisfaction that counts. Regardless of whether I believe or not, whether I am a Christian or not, I would play my part in the collective building of the cathedral.

DRAMA

AN IMITATION OF LIFE

Drama is translated from a Greek word meaning "to act," and "to act" in drama has come to mean "to imitate life." The relationship between dramatic action and the life it is supposed to imitate has long been the concern of dramatic theory and criticism, for although it imitates life, great drama must infuse realism into the imitation. Yet realism has its limits; there is a barrier between play and audience that must not be breached. Realism has thus become central to most dramatic concern, but it is by itself not a sufficient basis for judging drama. The questions of realism and mimesis (the quality of imitation) are dealt with more specifically in later portions of this lesson.

In this lesson we begin by exploring something of the long history and traditions of drama. It is thought that perhaps drama began in the oral retelling of myths and heroic folk legends by primitive peoples and in rituals and worship intended to enhance the hunt or placate the gods. Steps of primitive dances told stories of mystic rites. These rites were acted and reenacted, probably in forest clearings or before crude altars. The concept of a theater came with emergence of these rites as entertainment, and theaters are known to have existed in Greece as early as 700 B.C. It is also thought likely that tragedy was the first distinct form of drama to emerge from primitive beginnings, probably inspired by the deaths of rulers, kings, or queens.

Drama has since appeared in many forms, but its essence remains the same: humankind's unending conflicts with fate, nature, neighbor, world, and self. The earliest of written dramatic works still in existence contain these very themes.

The television portion of this lesson allows us to see recreations of important moments in the history of drama. From ancient Greece, we see Sophocles's great tragedy, *Oedipus Rex*, and Aeschylus's *Agamemnon*. Development of drama as a truly great art languished following the contributions of the Greeks, but drama of a sort did flourish in the Middle Ages in the form of mimes, jugglers, minstrels, dramatizations of Biblical stories, and the so-called morality plays, which were encouraged by the church to help spread the Christian religion. The Renaissance and the Elizabethan Age, with their de-emphasis on religion and their renewed interest in the individual, ushered in a second Golden Age of drama, giving us such playwrights as Marlowe, Molière, and Shakespeare. We glimpse excerpts from Shakespeare's *Julius Caesar*, *Macbeth*, and *Henry V*, and we are ushered into the world of modern drama with Henrik Ibsen's *A Doll's House*.

Two questions are posed for us in this lesson: What is comedy and what is tragedy? Readings in both this lesson and the next will reveal how difficult it is to arrive at a precise definition of these two genres of the art of drama. However, our television host, Maya Angelou, offers two excellent working definitions: "Comedy," she says, "laughs affectionately at the foibles of individuals. Tragedy exalts the worth of individuals, even in their struggles to overthrow a conventional order."

Readings assigned for this lesson explore the issue of realism thoroughly, and particularly the use of archetypes in creating dramatic realism. Archetypes are defined as patterns of human experience that seem to appear again and again throughout human history and throughout literature and drama. Again and again we see recurring such themes as betrayal, loss of innocence, and quest for self. We read a synopsis of Shakespeare's *Romeo and Juliet* because it suggests many qualities of tragedy and realism that typify good drama. Several archetypes are clearly evident in this tragedy, which still has the power to move modern audiences. The tragic young couple is the archetype of the star-crossed lovers whose fates are sealed; there is a symbolic conflict between light and dark, and an archetypal union of sex and death as the play ends.

This introduction to drama might imply that this art has remained essentially unchanged from Greece to modern times, and it is true that our attention to certain compelling aspects of drama show that the importance of the individual character, of conflict, and of the deepest human experiences have remained paramount. However, changes in drama have evolved in part from our own changing perception of ourselves and the universe in which we live. For example, in our twentieth-century civilization, we certainly view the cosmos and the dark impersonal forces of self and nature differently than did the Greeks or the Elizabethans. No longer does the hero of tragic drama have to be noble, as was once the case; he or she can be any one of us. Perhaps the classic plays of Sophocles and Shakespeare still appeal to us, however, because these playwrights made their characters and their conflicts so real that their imitation of life, mimesis, still serves us as a mimesis of life today.

LEARNING OBJECTIVES

ON COMPLETING YOUR STUDY OF THIS LESSON, YOU SHOULD BE ABLE TO:

1. Identify one characteristic of comedy and two characteristics of tragedy.
2. Name two outstanding ages of drama and a representative artist and play from each period.
3. Briefly summarize the plots of three plays studied in this lesson.
4. Appreciate the type of realism that is developed within a drama and suggest the limitations within which this realism must be presented.
5. Define an archetype and recognize an example of an archetypical pattern.

ASSIGNMENTS

BEFORE VIEWING THE PROGRAM:

Read the "Overview" and familiarize yourself with the "Learning Objectives" for this lesson.

Familiarize yourself with these terms now, noting how these brief descriptions are expanded in the lesson:

archetype: a pattern of events recurring to many individuals throughout time.
conflict: opposing desires or demands, as well as the actual struggle
fantasy: a play containing one unbelievable element
mimesis: having the quality of imitating life
realism: in a narrow sense, referring to a play in which the situation and characters reveal a high degree of probability
tragedy: the genre of drama that has, as its outcome, a painful or fatal resolution

Look over the "Aids for Study" for this lesson.

VIEW THE TELEVISION PROGRAM *Drama: An Imitation of Life."*

AFTER VIEWING THE PROGRAM:

In the textbook, Chapter 8, "Drama":
  • Read pages 239–246 (introductory section, "Realism," "The Nature of Drama," "Conventions of Drama," "Archetype," "Genres of Drama: Tragedy," and "Tragic Rhythm") and pages 249–252 ("Shakespeare's *Romeo and Juliet*").

Review what you have learned, using the "Aids for Study" again.

Evaluate your learning with the "Review Quiz," then check your answers with the "Answer Key" at the back of this study guide.

In accordance with your own interests or your instructor's assignment, complete selected "Additional Activities."

AIDS FOR STUDY

1. What was Maya Angelou's description of comedy? Although no examples of comedy were presented in this lesson, can you relate her description to familiar modern-day comedies, either on stage or on film?

2. What was Maya Angelou's description of tragedy? Compare this with the characteristic noted in the assignments for this lesson and with the discussion of Aristotle's pathos in Chapter 8. At first glance, these two concepts may seem unrelated. Yet, are both of these elements (individual worth, suffering) present in *Oedipus Rex* and *Romeo and Juliet*?

3. Who wrote *Oedipus Rex*? In what age of history was it written and first performed? What other types of drama were written in this period? What was the most important conflict portrayed in this play?

4. Reflect on the concept of mimesis (imitation of life), using the Perception Key, "Varieties of Imitation" (textbook page 240). How has the word "realism" developed a specialized meaning in present-day discussion of drama? Can you suggest the limits of realism in drama with which you would be comfortable?

5. What is meant by archetype? The authors of the textbook state that these are structural patterns, related to mythic interpretations of experience, but where do they feel these archetypes originate? How does Maud Bodkin describe the archetypes? With what does Northrop Frye associate the archetypes? What are one or more archetypical patterns suggested in the description of *Romeo and Juliet*?

6. Do you feel that there could be deeply ingrained, subconscious "memories" such as the archetypes carried in every human's being? If not, how do you explain the continuing popularity of certain plays and certain themes in drama? If so, do you feel than an archetypal pattern is, on the subconscious level, as "real" as realistic settings, characterizations, and actions? In other words, does "realism" depend only on the outward aspects of the drama?

REVIEW QUIZ

Select the one best answer.

1. Which of the following is identified as a characteristic of comedy in the television program?
   a. Comedy exalts the worth of individuals.
   b. Comedy places the characters in difficult situations resulting from flaws in their own characters.
   c. Comedy laughs affectionately at the foibles of individuals.
   d. Comedy reveals the strengths and weaknesses of individuals.

2. Which of the following was identified as a characteristic of tragedy in the television program?
   a. Tragedy exalts the worth of individuals.
   b. Tragedy places characters in difficult situations resulting from flaws in their own character.
   c. Tragedy laughs affectionately at the foibles of individuals.
   d. Tragedy reveals the strengths and weaknesses of individuals.

3. Which of the following is the best summation of Aristotle's description of pathos?
   a. reversal
   b. death
   c. suffering
   d. sorrow or loss

4. Two eras in which drama attained sophisticated development were the
   a. Roman and Elizabethan.
   b. Greek and Elizabethan.
   c. Roman and Medieval.
   d. Greek and Medieval.

5. Of the *earlier* of the two eras selected as the answer to Question 4, identify a play from that era (in the left column) and the author of that play (from the right column).
   a. *A Doll's House*
   b. *Romeo and Juliet*
   c. *Oedipus Rex*
   d. *Faust*
   e. Shakespeare
   f. Ibsen
   g. Molière
   h. Sophocles

6. Of the *later* of the two eras selected as the answer to Question 4, identify a play from that era (in the left column) and the author of that play (from the right column).
   a. *A Doll's House*
   b. *Romeo and Juliet*
   c. *Oedipus Rex*
   d. *Faust*
   e. Shakespeare
   f. Ibsen
   g. Molière
   h. Sophocles

7. The manner in which drama seeks to imitate life is best described as
   a. realism.
   b. mimesis.
   c. fantasy.
   d. pathos.

8. Which of the following is not a description of archetype patterns?
   a. structural patterns that seem to have their origins deep in our culture or psyche
   b. faithful reproduction of characterizations, scenery and sets, and actions of an actual historical occurrence
   c. subconscious memory of numberless experiences of the same type
   d. linked with the four natural seasons and the pattern of agricultural growth and decay

9. An archetypal pattern in *Romeo and Juliet* is
   a. conflict between two powerful groups.
   b. lovers who are not permitted to love.
   c. feelings of love and hate towards one's parents.
   d. struggle for freedom from bondage.

10. The tragedy of *Oedipus Rex* is
    a. being overcome by a trusted lieutenant.
    b. his despair upon discovering that he murdered his own father and married his own mother.
    c. the lover who is not permitted to marry his love.
    d. the legal and divine requirement that he kill his own mother.

ADDITIONAL ACTIVITIES

1. Read the complete script of *Romeo and Juliet* or *Oedipus Rex*, or if a rare coincidence occurs, and either of these plays or another classic tragedy is presented on stage in your area, by all means see it. Discuss whether or not the play contains both characteristics of tragedy suggested in Learning Objective 1 and Questions 2 and 3 of the "Review Quiz." Identify lines and actions that seem to indicate an archetypal structure (or, at least, a pattern that has repeatedly occurred in drama and in life throughout history.)

2. Discuss realism and mimesis. If possible, select an example of realistic drama in the narrow sense discussed in the text that you have seen on stage and describe it briefly. In what ways did it condense action or otherwise change absolute realism in order to achieve its effect? (If you prefer, discuss a television or film drama rather than a staged one). Select a second example that is obviously not realistic in the narrow sense, either because it contains a fantasy element or does not portray a "realistic" conflict or setting. Describe it briefly and discuss whether or not you think it is indeed an "imitation of life."

3. Select a modern tragic drama, perhaps by Tennessee Williams or Eugene O'Neill, for reading. Discuss elements or characteristics you perceive in this work that are similar to those studied in this lesson. Do you find any characteristics in this drama that differ from *Romeo and Juliet* or *Oedipus Rex*? Perhaps you may find significant differences in the type of leading character presented or the type of struggle or conflict he or she undergoes.

DRAMA

NUCLEUS OF A STORY

In his *Poetics*, which is still the most respected discussion of literature ever presented, Aristotle analyzed tragedy and defined six elements as being essential to this particular art form. These elements are plot, character, diction, thought, spectacle, and music. Fate, too, is an important part of classical drama, and classical drama must have a certain rhythm blended of three requirements. A dramatic reversal or serious event must befall the hero; the hero must recognize or perceive some truth; and the hero must endure suffering or passion.

As we will learn in this lesson, not all of Aristotle's elements and qualities are necessary to modern drama. Some play a minor role, while others are ignored entirely. For example, fate is no longer considered essential to tragedy because our understanding of humankind and the universe has changed. No longer is humankind thought to be bound by fate into a "large scheme of cosmic and religious events."

However, two of Aristotle's tragic elements—character and plot— are as essential as ever to drama today. Those elements were considered in some detail through a careful analysis of Shakespeare's *Romeo and*

Juliet in the previous lesson. In this lesson, we take a brief look at tragic elements in Shakespeare's *King Lear* and Arthur Miller's modern tragedy, *Death of a Salesman.*

The two great ages of tragedy were the Greek and Elizabethan eras, and the textbook describes the principal physical features of the theaters in which tragedies of these times were staged. In contrast to most present-day theater stages, which are traditionally framed and separated from the audience, Greek and Elizabethan stages extended out into the audience and were not definitely separated from the playgoers. In this respect, they were rather more akin to today's theater-in-the-round. We are asked to consider whether the increased separation of audience and play in present-day theaters lessens the impact of tragic drama.

Although it is not known whether Aristotle analyzed comedy in a treatise, the Greek philosopher did observe that comic characters need not be noble men and women (as did tragic heroes) because "comedy is an imitation of men who are inferior, but not altogether vicious." He also pointed out that comedy, unlike tragedy, could have multiple plots. Comedy, therefore, is no less complex than tragedy. In this lesson, Molière's comedy *The Misanthrope* is used to illustrate Aristotle's element of character.

The Old Comedy and New Comedy of Aristotle's Greece contained most of the elements that still delight comedy audiences today. Old Comedy such as *Lysistrata* and *The Clouds* was farcical and satirical, rather than savage in its attacks upon the foibles and weaknesses of others. New Comedy, more sophisticated, more gentle, and more concerned with the limitations of social custom and social restrictions, developed into the "comedy of manners," which remains a popular dramatic form today. Menander's *The Flatterer* and *The Grouch* are examples of Greek New Comedy.

In the television component of this lesson, George Bernard Shaw's *Pygmalion* is chosen to illustrate those key elements so necessary to drama as a successful imitation of life. As the program notes, in the opening scene of *Pygmalion* we are presented with recognizable people, a familiar situation (people caught in the rain), and developments that foretell a story—the nucleus of a dramatic story. In the chance meeting of Eliza, the saucy flower girl, and Henry Higgins, the smug phonetics expert, we get a definite impression of strong characters. There is immediate conflict between these characters, and out of this conflict a plot is deftly woven. Higgins bets his friend Colonel Pickering that he can make a "duchess out of this draggletailed guttersnipe" (Eliza) and "in six months take her anywhere and pass her off as anything." For her part, Eliza wishes to become a "proper-speaking lady in a flower shop." So a bargain is struck, and a memorable play results. In a way, each character gets what he or she wanted, but the play ends unsatisfactorily nonetheless, without a clear resolution.

The television commentator notes that *Pygmalion* is neither purely comedy nor purely tragic. The play is described as a tragicomedy, a blend of the two genres, because of the manner in which Shaw chose to end the play. (It should be interesting to you to decide whether or not you agree with the classification of this play as tragicomedy.)

Tragicomedy is not new to drama; many of Shakespeare's tragedies had comic endings, and his comedies sometimes have sad endings. As a genre, it is commonly used today (Beckett's *Waiting for Godot* is a familiar example), but its acceptance as a genre was somewhat belated precisely because Aristotle did not recognize it as an established genre. It was also considered to be an inferior mishmash of two pure genres. Unlike pure tragedy or pure comedy, however, tragicomedy does not deliver a neatly wrapped resolution with which to end the play. Tragicomedy often deals in irony, and denouement tends more toward ambiguity and unanswered questions. Perhaps, as the textbook suggests, such a mixing of genres actually makes the drama more true to life.

LEARNING OBJECTIVES

ON COMPLETING YOUR STUDY OF THIS LESSON, YOU SHOULD BE ABLE TO:

1. Name the elements of tragedy as identified by Aristotle.
2. Describe an organic plot and an episodic plot.
3. Appreciate the importance of belief in fate, or an organized cosmic order, to classical tragedy.
4. List the three critical moments of "tragic rhythm" as described in the textbook.
5. Give contemporary (modern) examples that parallel Old Comedy and New Comedy.
6. Distinguish between tragedy, comedy, and tragicomedy.
7. Define "type character."
8. Describe the differences among the Greek, Elizabethan, and modern theaters.

ASSIGNMENTS

BEFORE VIEWING THE PROGRAM:

Read the "Overview" and familiarize yourself with the "Learning Objectives" for this lesson.

Familiarize yourself with these terms, consulting a dictionary or encyclopedia:

> denouement
> genre
> proscenium
> theater-in-the-round

Look over the "Aids for Study" for this lesson.

VIEW THE TELEVISION PROGRAM *"Drama: Nucleus of a Story."*

AFTER VIEWING THE PROGRAM:

In the textbook, Chapter 8, "Drama":
- Read pages 246–249 ("The Tragic Stage"), pages 253–256 ("Genres of Drama: Comedy" and "Old and New Comedy"), pages 261–262 ("Genres of Drama: Tragicomedy or the Mixed Genre"), and page 265 (Perception Key "Tragicomedy").
- Review pages 244–246 ("Genres of Drama: Tragedy" and "Tragic Rhythm").

Review what you have learned, using the "Aids for Study" again.

Evaluate your learning with the "Review Quiz," then check your answers with the "Answer Key" at the back of this study guide.

In accordance with your own interests or your instructor's assignment, complete selected "Additional Activities."

AIDS FOR STUDY

1. What are Aristotle's six elements of tragedy? Would these six elements also be important to a modern comedy or musical?

2. What type of drama is presented as typical of an organic plot? Do you know other examples of the episodic plot than those given in the textbook? What type of plot is usually found in television drama?

3. Why does the individual character seem so important in tragedy? For what two reasons do the authors of the textbook feel that classical tragedy is not possible now?

4. What are the three critical moments of Aristotle's tragic rhythm? Can you identify these moments in any recent dramatic production you have seen on stage? On film? On television?

5. Do you agree with Aristotle that "tragedy without character-ization is possible?" Have you seen a dramatization in which characters are not important, although the event is tragic?

6. How does the proscenium stage differ from the Greek and Elizabethan stages? Do you feel that greater separation from the audience lessens the impact of tragedy on the audience? If not, why does theater-in-the-round enjoy continued popularity? If so, why do classical and Shakespearian tragedies enjoy popularity today?

7. What are the characteristics of Old Comedy? Of New Comedy? In which is plot probably more important? In which is character probably more important? In what types of modern comedy do we see reflections of the Old Comedy? In what types of modern comedy do we see reflections of the New Comedy? Into which category do most of television's situation comedies seem to better fit?

8. What is a type character? How does a type character differ from a true stereotype? What examples of type characters are presented in the text? Can you add other examples from modern stage drama, films, or television drama?

9. Complete the Perception Key "Old and New Comedy"(textbook pages 255–256). In particular, after performing this exercise, do you feel all comedy requires social comment or criticism?

10. Do you agree with the description of *Pygmalion* as a tragicomedy? Why? Do you think Shaw saw his play as tragicomedy? Try to explain how Shaw resolved *Pygmalion*.

REVIEW QUIZ

Select the one best answer.

1. Which of the following contains an element *not* listed by Aristotle as a part of tragedy?
   a. plot, character, spectacle
   b. character, diction, thought
   c. plot, character, music
   d. plot, rhythm, character

2. An example given of an organic plot is the
   a. love story drama.
   b. mystery drama.
   c. musical drama.
   d. all of the above.

3. An episodic plot would have
   a. a sequence of events leading to a logical solution.
   b. much talk by characters but no inevitable conclusion.
   c. very little characterization.
   d. a strong denouement.

4. In classical tragedy, such as described by Aristotle, the tragic action
   a. must come from the strengths and weaknesses of the character.
   b. grows out of the situation.
   c. is a result of mere chance.
   d. does not require important characters at the center of the drama.

5. The textbook authors feel that tragedy has less impact today because
   a. a noble or royal person cannot be tragic.
   b. modern concepts of sin, guilt, and fate differ from the older concepts.
   c. all modern drama requires type characters to facilitate the drama.
   d. modern audiences prefer comedy to tragedy, but audiences in former ages liked tragedy.

6. The "tragic rhythm" as described by Aristotle includes
   a. reversal, recognition, pathos.
   b. purpose, passion, perception.
   c. reversal, passion, suffering.
   d. purpose, recognition, pathos.

7. The Old Comedy is reflected in which type of modern comedy?
   a. comedy of manners
   b. musical comedy
   c. burlesque
   d. all of the above

8. The New Comedy is reflected in which type of modern comedy?
   a. comedy of manners
   b. farce
   c. burlesque
   d. all of the above

9. A character who displays often-repeated characteristics in comedy is known as
   a. an archetypal character
   b. a heroic character
   c. a blocking character
   d. a type character

10. The Greek theater differed from the modern theater because
    a. drama was then performed only at night.
    b. the stage was more separated from the audience by a frame or screen.
    c. the stage extended more into the audience.
    d. there was no actual stage for the performance.

11. Some critics claim *Pygmalion* is a tragicomedy because
    a. Eliza and Higgins marry and live happily thereafter.
    b. Shaw left the conclusion in doubt.
    c. Shaw married Eliza off to someone of her own class.
    d. Higgins won the bet but lost Eliza.

ADDITIONAL ACTIVITIES

1. Using the terms from Aristotle, identify the aspects of tragic rhythm in a drama with which you are already familiar. (You may wish to use one studied in conjunction with the preceding lesson.) If one or more of these aspects are not identifiable, do you still feel justified in classifying the play as a tragedy? If all elements can be identified, do you find any other aspects of the drama that clearly identify it to you as tragedy?

2. If you watch situation comedy or drama on television frequently, identify one or more "type characters" from each program you watch for one week. Do any of them resemble those listed in the textbook? How many others do you find? Are television writers successful in keeping these type characters from becoming stereotypes?

3. Discuss the use of a subplot in a current popular stage or musical comedy. Discuss whether or not the subplot seems suited only to the genre of comedy, as the textbook authors and many critics have suggested. Does the subplot in your selection have a particular relationship to the main plot? Describe it and discuss whether or not such a relationship is necessary to good dramatic artistry. Finally, give your opinion as to whether the comic or dramatic value of the subplot is significant enough to serve as the basis for a dramatic work of its own.

LESSON 8

DRAMA

MEANING FOR EVERY AGE

In the preceding two lessons, we surveyed the origins and development of drama from primitive rites, and we examined the elements and qualities that have come to characterize good drama. In this lesson, we will consider how drama offers meaning through these elements and form, and we will do so primarily by looking at the works of Shakespeare, whose forty-seven plays—all written before 1616—have had a timeless meaning for every age. We also briefly study Molière's *The Misanthrope*, a comedy of manners that stands as a sort of harbinger of modern comedy.

At first, Puritan England did not permit "play acting," so the theaters were situated outside of London on the bank of the Thames River. Of crude, open-air construction, they resembled the inns commonly seen in the countryside. Scenery and stage props were virtually nonexistent, and since drama depends upon illusion, much had to be left to the playgoers' imaginations. Considering the physical appearance of the stage and its lack of equipment, good plays of the era may have been forced to lean heavily on such elements as character, plot, and conflict.

Shakespeare probably first entered this world of the "theater" as an actor, then as writer of his own plays. Lacking setting and props to help create illusion, he drew heavily upon all the elements and qualities of both tragedy and comedy in his successful effort to give meaning to his plays. *Hamlet, Romeo and Juliet*, and *King Lear* are tragedies that have timeless appeal to audiences; *Midsummer Night's Dream, Much Ado About Nothing*, and *The Taming of the Shrew* are matchless comedies, the themes of which are still being copied. The playwright's use of archetypes to create realism and meaning is readily seen in *Romeo and Juliet*, in which birth and death could be added to archetypes noted earlier; in *Hamlet*, in which the ill-fated prince searches for himself; in *Lear*, in which old age is associated with winter; and in *Midsummer Night's Dream*, in which summer is linked with romance, and the play— true to good comedy—ends in multiple marriages.

In the television program, we get a fascinating look at the theater of Shakespeare's time, and we see examples of his imaginative use of the limited resources of the Elizabethan stage in giving meaning to his magnificent plays. We will see moments from *Hamlet, Romeo and Juliet, Midsummer Night's Dream*, and *Henry V*, which is neither strictly comical nor tragic but a historical play that embodies something of an archetype in the young prince who thinks he can be a better and nobler king if he first plays the part of an irresponsible, fun-loving commoner whose companions are little better than thieves. We should particularly note the appearance of the Elizabethan stage and note the description of its evolution from a typical inn courtyard.

A careful study of Molière's *The Misanthrope*, which has additional elements of harsh satire and a conclusion that does not completely resolve the problem within the play, is intended to prepare us for understanding and participating in modern comedy.

LEARNING OBJECTIVES

ON COMPLETING YOUR STUDY OF THIS LESSON, YOU SHOULD BE ABLE TO:

1. Describe the general structure and arrangement of the Elizabethan theater and give examples of how various structures of the theater were used in a drama.

2. Define the terms "aside" and "soliloquy," explaining what each represents in a drama.

3. Explain the frequent use of the "chorus" and the "epilogue" in Elizabethan drama.

4. Identify elements of New Comedy and Old Comedy in *The Misanthrope*.

5. Explain how the conclusion of *The Misanthrope* is not in the tradition of its genre.

6. Appreciate the quality of comedy that enables us to laugh at our own faults.

ASSIGNMENTS

BEFORE VIEWING THE PROGRAM:

Read the "Overview" and familiarize yourself with the "Learning Objectives" for this lesson.

In the textbook, Chapter 8, "Drama":
  • Review pages 242–244 ("Archetype") and pages 255–256 (Perception Key "Old and New Comedy").

Consult a dictionary or an encyclopedia for the meaning of the following terms as they relate to drama or the stage:

  apron
  aside
  satire
  soliloquy

Look over the "Aids for Study" for this lesson.

VIEW THE TELEVISION PROGRAM *"Drama: Meaning for Every Age."*

AFTER VIEWING THE PROGRAM:

Review the program, using the "Aids for Study," Questions 1 through 4.

In the textbook, Chapter 8, "Drama":
 •Read pages 256–261 ("Molière's *Misanthrope:* Comedy of Manners
  with a Twist").

Review your reading using the "Aids for Study," Questions 5 through 9.

Evaluate your learning with the "Review Quiz," then check your answers
with the "Answer Key" at the back of this study guide.

In accordance with your own interests or your instructor's assignment,
complete selected "Additional Activities."

AIDS FOR STUDY

1. Describe the overall design of the Elizabethan theater. How
    did scenes alternate between the apron stage and the recessed
    stage? How was the balcony employed? How were the side
    windows used?

2. What uses of the curtains were demonstrated in this program?
    Do you feel that audiences today would have difficulty
    accepting a simple stage curtain as "city gates?" On the other
    hand, do such devices help the audience maintain the necessary
    "psychic distance"? See the section on "Realism" (textbook
    pages 239–241) to participate in viewing a play.

3. What is an "aside"? Do you feel audiences automatically accept
    such an acting device, or do they have to be taught that an aside
    is meant to be heard by them alone? How may the other actor(s)
    on the stage assist in the illusion of the aside? How does a
    "soliloquy" differ from an aside? In the examples shown in this

program, which was associated with a comical sequence? Which with a serious or seemingly tragic sequence?

4. What example of a chorus was demonstrated in this program? How did the chorus "set the stage" for the audience? What was the purpose of the epilogue from *Midsummer Night's Dream*? What is often used in modern theater to perform the functions of chorus and epilogue?

5. What, according to your study in earlier assignments, were the differences between Old Comedy and New Comedy? What element of Old Comedy is evident in *The Misanthrope*? Who or what is being satirized?

6. What are the New Comedy aspects of *The Misanthrope?* Even though the society portrayed in this play is "fantastic," how does it relate to actual society? What are the "type characters" portrayed in this play?

7. What type of ending is typical of the comedy of manners? How does the ending to *The Misanthrope* differ? What are some of the effects of this unresolved ending?

8. The textbook describes the plot of *The Misanthrope* as "very thin." Why does the play seem, then, to have so much appeal?

9. Does *The Misanthrope*, as summarized in the textbook, provoke your thought about the society we live in? What values in our own culture are reflected in some way in this play?

REVIEW QUIZ

Select the one best answer.

1. In the Elizabethan theater, the portion of the stage extending into the audience was called the
   a. alcove.
   b. balcony.
   c. apron.
   d. recess.

2. The curtain and balcony in Elizabethan theater were
   a. rarely used.
   b. suitable only for special scenes, such as the balcony scene in *Romeo and Juliet.*
   c. adapted to represent a wide variety of settings.
   d. used exclusively by the chorus and epilogue.

3. An aside is
   a. the thoughts of a character, shared with the audience while others are on stage.
   b. an extended speech given while the character alone is on stage.
   c. the windows situated at the edge of the stage.
   d. a whispered conversation between two characters.

4. The soliloquy given as an example in the program was
   a. designed for comedy relief.
   b. serious, even tragic, in its tone.
   c. spoken to several other characters.
   d. given to conclude the play.

5. The chorus presented as an example in the program
   a. consisted of a group of actors.
   b. was responsible for holding the scripts and prompting.
   c. appeared at the conclusion of the play.
   d. appeared to describe the setting for the audience.

6. *The Misanthrope* has elements of the Old Comedy
   a. in the harshness of its attack.
   b. in the love story theme.
   c. in its emphasis upon character.
   d. because it causes laughter without causing reflection or thought.

7. The elements of New Comedy in *The Misanthrope* include all of the following except
   a. the love story theme.
   b. careful dissection of weaknesses.
   c. harsh attacks on individuals.
   d. presence of type characters.

8. The ending of *The Misanthrope*
   a. is typical of the comedy of manners.
   b. does not resolve the question of whether Alceste and Célimène will marry.
   c. resolves the question of compromising with a society based on artificial politeness and manners.
   d. reassures the audience that Alceste and Célimène will marry.

9. In *The Misanthrope,*
   a. plot development is more important than character development.
   b. character development is more important than plot development.
   c. neither plot nor character development is important.
   d. both plot and character are extensively developed.

10. An element of serious thought found in *The Misanthrope*
    a. is the acceptance of "fate" as a dominant force in governing people's lives.
    b. is in the similarity of the characters to ourselves.
    c. is in the questions it raises about the desirability of marriage.
    d. none of these.

ADDITIONAL ACTIVITIES

1. Discuss whether or not, in your opinion, the story presented in *The Misanthrope* would lend itself to film. What additional elements would you suggest adding to make it more acceptable to filming?

2. If you have attended a stage presentation recently, discuss the arrangement and structure of the stage and describe how the various parts of the stage were used to represent a variety of scenes and settings.

3. Read or attend a current comedy and discuss the play following the questions in the Perception Key on Comedy (textbook pages 260–261). In particular, try to identify whether or not character development is an important part of the comedy, humor, or thought-provoking aspects of the play. Are these elements of satire or harsh attacks on individuals or society as a whole?

LESSON 9

DRAMA

GREAT AGE AHEAD?

As noted earlier, criticism and the development of our critical skills
enable us to participate with art more intensely and with greater
enjoyment. We often rely on others to describe, interpret, and evaluate art
for us, but we need to learn from experienced critics how to be good critics
ourselves, for we cannot always have a critic-instructor beside us
whenever we have an opportunity to participate with a work of art. In
this lesson, then, we will explore some directions in which to expand our
critical skills in the areas of description and interpretation, and we will
apply these skills to drama in particular.

Some general guidelines are suggested by the Martin and Jacobus
textbook to help us in developing our critical abilities. An earlier lesson
introduced three approaches to criticism: description, interpretation, and
evaluation. Descriptive criticism involves attention to the form itself,
and our attention is guided to elements of form, texture, and structure.
Form refers to the interrelationship of part to part and part to whole; the
connection of these parts is texture; and structure is concerned with
totality of work. Interpretive criticism concentrates on the content of the

work; it is a search for meanings to be discovered in the work. Interpretation becomes more meaningful, however, if we are familiar with the subject matter that provides the material for the work, as well as with its form, texture, and structure. Personal background and knowledge also become more important when we attempt to interpret.

Tragicomedy is a comparatively recent form to emerge in the art of drama. Some enlightening descriptions of this type of drama are offered in the text, together with some challenging interpretations of its appeal to the present age. Discussion of one play from the modern period, *Waiting for Godot,* may help us better appreciate the form and content of modern drama.

An additional assignment for this unit involves criticism of drama that is centered in social problems. George Bernard Shaw, himself a famous playwright who did not shun social problems, described the problem play for us by naming several significant examples in his article "The Problem Play—A Symposium." He sought a meaning in the preoccupation of some writers with current social concerns.

On reflection, it may seem that Shaw's criticism is more centered on society than on drama in this article. Certainly he identified shortcomings of society as he perceived them. However, he also gave us a measure to suggest the difference between a great writer and a minor one, and the article may well enhance our perception of the difference between "contemporary" or current conflict and eternal or inevitable conflicts.

The television program for this lesson provides critical comment on drama. You should complete much of the reading assignment in this lesson before viewing the program so that you can note the type of criticism being presented.

Martin and Jacobus conclude their critical discussion of drama with the opinion that a great new age of drama may soon be upon us. Should impending events prove them right, we shall be observers and participators in very exciting times indeed.

LEARNING OBJECTIVES

ON COMPLETING YOUR STUDY OF THIS LESSON, YOU SHOULD BE ABLE TO:

1. Select the appropriate definitions for descriptive criticism and interpretive criticism.
2. Suggest why interpretive criticism requires more knowledge than descriptive criticism.
3. Define "detail relationship" and "structural relationship."
4. Anticipate varying interpretations from different critics.
5. Recognize an example of interpretive criticism.
6. Suggest a reason for the treatment of social problems in a drama.
7. Apply descriptive or interpretive criticism to a play of your choice.

ASSIGNMENTS

BEFORE VIEWING THE PROGRAM:

Read the "Overview" and familiarize yourself with the "Learning Objectives" for this lesson.

Look over the "Aids for Study" for this lesson.

Consult a dictionary, an encyclopedia, or your textbook to acquaint yourself with these terms:

> Aristotle's dianoia
> dramatic irony
> mixed genre
> "portable" thought

In the textbook, Chapter 3, "Being a Critic of the Arts":
*   •Read pages 49–57 ("Kinds of Criticism," "Descriptive Criticism," and "Interpretive Criticism").

In the textbook, Chapter 8, "Drama":
- •Review pages 261–262 ("Genres of Drama: Tragicomedy or the Mixed Genre").
- •Read pages 262–268 ("*Waiting for Godot*," Experimental Drama," and "Summary").

Attend a play, or read the script of a play of any length.

VIEW THE TELEVISION PROGRAM *"Drama: Great Age Ahead?"*

AFTER VIEWING THE PROGRAM:

In the study guide:
- •Read pages 99–105 ("The Problem Play—A Symposium," by George Bernard Shaw).

Review what you have learned, using the "Aids for Study" again.

Write a descriptive or interpretive criticism of the play you selected for attending or reading. As guidelines, you may consider the following questions:

What are significant features of the structure of the play?
Which of Aristotle's six elements (listed in the text discussion of tragedy) are strongest in this play; which are weakest?
Do the characters, situations, reversals, or resolutions imply meanings to you? What are they?
Can you classify this play according to the types discussed: tragedy, comedy, tragicomedy, or experimental? What aspects of the play cause you to classify it this way?

Evaluate your learning with the "Review Quiz," then check your answers with the "Answer Key" at the back of this study guide.

In accordance with your own interests or your instructor's assignment, complete selected "Additional Activities."

1. What is descriptive criticism? How may improved descriptive skills increase our enjoyment of art?

2. What is interpretive criticism? Why is it more subjective than descriptive criticism? What knowledge is required before one can interpret meaningfully?

3. Define "structural detail," explaining how it relates to overall form. Try to use sculpture as one example in defining this term and drama as another example. Would you feel that plot is a part of structure? Is the dialog example from *Waiting for Godot* (textbook page 263) an example of structure?

4. Explain the relationship of tragicomedy to dramatic irony.

5. What is the meaning implied by the circumstances of the leading characters in *Waiting for Godot*, according to the textbook? How does this meaning reveal something about life? Do you feel you would enjoy watching this play more if you became aware of this interpretation before the performance or during the performance?

6. In his essay, Shaw identifies the quality of the dramatist who he feels will adapt social problems as material for drama. What is this quality? What does Shaw feel is necessary to a dramatic work if it is to be enjoyed after the social problem it presents is resolved?

7. In Shaw's article, select comments that are chiefly descriptive and comments that are chiefly interpretive.

REVIEW QUIZ
_____

Select the one best answer.

1. Descriptive criticism may be defined as
    a. identifying the strengths and weaknesses of a written
        description of a work of art.
    b. description of the meanings implied by a work of art.
    c. detailed description of all important characteristics of a work
        of art.
    d. a description that determines the value or worth of a work of
        art.

2. Interpretive criticism may be defined as an explanation of
    a. the strengths and weaknesses of a work of art.
    b. the meanings implied in a work of art.
    c. all important characteristics of a work of art.
    d. the value or worth of a work of art.

3. Interpretive criticism is more demanding than descriptive criticism
    because
    a. one must know the value or worth of the work.
    b. one should be an artist—experienced in the form and its
        elements—to interpret the work.
    c. one must be familiar with the subject matter in order to interpret
        the work.
    d. everyone should agree on the meaning of a work of art.

4. A "detail relationship" is the
    a. connection of one part of form to another part of form.
    b. connection of one part of form to the whole form.
    c. surface pattern of a form.
    d. outline of a form.

5. Interpretive criticism by individuals may differ because
    a. the same element may suggest different meanings to different
        people.
    b. some individuals cannot determine meanings from a work of art.
    c. people hold differing opinions about the worth of a work of art.
    d. interpretation is always objective.

6. An interpretive criticism of a drama would
   a. describe most or all of the significant elements.
   b. judge whether or not the work would be enjoyed in future generations.
   c. explain the meanings implied by the elements of the work.
   d. describe the detail and structure of the work.

7. Which of the following is an example of interpretive criticism given in the textbook?
   a. discussion of detail and structure of two primitive face masks
   b. the suggested meaning of the situation of the two major characters in the play *Waiting for Godot*
   c. the description of the plot and major characters of *Romeo and Juliet*

8. Social problems, according to George Bernard Shaw, are made into subject matter of drama by
   a. both great and minor writers.
   b. only minor writers.
   c. chiefly great writers.
   d. only inferior writers.

9. Shaw thought that social problems, as subject matter of drama, are
   a. legitimate material, since drama may portray any conflict between human feelings and circumstances.
   b. legitimate material, but that the writer is politically motivated.
   c. used by writers who do not understand the eternal and inevitable conflicts between human feelings and circumstances.
   d. used only from a desire to please the audience.

10. In Shaw's opinion, the dramas that will survive the test of time are those that
    a. present a satisfactory solution to a social problem.
    b. deal with social problems that have been resolved.
    c. deal with conflicts of permanent or universal interest.
    d. deal most directly with the immediate concerns of its contemporary era.

ADDITIONAL ACTIVITIES

1. Select a current review of a drama from a large-circulation newspaper or magazine. Summarize the review briefly, and discuss the following questions:
    a. Did the critic see elements or meanings in the drama that you might have overlooked had you seen the play?
    b. Is the criticism primarily descriptive, primarily interpretive, or would you have to classify it differently? Explain.
    c. Within the review, find both a descriptive and an interpretive example or statement.

2. Summarize the comments of one guest critic on the television program. Discuss the following:
    a. Did he suggest any perceptions that were new to you?
    b. List the elements of drama he described.
    c. From what characteristics of a play or from a style of drama did he draw meanings or present interpretations?

3. Contrast your experiences in participating in a film or a stage drama. Suggest differences in your own critical approach to each of these arts.

No one in the modern theater is a more eloquent defender of the social drama than George Bernard Shaw (1856–1950). His plays exemplify the drama that deals with social problems at its most engaging, if not necessarily at its most profound. In his prefaces to his plays, Shaw explained what he was doing, always with charm, and often with a crackling, crusading zeal for social, political, and economic justice that continues to be moving even in areas in which justice has long since had its due in almost precisely the terms that Shaw demanded. A learned, witty, and persuasive theater critic and theorist, he is never better than when his crusade for justice in society is joined to his crisp criticism of those playwrights either too dull or too timid to crusade for justice in their own works. In this short statement Shaw sums up, in effect, his own achievement in the social drama as well as Henrik Ibsen's. He not only asserts his principles but does so with such clarity and logic that even the most dogged opponent of the drama of social consciousness must pause long and think hard before rejecting any part of the argument, the principle, or the drama.

THE PROBLEM PLAY—A SYMPOSIUM

(Should social problems be
freely dealt with in drama?)

The Humanitarian VI, May, 1895

George Bernard Shaw

I do not know who asked the question, Should social problems be freely dealt with in the drama?—some very thoughtless person evidently. Pray what social questions and what sort of drama? Suppose I say yes, then vaccination being a social question, and the Wagnerian music drama being the one complete form of drama in the opinion of its admirers, it will follow that I am in favor of the production of a Jennerian tetralogy at Bayreuth.[1] If I say no, then, marriage being a social question, and also the theme of Ibsen's *Doll's House*, I shall be held to condemn that work as a violation of the canons of art. I therefore reply to the propounder that I am not prepared to waste my own time and that of the public in answering maladroit conundrums. What I am prepared to do is to say what I can with the object of bringing some sort of order into the intellectual confusion which has expressed itself in the conundrum.

---

[1]Shaw's fanciful set of plays, designed for performance at Wagner's festival city of Bayreuth, is based on the achievement of Dr. Edward Jenner (1749–1823), the English physician who discovered the vaccination.

Social questions are produced by the conflict of human institutions with human feeling. For instance, we have certain institutions regulating the lives of women. To the women whose feelings are entirely in harmony with these institutions there is no Woman Question. But during the present century, from the time of Mary Wollstonecraft [English feminist, 1759–1797, mother by William Godwin of Shelley's wife Mary] onwards, women have been developing feelings, and consequently opinions, which clash with these institutions. The institutions assumed that it was natural to a woman to allow her husband to own her property and person, and to represent her in politics as a father represents his infant child. The moment that seemed no longer natural to some women, it became grievously oppressive to them. Immediately there was a Woman Question, which has produced Married Women's Property Acts, Divorce Acts, Woman's Suffrage in local elections, and the curious deadlock to which the Weldon and Jackson cases have led our courts in the matter of conjugal rights. When we have achieved reforms enough to bring our institutions as far into harmony with the feelings of women as they now are with the feelings of men, there will no longer be a Woman Question. No conflict, no question.

Now the material of the dramatist is always some conflict of human feeling with circumstances; so that, since institutions are circumstances, every social question furnishes material for drama. But every drama does not involve a social question, because human feeling may be in conflict with circumstances which are not institutions, which raise no question at all, which are part of human destiny. To illustrate, take Mr. Pinero's *Second Mrs. Tanqueray* [most famous of the characters of the English playwright Sir Arthur Wing Pinero, 1855–1934, in the play of the same name]. The heroine's feelings are in conflict with the human institutions which condemn to ostracism both herself and the man who marries her. So far, the play deals with a social question. But in one very effective scene the conflict is between that flaw in the woman's nature which makes her dependent for affection wholly on the attraction of her beauty, and the stealthy advance of age and decay to take her beauty away from her. Here there is no social question: age, like love, death, accident, and personal character, lies outside all institutions; and this gives it a permanent and universal interest which makes the drama that deals with it independent of period and place. Abnormal greatness of character, abnormal baseness of character, love, and death: with these alone you can, if you are a sufficiently great dramatic poet, make a drama that will keep your language alive long after it has passed out of common use. Whereas a drama with a social question for the motive cannot outlive the solution of that question. It is true that we can in some cases imaginatively reconstruct an obsolete institution and sympathize with the tragedy it has produced: for instance, the very dramatic story of Abraham commanded to sacrifice his son, with the interposition of the angel to make a happy ending; or the condemnation of Antonio to lose a pound of flesh, and his rescue by Portia at the last moment, have not completely lost their effect nowadays—though it has been much modified—through the obsolescence of sacrificial rites, belief in miracles, and the conception that a debtor's person belongs to his creditors. It is enough that we still have paternal love, death, malice, moneylenders, and the tragedies of criminal law. But when a play depends entirely on a social question—when the struggle in it is between man and a purely legal institution—nothing can prolong its life beyond that of the institution. For example, Mr. Grundy's *Slaves of the Ring* [a play of the utmost inconsequence by a sentimental and melodramatic playwright (Sydney Grundy, 1848–1914) of the same merit], in which the tragedy is produced solely by the conflict between the individual and the institution of indissoluble marriage, will not survive a rational law of divorce, and actually fails even now to grip an English audience because the solution has by this time become so very obvious. And that irrepressibly popular play *It's Never Too Late To Mend* will hardly survive our abominable criminal system. Thus we see that the drama which deals with the natural factors in human destiny, though not necessarily better than the drama which deals with the political factors, is likely to last longer.

It has been observed that the greatest dramatists show a preference for the non-political drama, the greatest dramas of all being almost elementarily natural. But so, though for a different reason, do the minor dramatists. The minor dramatist leads the literary life and dwells in the world of imagination instead of in the world of politics, business, law, and the platform agitations by which social questions are ventilated. He therefore remains, as a rule, astonishingly ignorant of real life. He may be clever, imaginative, sympathetic, humorous, and observant of such manners as he has any clue to; but he has hardly any wit or knowledge of the world. Compare his work with that of Sheridan, and you feel the deficiency at once. Indeed, you need not go so far as Sheridan: Mr. Gilbert's *Trial by Jury* is unique among the works of living English playwrights, solely because it, too, is the work of a wit and a man of the world. Incidentally, it answers the inquiry as to whether social questions make good theatrical material; for though it is pointless, and, in fact, unintelligible except as a satire on a social institution (the breach-of-promise suit), it is highly entertaining, and has made the fortune of the author and his musical collaborator. *The School for Scandal*, the most popular of all modern comedies, is a dramatic sermon, just as *Never Too Late to Mend*, the most popular of modern melodramas, is a dramatic pamphlet: Charles Reade [1814–1884, author of *Never Too Late to Mend*, an English novelist who moved his own works and others' (such as Tennyson's *Dora* and Zola's *L'Assomnoir*) onto the stage with some box-office and critical success but little theatrical skill] being another example of the distinction which the accomplished man of the world attains in the theatre as compared to the mere professional dramatist. In fact, it is so apparent that the best and most popular plays are dramatized sermons, pamphlets, satires, or bluebooks, that we find our popular authors, even when they have made a safe position for themselves by their success in purely imaginative drama, bidding for the laurels and the percentages of the sociologist dramatist. Mr. Henry Arthur Jones [1851–1921, along with Shaw and Pinero, one of the top English playwrights at the turn of the century; admired by Shaw as a social portraitist in the theater] takes a position as the author of *The Middleman* and *The Crusaders*, which *The Silver King*, enormously popular as it was, never could have gained him; and Mr. Pinero, the author of *The Second Mrs. Tanqueray* and *The Notorious Mrs. Ebbsmith*, is a much more important person, and a much richer one, than the author of *Sweet Lavender* [a highly sentimental play by Pinero]. Of course, the sociology in some of these dramas is as imaginary as the names and addresses of the characters; but the imitation sociology testifies to the attractiveness of the real article.

We may take it then that the ordinary dramatist only neglects social questions because he knows nothing about them, and that he loses in popularity, standing, and money by his ignorance. With the great dramatic poet it is otherwise. Shakespeare and Goethe do not belong to the order which "takes no interest in politics." Such minds devour everything with a keen appetite—fiction, science, gossip, politics, technical processes, sport, everything. Shakespeare is full of little lectures of the concrete English kind, from Cassio on temperance to Hamlet on suicide. Goethe, in his German way, is always discussing metaphysical points. To master Wagner's music dramas is to learn a philosophy. It was so with all the great men until the present century. They swallowed all the discussions, all the social questions, all the topics, all the fads, all the enthusiasms, all the fashions of their day in their non-age; but their theme finally was not this social question or that social question, this reform or that reform, but humanity as a whole. To this day your great dramatic poet is never a socialist, nor an individualist, nor a positivist, nor a materialist, nor any other sort of "is," though he comprehends all the "isms," and is generally quoted and claimed by all the sections as an adherent. Social questions are too sectional, too topical, too temporal to move a man to the mighty effort which is needed to produce great poetry. Prison reform may nerve Charles Reade to produce an effective and businesslike prose melodrama; but it could never produce *Hamlet*, *Faust*, or *Peer Gynt*.

It must, however, be borne in mind that the huge size of modern populations and the development of the press make every social question more momentous than it was formerly. Only a very small percentage of the population commits murder; but the population is so large that the frequency of executions is appalling. Cases which might have come under Goethe's notice in Weimar perhaps once in ten years come daily under the notice of modern newspapers, and are described by them as sensationally as possible. We are therefore witnessing a steady intensification in the hold of social questions on the larger poetic imagination. *Les Miserables*, with its rivulet of story running through a continent of essays on all sorts of questions, from religion to main drainage, is a literary product peculiar to the nineteenth century: it shows how matters which were trifles to Aeschylus become stupendously impressive when they are multiplied by a million in a modern civilized state. Zola's novels are the product of an imagination driven crazy by a colossal police intelligence, by modern hospitals and surgery, by modern war correspondence, and even by the railway system—for in one of his books the hero is Jack the Ripper and his sweetheart a locomotive engine. What would Aristophanes have said to a city with fifteen thousand lunatics in it? Might he not possibly have devoted a comedy to the object of procuring some amelioration in their treatment? At all events, we find Ibsen, after producing, in *Brand*, *Peer Gynt*, and *Emperor and Galilean*, dramatic poems on the grandest scale, deliberately turning to comparatively prosaic topical plays on the most obviously transitory social questions, finding in their immense magnitude under modern conditions the stimulus which, a hundred years ago, or four thousand, he would only have received from the eternal strife of man with his own spirit. *A Doll's House* will be as flat as ditchwater when *A Midsummer Night's Dream* will still be as fresh as paint; but it will have done more work in the world; and that is enough for the highest genius, which is always intensely utilitarian.

Let us now hark back for a moment to the remark I made on Mr. Grundy's *Sowing the Wind*:[2] namely, that its urgency and consequently its dramatic interest are destroyed by the fact that the social question it presents is really a solved one. Its production after *Les Surprises de Divorce* (which Mr. Grundy himself adapted for England) was an anachronism. When we succeed in adjusting our social structure in such a way as to enable us to solve social questions as fast as they become really pressing, they will no longer force their way into the theatre. Had Ibsen, for instance, had any reason to believe that the abuses to which he called attention in his prose plays would have been adequately attended to without his interference, he would no doubt have gladly left them alone. The same exigency drove William Morris in England from his tapestries, his epics, and his masterpieces of printing, to try and bring his fellow-citizens to their senses by the summary process of shouting at them in the streets and in Trafalgar Square. John Ruskin's writing began with *Modern Painters*; Carlyle began with literary studies of German culture and the like: both were driven to become revolutionary pamphleteers. If people are rotting and starving in all directions, and nobody else has the heart or brains to make a disturbance about it, the great writers must. In short, what is forcing our poets to follow Shelley in becoming political and social agitators, and to turn the theatre into a platform for propaganda and an arena for discussion, is that whilst social questions are being thrown up for solution almost daily by the fierce rapidity with which industrial processes change and supersede one another through the rivalry of the competitors who take no account of ulterior social consequences, and by the change in public feeling produced by popular "education," cheap literature, facilitated travelling, and so forth, the political machinery by which alone our institutions can be kept abreast of these changes is so old-fashioned, and so hindered in its action by the ignorance, the apathy, the stupidity, and the class feuds of the electorate, that social questions never get solved until the pressure becomes so desperate that even governments recognize the necessity for moving. And to bring the pressure to this point, the poets must lend a hand to the few who are willing to do public work in the stages at which nothing but abuse is to be gained by it.

---

[2]Evidently a slip for *Slaves of the Ring*, mentioned above. This play was the subject of Shaw's first contribution to *The Saturday Review* as dramatic critic (January 5, 1895.) He had printed on March 23, 1895, a comment on a revival of *Sowing the Wind*, which he found better than Grundy's usual product.

Clearly, however, when the unhappy mobs which we now call nations and populations settle down into ordered commonwealths, ordinary bread-and-butter questions will be solved without troubling the poets and philosophers. The Shelleys, the Morrises, the Ruskins, and Carlyles of that day will not need to spend their energies in trying to teach elementary political economy to other members of the commonwealth; nor will the Ibsens be devising object lessons in spoiled womanhood, sickly consciences, and corrupt town councils, instead of writing great and enduring dramatic poems.

I need not elaborate the matter further. The conclusions to be drawn are:

1. Every social question, arising as it must from a conflict between human feeling and circumstances, affords material for drama.

2. The general preference of dramatists for subjects in which the conflict is between man and his apparently inevitable and eternal rather than his political and temporal circumstances, is due in the vast majority of cases to the dramatist's political ignorance (not to mention that of his audience), and in a few to the comprehensiveness of his philosophy.

3. The hugeness and complexity of modern civilizations and the development of our consciousness of them by means of the press, have the double effect of discrediting comprehensive philosophies by revealing more facts than the ablest man can generalize, and at the same time intensifying the urgency of social reforms sufficiently to set even the poetic faculty in action on their behalf.

4. The resultant tendency to drive social questions on to the stage, and into fiction and poetry, will eventually be counteracted by improvements in social organization, which will enable all prosaic social questions to be dealt with satisfactorily long before they become grave enough to absorb the energies which claim the devotion of the dramatist, the storyteller, and the poet.

MUSIC

AGE-OLD SEARCH FOR MEANING

OVERVIEW

In an earlier lesson about film, we are asked to consider whether popular entertainment can be considered a true art form. Music, too, is a form of popular entertainment, yet why does no one seem to question its place among the arts? It is true that folk, jazz, and rock are not usually thought of as art in the same sense as Bach and Beethoven; even so, a little objective exploration will reveal that even the "Top 40" tunes listed by *Billboard Magazine* each week are basically composed according to theories and techniques of music that are centuries old.

This lesson focuses upon the history and development of music in all its forms. Music in some form has existed since prehistoric times. Indeed, it is suggested that music may be the primordial art form—the form in which men and women first expressed their feelings and longings about the mysteries of life and the way in which they first questioned the meanings of things. Music may have evolved first from sounds uttered for pure pleasure and from sounds uttered in imitation of nature, then finally perhaps from these to heretofore unspoken sounds of human questioning.

As technology allowed, music became both an expression of humankind's unceasing quest for self and the individual's growing awareness of self.

Like drama, music may have had its *formal* beginning in ritualism and religious observance. The Gregorian chant heard in the television program is typical of the early use of music in ritual and religion. Ritual music acquired drama and power in the twelfth and thirteenth centuries, as did architecture, which abandoned the old domed, basilican forms for the bolder Romanesque round arches and massive walls. In fact, some historians see a close relationship between developing styles of music and architecture in the Middle Ages.

The Medieval period also saw the first stirrings of the development and spread of music into Western culture. The Italian monk Guido and the written notation system he devised that made it possible to write down music opened the way for the average musician to understand music and, in turn, instruct others in it. Before Guido, music had been learned largely by ear. Guido's achievement was perhaps as important to the subsequent spread and development of music as was the concept of written language to literature.

With the Renaissance (1300–1600) came polyphonic music—music with harmony. We hear music of Palestrina from this period, and the textbook suggests several approaches to listening to this music. The motet and the madrigal are the outstanding vocal forms to emerge from this period.

Following the Renaissance came a period known as the Baroque and its offspring, the Rococo, periods typified by increasing musical complexity and ornamentation. In these years, development in musical technique almost surpassed the technology of musical instruments, but advances in the construction of instruments soon led to the development of the orchestra. The opera, which first appeared in these eras, developed from a relatively simple to a highly ornate form. In the television program we hear examples from Monteverdi's *Poppea*, written while opera was still in its infancy, and from *Don Giovanni*, a work still part of standard repertory. We also hear excerpts from Bach's Brandenburg Concertos and the *St. Matthew Passion*.

The Classic period is characterized for us as the Age of Revolution, and Beethoven is described for us as perhaps the greatest of composers of this period. This was the age of the symphony, the sonata, and the concerto.

In the years called the Romantic period (1830–1900), musical forms became somewhat freer, and program music associated with specific objects or events came into vogue.

The Modern era is seen, in part, as one of experimentation. New approaches to tonality and music theory are applied, and technology is making new forms of music possible, especially electronic music. It is possible that this new technological age may someday be considered as significant as the work of Stradivarius and Guenarius in the seventeenth century in developing the art of instrument construction to near-perfection.

As a final note, we consider seriously and sympathetically the field of "popular music" along with other eras and genres of music. Even though we lack a technical knowledge of music, the descriptions of the accomplishments and styles of each era should suggest to us the many periods to which popular music is indebted. We may also be surprised to learn that popular music is not so experimental or innovative as is some serious modern music (some of it many years old).

For most of us, no matter what our musical tastes, there are new horizons of music to encounter for the first time. Perhaps it is new music made possible by electronic instruments, or perhaps it is music from another period originally composed to express the realities of another time and place. Either may convey meaning to us, giving enjoyment just as timeless to us and just as meaningful as was the enjoyment of the baby singing to itself in the opening moments of the television presentation.

LEARNING OBJECTIVES

ON COMPLETING YOUR STUDY OF THIS LESSON, YOU SHOULD BE ABLE TO:

1. Identify the years and some composers associated with several musical periods.
2. Describe the various approaches to harmony and consonance typical of different eras of music.
3. Identify some developments in musical form and technique associated with the Baroque period.
4. Appreciate the scope of musical history and the wealth of listening experiences available from all periods of Western music.
5. Appreciate the lasting popularity of the opera form.

ASSIGNMENTS

BEFORE VIEWING THE PROGRAM:

Read the "Overview" and familiarize yourself with the "Learning Objectives" for this lesson.

Consult a dictionary or encyclopedia to acquaint yourself with these terms:

> Baroque
> Classic period (literature, music)
> consonance
> dissonance
> Gothic period
> monody
> polyphony
> Romantic period (literature, music)

Look over the "Aids for Study" for this lesson.

In the study guide:
> •Read "A Brief Glossary of Styles and Genres—with Suggestions for Listening" (pages 114–131).

VIEW THE TELEVISION PROGRAM *Music: Age-old Search for Meaning."*

AFTER VIEWING THE PROGRAM:

In the textbook:
> •Review Chapter 2, "What Is a Work of Art" (pages 17–45) with particular attention to examples and descriptions referring to music.

Review what you have learned, using the "Aids for Study" again.

Evaluate your learning with the "Review Quiz," then check your answers with the "Answer Key" at the back of this study guide.

In accordance with your own interests or your instructor's assignment, complete selected "Additional Activities."

AIDS FOR STUDY

1. What is monodic musical style? How was early Gregorian chant related to monodic music?

2. What development in the Medieval years made it possible to write out exact musical pitches and melodies, freeing a musician from having to memorize all music?

3. What musical forms for the human voice are distinctively associated with the Renaissance? Which of these was essentially religious in character? Which was essentially secular?

4. As a period of musical history, the Renaissance covers which years? Which of the composers listed in "A Brief Glossary of Styles and Genres" was discussed in the television program? Why was his music especially favored by the Church?

5. What is especially characteristic of Renaissance music in its use of harmonious, pleasing combinations of notes?

6. What relationship do some historians see between the development of architecture and the development of music during the Medieval period? Try to recall a specific example.

7. What years are designated as the Baroque era? Which two makers of musical instruments are important to this period, and what is the significance of their work? Which new musical-dramatic form first appeared in this period? Of the Baroque composers listed in the Glossary, which is mentioned especially in the television program?

8. What is especially characteristic of the use of melodic lines in Baroque music? How does the use of consonance and dissonance in this era differ from most Renaissance music?

9. How is the Classic age of music described in the television program? What political and social events from this era are best remembered? Which composer of this period is selected for discussion in the television program?

10. In what ways does the music of the Classic era surpass the mus
of the Baroque in complexity and sophistication? How is
dissonance employed more fully in this period?

11. What are the years assigned to the Romantic age of music?
Which composer of this period is mentioned as combining music,
drama, and literature?

12. Describe how the Romantic composers used harmony to a greater
extent than did Classic composers, yet emphasized dissonance
even more than the preceding era.

13. When is the Modern musical era said to have begun? What new
trend, which has become possible only in this era, was
demonstrated during the television program? Name one composer
who uses this new medium. Who are composers of a neoclassic
style? What two composers are mentioned who no longer employ
a single "tonal center" for their music? To what extent is
dissonance employed in modern music?

14. Contrast the use of harmony and dissonance in today's "popular
music" with the use of these elements in much of the music
discussed under "The Modern Era."

REVIEW QUIZ

Select the one best answer.

1. The Modern era of music began about
   a. 1800.
   b. 1850.
   c. 1900.
   d. 1950.

2. Which of the following was characteristic of the Renaissance?
   a. motets and madrigals
   b. symphonies and operas
   c. romances and variations
   d. concertos and symphonies

3. The Baroque era is considered to have begun about
   a. 1300.
   b. 1600.
   c. 1750.
   d. 1850.

4. Which of the following is a composer of the Renaissance?
   a. Bach
   b. Beethoven
   c. Palestrina
   d. Berlioz

5. Which of the following periods contains music that employs some dissonances, but relies mainly on consonances and melodic line?
   a. Modern
   b. Romantic
   c. Classic
   d. Baroque

6. The music of which of these eras employs dissonance extensively, sometimes ending a work without resolving into consonance?
   a. Modern
   b. Romantic
   c. Classic
   d. Baroque

7. Which of the following is a composer of the classical period?
   a. Bach
   b. Beethoven
   c. Palestrina
   d. Ives

8. Which of the following identifies two developments in musical history that occurred in the Baroque?
   a. development of the large symphony orchestra and the opera
   b. development of excellent musical instruments and the madrigal form
   c. development of musical instruments and the opera
   d. development of the large symphony orchestra and of the symphony form

9. In which era was instrumental music extensively composed that attempted to interpret an object or a literary work?
   a. Classic
   b. Romantic
   c. Modern
   d. Baroque

10. Which of the following is *not* characteristic of the Modern era of music?
   a. extensive use of dissonance
   b. music composed without "tonal center"
   c. electronic music
   d. extensive employment of harmonies

ADDITIONAL ACTIVITIES

1. From the perception keys for each of the periods of music listed in the Glossary of Styles and Genres, select one for a period with which you have not been previously acquainted. Follow the directions of the perception key, listening to at least one work from the period. Discuss which characteristics of this period, as described in the Glossary, were most evident to you from your listening.

2. From the information presented in the television program and the Glossary of Styles and Genres, summarize the history of music both as a development in use of melody and as a development of the use of consonance and dissonance. Comment on whether or not you feel audiences may become more accustomed to dissonances, atonal music, or polytonal music.

3. Comment on the development of opera form, giving your opinion as to why it has continued in popularity through several periods of music. If you are familiar with any classic, romantic, or modern opera, discuss the elements of drama that may contribute to the continuing popularity of opera.

A BRIEF GLOSSARY OF STYLES AND GENRES —WITH SUGGESTIONS FOR LISTENING

F. David Martin
Lee A. Jacobus

As a way of helping interested listeners, this glossary of musical styles should serve as a guide to different styles of music. All the compositions that are named are available on record and are in the *Schwann Record Guide*. No specific recording is suggested, since recordings come into and go out of print with such rapidity that such suggestions often become obsolete.

RENAISSANCE: 1300–1600

Guillaume Dufay (1400–1474), hymns and songs. Josquin Des Pres (ca. 1440–1521), *Missa Pange Lingua, Missa L'Homme Arme*, motets. Giovanni Palestrina (1525–1594), Magnificat, *Missa Sine Nomine*, motets. Roland de Lassus (1532–1594), *St. Matthew Passion*, motets, and madrigals. Giovanni Gabrieli (1551–1612), assorted canzoni for brass instruments,

madrigals, and motets. Carlo Gesualdo (1560–1613), madrigals and
motets.

Much of the instrumental music of the Renaissance was composed for
dancers, although some was also composed for use in the church. The
dance pieces of the Renaissance are still among the most delightful of
any period. The slow pavanne, the more frenetic morris dance, and the
speedy galiard are still being danced. The music composed for such dances
naturally correlates with the needs—in terms of tempo and contrast—of
the dances themselves. Some of the composers named above wrote music
for the dance, and the best way to listen to it is to find an anthology
record such as *Dance Music of the Renaissance* (Musical Heritage Society,
Inc., Tinton Falls, N.J.).

The instrumental music composed for religious purposes seems
designed for churches—such as Giovanni Cabrieli's antiphonal (meaning
sounds opposite or answering one another) pieces for brass, in which one
brass chorus in one cross section of a church would answer another chorus
in the opposite section. The resounding echoes from the church stonework,
with the persistence of partials as well as primary tones, produced
unexpected timbres and unexpected consonant-dissonant combinations.
This music is still played today and is still exciting to hear.

But the music written for the voice in the Renaissance probably seems
more significant to us now than that written for instruments, brilliant as
the instrumental writing is. The masses of Des Pres and Palestrina—as
well as those by Dufay, whose *Missa L'Homme Arme* is almost as well
known as Des Pres' on the same theme—are the most ambitious
compositions of the period. Setting the words of the mass to music
involves a careful attention to the meaning of those words and a careful
interpretation in musical terms of that meaning. Consequently, it is
always wise to read the words of the mass before listening to a mass of
any period.

Madrigals—songs written in the native or vernacular language
rather than in Latin—were immensely popular throughout the entire
Renaissance. Roland de Lassus' madrigals are exceptionally influential
and beautiful. Most important Renaissance composers wrote madrigals,
and many contemporary singing societies include them in their
repertory—consequently many may sound familiar. Motets were also
words set to music but usually Latin words. The form was contrapuntal,
with an organ on bass line and the words sung in the upper registers.

LISTEN FOR:

1. Smooth consonance and very little dissonance except for occasional accent.
2. Careful attention paid to the text, with the music, especially its rhythms, usually imitative to some extent of the words.
3. Relatively conservative and restricted use of dynamics except occasionally in some instrumental music.
4. A smooth, sonorous quality to the voices, with careful distinctions between soprano, alto, tenor, and bass, emphasizing the beauty of the voices, their contrasts, and their blending.
5. Relatively slight tension building, with very quick release in treatment of themes—theme one, usually a few measures, will come to a resting point just as theme two, often very similar in quality, begins. This pattern repeats throughout.
6. Slight use of contrasts, relatively restricted range of pitch.

PERCEPTION KEY RENAISSANCE MUSIC

1. Listen to a Renaissance composition for instruments and one for voices. Compare them by means of descriptive analysis for their uses of musical elements. Which seems to you to be more imaginative or successful in the handling of timbres, tempos, contrasts, dynamics, and musical tension?
2. Listen to a song written by Byrd (1540–1623), Morley (1557–1602), or Dowland (1560–1626). How carefully integrated is the music with the text? What techniques were used by the composer to make the music congruent with the words? Was he successful? Be detailed in your discussion.

BAROQUE: 1600–1750

Claudio Monteverdi (1567–1643), *Carnival Songs, Vespers for the Blessed Virgin, Moral and Spiritual Pieces,* madrigals and incidental songs. Henry Purcell (1659–1695), *Masque: The Faerie Queene, King Arthur,* songs. Antonio Vivaldi (1675–1741), *The Four Seasons;* concertos for lute, flute, and many combinations of instruments. J. S. Bach (1685–1750), the Brandenburg Concertos, Mass in B Minor, *Art of Fugue, St. Matthew Passion, Well-tempered Clavier,* cantatas, fugues and concertos for various instruments. G. F. Handel (1685–1759), *Messiah, The Creation,* Concerto Grosso in D Major.

Madrigals and songs, as well as larger compositions for voice and instruments, continue to be important for the composers of this period. Most of these have a religious subject matter, but many do not. Purcell's writing is conspicuous for its treatment of secular English and Irish traditional material. Yet, masses and religious cantatas—as well as such church instrumental compositions as Bach's organ preludes—are consistently popular. The church's influence is all but imperceptible in the concertos of Vivaldi, Bach, and Handel, in which the subject matter is certainly not religious but much more the kind of subject matter we associated with pure music, that of feeling abstracted from specific objects or events.

Purcell, Bach, and Handel are products of the Reformation, the splitting away of the Protestant churches from Catholicism. The Protestants needed religious music, although they wanted it to be of a less gaudy nature than Catholic music. Yet, Protestant church music sounds very much the same to our ears as Catholic music even though much Protestant music was based on religious hymns written by such men as Martin Luther. The rapid increase of wealthy families in this period made it possible to support a secular music designed not to uplift the audience in a religious sense but simply to entertain its sensibilities. The more purely instrumental music, as well as Monteverdi's songs and the vocal works of Purcell, were often designed to attend to the needs of a nonchurchly audience.

As a consequence, Baroque music tended to be more richly ornamented, brilliant, and vigorous than the simpler—relatively speaking—Renaissance compositions. It is also more ambitious and sometimes more superficial.

LISTEN FOR:

1. Considerable tension in the drive of tempos, although not necessarily much variety in tempos within a composition.
2. Virtuosity in melodic lines, with ingenious counterpoint and carefully sustained melodic tension developed by the constant playing of one melodic line against another.
3. Considerable contrast achieved through varieties of pitch in a composition—though most Baroque music emphasizes the upper registers—and through varieties in timbres.
4. Contrast achieved through the pitting of one instrument against the orchestra, the concerto; or contrast achieved by pitting a small group of instruments against the orchestra, the concerto grosso.
5. Attention to structures such as rondo and theme and variations, indicating an attempt to explore the resources of thematic material.
6. Interesting uses of harmony, particularly in the passions and cantatas of Bach and in the oratorios of Handel (dramatic musical compositions closely related to opera, but without the addition of the spectacle of acting.)
7. Greater tolerance of dissonances, particularly those that involve more than two dissonant tones.

PERCEPTION KEY BAROQUE MUSIC

1. Listen to two compositions, one religious, such as Bach's *St. Matthew Passion* or Monteverdi's *Vespers for the Blessed Virgin*, and one which is secular, such as Vivaldi's *The Four Seasons*, or Purcell's *Masque: The Faerie Queene*. Begin by describing the general impressions they give you. Do you detect a religious subject matter in the religious composition? Do you detect the secular nature of the nonreligious composition? What uses of tempos, dynamics, timbres, and contrasts do the compositions share? What uses seem more peculiar to each? Can secular music be distinguished from religious music by reference to their use of musical elements?

2. Listen to at least one concerto or concert grosso. Describe it as carefully as possible in terms of its use of melodic material, its concerns for counterpoint, its interest in harmony, and the means by which it achieves contrast and tension. Is tension relieved at the points of arrival—the endings of musical phrases or sections of the composition—by means of the cadences we described in discussing a sense of ending in Question 3 of the perception key [textbook page 281 on "Swing Low, Sweet Chariot"?

CLASSIC: 1750–1830

Franz Josef Haydn (1732–1809), Symphony in G major, No. 94, the *Surprise;* Symphony in D major, No. 101, the *Clock;* String Quartet No. 2 (Opus-76—which contains six fine quartets); *The Seven Last Words of Christ.* Wolfgang Amadeus Mozart (1756–1791), *Requiem,* Symphony in C major, the *Jupiter;* Concerto for Piano, No. 21 in C major; *Eine Kleine Nachtmusik* (or Serenade in G major). Ludwig van Beethoven (1770–1827), Symphony No. 5 in C minor; Symphony No. 6 in F major, the *Pastorale;* Symphony No. 9 in D minor, the *Chorale;* the Rasumovsky Quartets (Nos. 1, 2, 3).

Although most of the classic composers produced some religious music, it was not their principal activity. Haydn's Mass in D minor, for Lord Nelson, may be as political as it is religious. Yet, Mozart's *Requiem* may be the greatest ever written, and Beethoven's *Missa Solemnis* compares well with the masses of the great ages of religion. But these are limited examples. Haydn's 104 symphonies were written to amuse a small courtly audience that demanded new musical material for its weekly concerts. Mozart wrote for a broader musical audience that included the bourgeosie, not just the aristocrats. Their taste was not for religious music.

Classic composers built on the tonal experiments of the Baroque. They developed, for example, the sense of keyness and key interrelationship that Bach clearly valued. They also developed the vertical chordal texture that is usually lacking in most Baroque music, which emphasized counterpoint. Their harmony is basically triadic, as described in the section on tonal music, which builds on three-note chords and their variants—such as C-E-G in the key of C. The classic composers also developed the larger structures with predetermined repetitive structures, such as the sonata form, the rondo, and the minuet.

The melodic lines in classic compositions are often long and sustained, and they have a highly distinct quality to them that makes them more recognizable than most Baroque melodies. In Bach's Brandenburg Concerto No. 2 you will hear many melodies, but you will tend to be attracted to the texture of the sounds: the tone colors, dynamics, and contrapuntal effects. A classic composition calls attention to its structural qualities, since the textural elements of harmony and dynamics are controlled by the demands of strong key-based chords to "back up" the melodies as prescribed by the structure.

The texture of Beethoven's Symphony No. 5 does not closely resemble that of the *Brandenburg Concerto No. 2.* For one thing, our ear hears elements in the Beethoven that are clearly building blocks. The most famous motif in the symphony [shown below] is stated first by all the

Beginning motif from Beethoven's Symphony No. 5.

strings and the clarinets, then by second violins alone, then first violins, then violas, and on and on until another motif based on this first one appears. Then the original motif finds its way into the background sounds, which we have to strain to listen for until we begin to understand the motif is not there just to be listened to in isolation: It is there as a clearly identifiable unit that helps build the structure.

LISTEN FOR:

1. A dramatic variety in use of tempos, even within a small section of a composition.
2. Strong, well-highlighted melodies that are sometimes sustained for a relatively long time.
3. Melodic material, such as the beginning motif in Beethoven's Symphony No. 5, that contributes as a building block to the structure of the work.
4. Contrast achieved by means of opposing timbres of different families of instruments: strings, brasses, woodwinds, and percussion all taking clearly identifiable roles in a piece for orchestra.

5. Great dynamic range, particularly in Beethoven and the music of the later part of the period; less of a dynamic range in Haydn, although his experiments—in the *Surprise* Symphony, for instance—are interesting.
6. Full development of forms such as the rondo, the sonata form, theme and variations.
7. Full triadic harmony, with emphasis on exploiting the "keyness" of the scale employed; dependence on a strong tonic center and the exploitation of the contrast of related keys.
8. Strong dissonant passages preparing for powerful resolutions of cadential consonance; dissonance for emphasis and dramatic purposes.

PERCEPTION KEY CLASSIC MUSIC

1. Listen closely to a symphony of Haydn. Describe each movement of the symphony in terms of its uses of basic musical elements. Can you determine the kinds of general feelings that might be revealed and evoked by each of the movements? Are they contrasted from movement to movement? What are the principal means of contrast used from movement to movement? Which movements seem to have the most in common in their uses of musical elements?
2. Listen to the last movement of Haydn's *Clock* Symphony, Mozart's *Jupiter* Symphony, and Beethoven's *Pastorale* Symphony. Which of these seems most clearly to have feeling as part of its subject matter? Is the sound of the clock a part of the subject matter of the Haydn symphony? Are the sounds of nature part of the subject matter of the Beethoven symphony? What kinds of insight, if any, are revealed to you by each of these works? In answering this question, refer to the musical elements that influence your conclusions.

ROMANTIC: 1800–1900

HECTOR BERLIOZ (1803–1869), *Symphony Fantastique, Romeo and Juliet, Roman Carnival Overture, Requiem.* Felix Mendelssohn (1809–1847), Concerto in E minor for Violin, *Incidental Music for A Midsummer Night's Dream;* Symphony No. 4, the *Italian.* Frederick Chopin (1810–1849), preludes or waltzes for piano. Johannes Brahms (1833–1897), Symphony No. 1 in C minor; *Variations on a Theme by Haydn;* Concerto for Violin and Orchestra; Double Concerto for Violin, Cello, and Orchestra; *Hungarian Dances.* Peter Tchaikovsky (1840–1893), *Swan Lake, The Nutcracker Suite,* Concerto No. 1 in B$^\flat$ minor for Piano, *Romeo and Juliet,* Symphony No. 4 in F minor.

The careful work of the classic composers in establishing cadential patterns, leading to strong rest points and even stronger ending points at the conclusion of compositions, is modified in the romantic style—particularly the later music of Wagner (his works are suggested for listening in the section on opera). In some of Wagner's music, the horizontal line of the melody seems to have no rest points at all. The melodies seem almost interminable, though some are clearly shaped and recognizable as they return again and again. Wagner also often used building-unit motifs—somewhat similar to those used by Beethoven in his Symphony No. 5—for example the "look motif" from *Tristan und Isolde,* and the "sword motif" from *The Ring of the Niebelungs.* Unlike Beethoven's, Wagner's motifs are associated with specific objects or events and are used to refer to or interpret them.

Reference to specific objects and events in romantic music is much greater, in general, than in classic music. In works such as the *Pastorale* Symphony, Beethoven begins the trend toward such reference. But romantic composers are vastly more ambitious in this regard than those who went before them. Berlioz and Tchaikovsky were not the only composers to dedicate a work to one of Shakespeare's plays or to try to make their musical composition refer to and interpret a piece of literature. The occasional marriage of music, literature, and dance, as in Tchaikovsky's *Swan Lake,* seems entirely easy and natural in the romantic period.

Some of the classic structures—such as the sonata form and the larger structure built on it, the symphony—persist in the works of Mendelssohn, Brahms, and Tchaikovsky in particular. But the expansion of the orchestra, with sometimes more than a hundred pieces, helped the romantic composer build the classic structures into something enormously expansive, with huge waves of sound that were all but impossible for classic composers who rarely had or needed huge orchestras. The size of the orchestra seems also to have affected the character of the concerto, with the solo instrument concentrating on extraordinary virtuosity as a help in balancing the relationship between a piano or violin, say, and the entire orchestra.

LISTEN FOR:

1. Careful use of tempos, particularly those that are extreme in speed, or, more frequently, extreme in slowness.
2. Melodic lines that are lengthy, often growing into new melodic lines without clear transitions.
3. Greater contrasts of dynamics than found in classic music, occasional bombast as in certain works of Berlioz and Tchaikovsky.
4. Interest in varieties of timbres on a grand scale, with choruses of instruments of a different family.
5. Appearance of less predetermined structures such as the nocturne, the aubade, the serenade, the capriccio, etudes, and sonatas that are not sonata-form compositions.
6. Harmonic texture strong, noticeable, and sustained; harmonies generally much more significant than in classic music in the sense that they are more obvious, more in competition with the melodic line for attention.
7. Greater emphasis and reliance on dissonances and lesser interest in consonance as a means of relieving tension.
8. Growing interest in exploring the capacities of music to refer to specific objects and events, and thus emphasis on program music and opera.

PERCEPTION KEY ROMANTIC MUSIC

1. After having read Shakespeare's *Romeo and Juliet,* listen to
    Berlioz's and Tchaikovsky's compositions of the same title. Is
    there a perceptible connection between the musical compositions
    and the play? Can you conclude that the compositions are
    interpretations of the play? Is it possible to decide which of the
    musical compositions is more faithful to the play, or which is
    more successful in its effort at interpretation?
2. Analyze the use of musical elements in a nonprogrammatic piece
    of Romantic music such as a concerto or a symphony. Describe
    carefully the use of tempos, melodic lines, harmonic qualities,
    dynamics, and anything else you believe is relevant. Does your
    description correlate with descriptions of the same piece made
    by other listeners?
3. Having performed the analysis in Question 2 above, do you feel
    confident in holding an opinion about the success of the
    composition? How do your opinions relate to those of others who
    have performed the same analysis? How do they relate to those
    who have not performed the analysis at all?

MODERN: 1900–PRESENT

Gustav Mahler (1860–1911), *Kindertotenlieder, Das Lied von der Erde,*
Symphony No. 8 in E$^\flat$, *Symphony of a Thousand;* Symphony No. 9 in D
major. Claude Debussy (1862–1918), *La Mer, Nocturnes, Clair de Lune,*
Children's Corner Suite. Richard Strauss (1864–1949), *Death and*
Transfiguration, Don Quixote, Till Eulenspiegel, Thus Sprach
Zarathustra. Ralph Vaughan Williams (1872–1958), Mass in G minor;
Symphony No. 1, *Sea;* Symphony No. 7, *Antarctica.* Arnold Schoenberg
(1874–1951), *Transfigured Night, Pierrot Lunaire.* Charles Ives (1874–
1954), *Three Places in New England, Holidays* Symphony. Maurice
Ravel (1875–1937), *Bolero,* Concerto in D major for the Left Hand (piano),
Rhapsodie Espagnole. Ernest Block (1880–1959), Schelomo, Rhapsody for
Cello and Orchestra. Bela Bartók (1891–1945), *Concerto for Orchestra;*
Miraculous Mandarin Suite; Music for Strings, Percussion, and Celesta.
Igor Stravinsky (1882–1971), *Firebird: Suite, Petrouchka, The Rites of*
Spring, Oedipus Rex, Symphony of Psalms. Edgar Varese (1885–1965),
Deserts, Ionization. John Cage (1912–   ), *Variation IV, Indeterminacy.*
Benjamin Britten (1913–1976), *Young Person's Guide to the Orchestra,*
War Requiem. Karl-Heinz Stockhausen (1928–   ), *Mikrophonie I for*

Tam-tam, 2 Microphones, & Filters, & Potentiometers. Krzysztof Penderecki (1933–), *Threnody for the Victims of Hiroshima, Dies Irae* (Auschwitz Oratorio).

Much of the music of the older composers of the modern period, such as Mahler, is close to the Romantics, continuing similar attitudes toward dissonance, rich harmonics, and program music. The younger composers often moved away from a tonal center. Like Schoenberg, they used atonality, an approach that treats all notes of a scale as equal in value, with no tonic, dominant, or mediant notes. Others, like Charles Ives, sometimes employed polytonality, in which melodic lines written in different keys were sounded together. The effect of having two strong key-based lines operating simultaneously can be very exciting. "July 4th" in Ives' *Holidays* Symphony is an interesting example, as one seems to hear two marching bands playing two different tunes marching toward, then through, one another. This actually was something Charles Ives once saw when he was a child watching his father's marching bands entertaining an audience in Danbury, Connecticut, on July fourth.

Some composers, such as Bartók, Stravinsky, and Paul Hindemith (1895–1963), developed a neoclassicism that tried to combine classic formal structures with the expansiveness of the Romantic approach to the use of mythic inspiration and literary sources. Their music has generally been well received, helping us to reevaluate the achievement of the classic composers.

Composers such as Luciano Berio (1925–) and Stockhausen have been working in the medium of electronic music and, sometimes, nontonal sounds or noises. Their work has been difficult for contemporary audiences to appreciate because it breaks so sharply with the traditions of the past. Some audiences treat their works as if they were not music at all. The absence of a strong tonal center and the use of noises have been enough to make it very difficult for some audiences to respond positively. The timbres achieved by electronic synthesizers have also been difficult for audiences used to the sounds of traditional musical instruments. One of the positive virtues of electronic music is the calling into question the perhaps dogmatic conception of music as having organized tones as its medium. When all sound is at the disposal of composers, their limits and their ambitions must be considerably different from those of their predecessors, who generally relied upon clearly defined scales and predetermined structures.

LISTEN FOR:

1. Wide variety of tempos, with strong accents and dramatic emphasis; sudden shifts and stops.

2. Melodic lines that resemble, in many cases, those of the Baroque—continuous, restless—and, in fewer cases, those of the classic period.

3. Fragmentation of melodic material in some cases, with themes that do not have the clearly perceptible beginning, middle, and end of traditional music; melodic lines that seem bits and pieces of sound, almost randomly organized, yet obviously linear—or horizontal—in their progress.

4. Considerable interest in timbres, even in the more traditional-sounding compositions, but extraordinary interest in electronic timbres and timbres of objects not ordinarily thought of as musical instruments.

5. Wide variety of structures borrowed from traditional music, but also structures that are not predetermined, that seem to develop and grow in accord with the musical potentialities.

6. Harmonies often similar to those of the Romantics, but much less concern for harmony as such—less reliance on harmony for overall orchestral color or for emphasis and ending.

7. Wide range of dynamics, but a tendency to be more abrupt, to shift dynamics without warning.

8. Preference for percussive effects and an expanded use of percussion instruments in all kinds of compositions.

9. More tolerance for dissonances, even to the extent of using them for the ending points of compositions; consonance does not necessarily resolve tensions nor dissonances create them.

10. Interest in nontonal sounds or noises.

PERCEPTION KEY MODERN MUSIC

1. Choose a piece of music such as the *Firebird: Suite, Ionization,* or *Threnody for the Victims of Hiroshima* and analyze it for its capacity to create, sustain, and resolve tension. What seem to be its resources, in terms of musical elements, for producing tension?

Are they vastly different from those of traditional music, or are they much the same?

2. Listen to a piece of music by any two composers listed as modern. Be sure their birth dates are a generation apart. Compare their treatment of specific musical elements—tempo, melody, harmony, dynamics, timbres, etc. How different are they? How do the chief differences affect your comparative evaluations of their works?

3. Choose a piece of electronic music and describe its use of musical elements. Are there any musical elements possessed by electronic music that are absent from traditional music? Explain the relative importance of each element used in the composition. Do others agree with your judgments?

OPERA

Claudio Monteverdi (1567–1643), *Orfeo*. W. A. Mozart (1756–1791), *The Marriage of Figaro, Don Giovanni, The Magic Flute*. Gaetano Donizetti (1797–1848), *Don Pasquale, Lucia di Lammermoor, Robert Devereux*. Vincenzo Bellini (1801–1835), *Norma, La Sonnambula*. Richard Wagner (1813–1883), *Tristan and Isolde, The Flying Dutchman, Tannhäuser, Lohengrin*, the "Ring" cycle—*Das Rheingold, Die Walküre, Siegfried, Götterdammerung*. Guiseppe Verdi (1813–1901), *Aida, Macbeth, Rigoletto, La Traviata, The Force of Destiny, Otello, Falstaff*. Georges Bizet (1838–1875), *Carmen*. Giacomo Puccini (1858–1924), *La Bohème, Madame Butterfly, Turandot*. Richard Strauss (1864–1949), *Der Rosenkavalier, Salome*. Scott Joplin (1868–1917), *Treemonisha*. George Gershwin (1898–1937), *Porgy and Bess*. Kurt Weill (1900–1950), *Threepenny Opera*. Gian-Carlo Menotti (1911–   ), *Amahl and the Night Visitors, The Medium*. Benjamin Britten (1913–1976), *Peter Grimes*. Krzysztof Penderecki (1933–   ), *The Devils of Loudun, Paradise Lost*. The Who, *Tommy* (1969).

Because opera depends on a dramatic narrative, which is usually called the "libretto" (little book), it refers to specific events. In a way, the music has a program, but the program is not separate from the composition, as it would be with *La Mer* or any other wordless piece of program music. Opera's program is its story line, which is acted, sung, and sometimes spoken. Most operas are not written in English, so many Americans have trouble following the narratives of Wagner, Verdi, or Bizet, for example. But even operas in English are sometimes difficult to follow, since the musical demands occasionally make clear articulation difficult. The problem can be solved, usually, only by acquainting oneself with the libretto–just as one must acquaint oneself with the program of a piece of program music.

The subject matter of opera is more obvious than the subject matter of a piece of nonprogrammatic music. Opera still uses all the basic elements of music, but those elements are closely wedded to the needs of the unfolding drama. Opera usually interprets highly dramatic situations, such as the resolution in face of torture that Grandier displays in Penderecki's *Devils of Loudun* or the heroism Treemonisha displays when she is challenged by voodoo forces in Scott Joplin's ragtime opera, the first opera by a black American. The musical character of great arias often becomes much clearer when one knows the dramatic necessities they are serving—which is to say that the significance of the aria is clearer when we have heard it in the total context of the opera's dramatic spectacle.

The Who's recent success with the rock opera *Tommy*—not to mention similar successes with *Jesus Christ Superstar* and *Godspell*—should serve to remind us that opera is a highly popular art and not something reserved for esoteric tastes. In many European cities opera stars such as Montserrat Caballé, Jon Vickers, Joan Sutherland, Sherrill Milnes, and Luciano Pavarotti are cheered like soccer or film stars. Non-European audiences also usually react warmly to opera when they are thoroughly acquainted with the story. That should always be a listener's first step before hearing an opera: read the libretto.

LISTEN FOR:

1. Uses of musical elements such as tempo, melodic lines, timbre, harmony, and dynamics that are characteristic of the periods in which the operas are written.
2. Efforts to fuse the musical materials to the text being sung, as in the masses of the late Renaissance and the early Baroque—but now with secular material of a highly dramatic nature in motets and madrigals.
3. Frequent use of orchestral dynamics to help evoke an emotional response to the dramatic situation on stage or, if not to evoke the response, to suggest it or interpret it on behalf of the characters.
4. Vocal coloration to express dramatic emotion on the part of the character.

5. Occasional exaggeration of the dramatic situation as an effort to highlight emotional values—sometimes called melodrama (literally, drama with music.)
6. Featuring the human voice at its most beautiful, sometimes at the expense of the narrative, as a way of demonstrating the virtuosity of opera's principal musical instrument: the voice.
7. Means of creating tension musically, particularly as moments of tension are timed to the needs of the narrative.
8. Because of the reference to specific events as the cause of feeling, emphasis on feeling as emotion and passion.

PERCEPTION KEY OPERA

1. Choose an opera in English: *Peter Grimes*, Ralph Vaughan Williams' *Pilgrims' Progress*, *The Medium*, or the last act of *Treemonisha*. Acquaint yourself with the libretto. After listening to the opera, identify the kinds of emotions and passions interpreted by the singers. How successful is the opera in clarifying these feelings?
2. In the opera you have chosen, what are the most basic means used to build tension? Compare them with the tension-building means you have discovered in nonoperatic music.
3. After acquainting yourself with the libretto or synopsis of a non-English-language opera, such as an opera of Wagner or Verdi, listen for the ease or difficulty with which it establishes and interprets feelings—in comparison with an English-language opera. Do you find the foreign language an insurmountable difficulty in understanding the emotional interpretations even after you have studied the libretto?
4. Take an opera of a given period—Renaissance, Classic, Baroque, Romantic, or modern—and evaluate the ways in which it has used the stylistic resources of that period for the purposes of interpreting a dramatic narrative. Do the resources of that stylistic period lend themselves to the purposes the opera puts them? Does the opera do those resources an injustice? Explain and be specific in referring to the resources in question.

CONTEMPORARY POPULAR MUSIC

This category includes folk, jazz, soul, Latin, calypso, rock, and country and western. Since popular music changes very rapidly, our suggestions for this section avoid naming specific groups or albums. The genres of popular music are primarily those named above, but even those are subject to change, as the periodic surfacing and disappearance of rhythm and blues would suggest. It is noteworthy that popular music, like most folk arts, tends to be conservative in its use of the basic elements of music. Most of the music we hear on the radio, for instance, is strong in establishing a tonal center and respecting the implications of a key-based scale. It is also conservative in its use of steady tempos—with some halving and doubling of tempo permitted but little variation of a radical sort. Even the strongly rhythmic Latin music usually establishes a complex rhythmic pattern at the outset and maintains it to the end of the piece. The structure of most popular pieces is also conservative, with precise limits to the number of measures permitted in the verse and chorus of the piece. Building a piece on twelve- or sixteen-bar (measure) units is normal. The result of this is somewhat akin to the result of writing sonnets: sometimes the form will strangle inspiration, sometimes it will intensify inspiration and permit the artist to create "better than he knew."

LISTEN FOR:

1. Powerful tonal center with clear and intense cadences leading to rest points and conclusions.
2. Usually a distinct melodic line with a clear and recognizable principal melody and a strongly contrasting secondary melody.
3. Reliance on the A-B-A' form in which the first section is contrasted with the second section, then repeated as a means of reinforcing the conclusion.
4. Occasional disregard for melodic line—as in some modern jazz and "hard" rock—in which the line is not clearly shaped or "memorable," but is reminiscent of the texture of Baroque counterpoint: the melodic line pushes onward with vigor, but without much clarity.
5. Various approaches to dynamics, with some pieces totally unchanging and others changing in response to the text being sung or in hopes of offering a contrast to an earlier section.

6. Relatively simple harmonies, usually based on the most clearly delineated chords of the basic key, such as the major triad and the seventh and ninth chords.

7. Various approaches to dissonance—sometimes following the lead of the Classic period and sometimes that of the modern period of music.

8. Reliance on repetition of theme, lyrics, and entire sections.

9. Use of electronically amplified volume as a significant element of the musical experience.

10. Exploration of feelings related to high energy, tension, restlessness, and moods such as those associated with the blues.

PERCEPTION KEY CONTEMPORARY POPULAR MUSIC

1. Select a piece of music from a popular style you admire—folk, jazz, soul, or whatever. Clarify its use of basic musical elements in such a way that you are satisfied you are describing the essential characteristics of that particular style.

2. Compare two different popular styles. How do they use rhythm, tempo, melody, timbre, harmony, dynamics, and dissonance? Are the two styles very different from one another, or are they more similar than might first be thought?

3. What kinds of feelings might be considered the subject matter of the pieces you have chosen to discuss? How does the music help reveal those feelings? Do other listeners agree with you?

MUSIC

EMOTION AND FEELING IN SOUND

OVERVIEW

Earlier in this course, we were challenged to examine our individual
tastes and preferences in the arts. It was suggested that one's preferences
at any given time should not be criticized. But if we do not allow our
tastes to grow and expand, we miss more than the delight of new
discoveries. We may even be denying ourselves an opportunity for greater
maturity. As we will learn in this lesson, music is perhaps the most
"abstract" of the arts, and its subject matter is more difficult to define
than, for example, drama or film. For this reason, it may be tempting to
let our tastes in music remain unchanged, to continue to enjoy only that
with which we are already comfortable.

   The overall objective of this lesson is to suggest elements to listen for
in music, for it it the interplay of these elements that creates meaningful
music. To do this, we will study several terms that describe some
important elements of this art—"tone," "timbre," "consonance," and
"dissonance." Possibly we already can pick out the rhythm and the
melody in a tune, yet we may not consciously recognize the importance of
the harmony or the dynamics in a work we've just heard for the first

time. These terms are simply a set of words to identify aspects of music that we may perhaps have heard for years, perhaps recognizing them and enjoying them even if we did not know the technical terms for them. Our hope is that music will be more meaningful to us as we consciously recognize more of the aspects of sound that the composer employs to communicate with us.

Music does communicate something to us. The textbook explores for us, in our further reading, what it is that music communicates: music communicates its subject matter. (We are referring here, of course, to the music itself, and not to the words that are sung with some works.) The titles of some music refer to definite objects or events, yet the works can be enjoyed even if one doesn't know the title. Some authorities, we will learn, think the sounds themselves are the only subject matter of music, while still others think that feelings and emotions are an integral subject of music.

Finally, we explore what is known as "tonal music," which is the type of music with which most of us are familiar. And we further consider some other approaches to music mentioned in the preceding lesson—atonal and polytonal music. Even those of us who are not familiar with music theory or a musical instrument will be able to appreciate the concepts underlying these contemporary departures from traditional music. Still another departure is called nontonal music, which employs sounds rather than tones as basic elements.

There is always a question of the origins of our enjoyment of music. Does it come from inherited traits within ourselves, or is it learned from our culture? Undoubtedly, there are elements of both in our responses to music. As we continue exploring music and learning to respond to previously unfamiliar elements and forms, perhaps many of us will discover more of the essential music within ourselves.

LEARNING OBJECTIVES

ON COMPLETING YOUR STUDY OF THIS LESSON, YOU SHOULD BE ABLE TO:

1. Define the following terms: noise, tone, timbre, consonance, dissonance, rhythm, tempo, melody, harmony, and dynamics.
2. Describe several significant features of musical forms that treat tonality in different ways.
3. List alternative subject matter that has been suggested for music.
4. Appreciate the interplay of elements that, together, create a meaningful musical work.

ASSIGNMENTS

BEFORE VIEWING THE PROGRAM:

Read the "Overview" and familiarize yourself with the "Learning Objectives" for this lesson.

Consult a dictionary to acquaint yourself with these terms:

> emotion
> scale (musical)
> tension (psychology)

Look over the "Aids for Study" for this lesson.

In the textbook, Chapter 9, "Music":
  •Read pages 305–315 ("Appendix," "Definitions," and "Basic Elements").

VIEW THE TELEVISION PROGRAM *"Music: Emotion and Feeling in Sound."*

AFTER VIEWING THE PROGRAM:

In the textbook, Chapter 9, "Music":
• Read pages 271–285 ("Hearers and Listeners," "Problems of
Analysis," "The Subject Matter of Music," "The Referential
Capacity of Music," "Feelings," "Feelings and Musical Structures,"
"Formalism," "Expressionism," "Sound," "Tonal Music,"
"Atonality," "Polytonality," and "Nontonal Music").

Review what you have learned, using the "Aids for Study" again.

Evaluate your learning with the "Review Quiz," then check your answers
with the "Answer Key" at the back of this study guide.

In accordance with your own interests or your instructor's assignment,
complete selected "Additional Activities."

AIDS FOR STUDY

1. How does a "tone" differ from "noise"? What is a "pure tone"?

2. What is a timbre? How does the text definition explain that a
note sounded on a violin, for example, will be distinctive from
the same note sounded on a trumpet?

3. Consonance and dissonance refer to what quality of sounds?
What are the strongest consonances? Why are dissonances also
important to musical composition?

4. How do "rhythm" and "tempo" differ? (You might find it
helpful to visualize a drummer. One aspect of the drummer's
playing is the speed with which the drums are struck. Another
aspect is the pattern of emphasis or accent placed on certain
beats in a series.)

5. Have you previously used the word "shape" to explain or
describe a melody? Does the first sentence of the textbook's
explanation adequately describe all melodies with which you
are familiar?

6. How is harmony related to consonance and dissonance? What is a cadence? How do chord harmonies provide the "building blocks" for cadences? Did it surprise you to learn that harmony is not as "universal" in music as melody and rhythm?

7. What does "dynamics" refer to? What are some of the ways composers employ dynamics?

8. Perform at least one of the perception keys in the textbook sections "Definitions" and "Basic Elements" (pages 305–315), preferably in an area of musical elements with which you are relatively unfamiliar. Can you select an aspect of music discussed in this portion of the textbook that you have heard previously, yet had not identified by name?

9. Do you agree with the textbook that "it is difficult for music to refer to specific objects and events"? In what three ways can music arouse our emotions? Do we listen to music just for the relationships of the tones themselves?

10. What is the tonic or tonal center in tonal music? Why do most compositions end on this tone?

11. Review the section on consonance again, if necessary, and explain which notes are most important in tonal music. How does atonal music differ from tonal music? How does polytonal music differ from tonal music?

Select the best definition or description for each term on the left from the list on the right.

Term	Description/Definition

d ____ 1. consonance

h ____ 2. tempo

b ____ 3. tone

i ____ 4. harmony

c ____ 5. timbre

e ____ 6. dissonance

j ____ 7. dynamics

f ____ 8. rhythm

g ____ 9. melody

a. any movement of air in waves

b. any sound dominated by one frequency or pitch

c. a sound made by the addition of partial tones to a primary tone

d. two or more tones sounded together with a resulting soothing or pleasant sound

e. two or more tones sounded together with a resulting sound that is rough and unpleasant

f. the time taken to play a given note and the stress placed on certain notes in a series

g. a group of notes played in sequence, having a definite shape

h. the speed with which a sequence of notes is played

i. a series of notes played simultaneously, usually in a chord

j. degrees of loudness and softness in a musical work

Select the one best answer.

10. The form of music that has a "home tone" usually ending the work is called
    a. tonal music.
    b. atonal music.
    c. polytonal music.
    d. nontonal music.

11. A form of music in which no one note is more important than any
other is called
   a. tonal music.
   b. atonal music.
   c. polytonal music.
   d. nontonal music.

12. The authors of the textbook feel that the subject matter of music
probably relates most closely to
   a. the sounds themselves.
   b. objects and events other than music.
   c. feelings and emotions.
   d. colors and rhythm.

ADDITIONAL ACTIVITIES

1. Listen again to the music you selected for use with one of the
perception keys from pages 305–315 of the textbook (suggested by
Aids for Study, #8). Describe what you hear in the music and
commment on other elements of music and how they were used by
the composer.

2. If possible, listen to a work that is not tonal in nature. Comment
on the apparent presence or absence of rhythm, harmony, or
melody in describing the work.

3. Select a work of serious music for listening. Try to identify visual
scenes or events that relate to the emotions this work calls forth.
If you have selected a work that by title or description relates to
something other than music (such as Debussy's La Mer), see if
your emotions and feelings are similar to those you would
experience in the actual setting. Write a brief description of your
actual emotional responses.

MUSIC

MEANING THROUGH STRUCTURE

All of us have probably responded strongly on listening to a particular piece of music. In such instances, the musical composition sounds natural and appropriate to us and evokes certain emotions and feelings. However, other levels, experiences, and meanings can be achieved through music; it is the purpose of this lesson to provide us with knowledge that will enhance our ability to respond to the various complexities and subtleties inherent in a musical composition.

The textbook explores the basic patterns and forms of music that composers have employed for centuries. An understanding of these forms is important because they link together what may seem to be dissimilar musical compositions. We can more fully participate in, and find more meaning in, a given piece of music if we know something of the structure and form of the composition and of how the composer has used that form to accomplish his or her purpose. The specific forms and patterns described in this lesson include:

Theme and Variations: One theme or melody with a refrain that is
   repeated after each contrasting episode or theme.

Rondo: A musical pattern with a refrain that is repeated after each contrasting episode or theme.

Fugue: A form of repetition in which a theme or statement is followed by, and contrasts at the same time with, the same theme in a related key.

Sonata: A three-section statement; the first section contains a main theme and secondary theme. The first section is followed by a development section, in which the themes are explored in a variety of ways. The final section is the recapitulation, a repetition of the statement, but usually in the tonic key.

Fantasia: A form representative of less demanding structures employed by composers in the nineteenth century and later. The pattern is determined within the work itself and is not necessarily repeated, as it is in the preceding forms.

Program Music: Music designed to evoke feelings and responses associated with events outside the music itself. It may be composed to convey a setting, relate a story, or depict a natural or historical event.

Symphony: In the broadest sense, a symphony is a sonata for orchestra, usually in four movements: sonata, allegro, minuet and trio, and finale. Far from being four loosely connected compositions, a symphony is usually designed as an organic whole, complete in itself and presented in its entirety.

The textbook also explores some of the notations given to indicate tempo, or pacing, because tempo is one of the unifying elements employed by the composer to achieve unity and continuity in a composition.

The television program concentrates exclusively on the work of Johann Sebastian Bach, today felt to be the greatest of the Baroque composers. The examples presented for us are evidence that, as the host suggests, Bach not only perfected the musical forms of his era but laid a basis for succeeding composers and even modern music.

The richness of Bach's music is hinted at by the variety of instruments employed in the program. Bach's Air on the G-String is played on a harmonica. The Third Suite for Lute is performed on the instrument for which it is composed. A contemporary jazz group plays a Bach composition, demonstrating further the universality of his music, and in contrast, two of Bach's works are performed on the harpsichord, chief keyboard–string instrument of his time. Bach's music is also performed on an electronic music synthesizer, one of the most contemporary of modern musical instruments. A chamber orchestra performs music from Bach's Second Flute Suite, while dancers provide an interpretation of the music in another art form. The final selection in the program is the Fantasia in C minor.

Music meanings, just as the meanings of other art forms we have explored, do not always lend themselves readily to language. One meaning may be found in Maya Angelou's comments on the program: [music that] "sounds natural and right," as Bach's music does to him. Other meanings are implicit in your own reactions to the music. Still other meanings may be found by examining closely how a composer uses elements to construct a work.

LEARNING OBJECTIVES

ON COMPLETING YOUR STUDY OF THIS LESSON, YOU SHOULD BE ABLE TO:

1. Select the correct description of these musical forms: theme and variations, rondo, fugue, sonata, fantasia, program music, and symphony.
2. Identify the correct meaning of basic tempo markings.
3. Identify the historical period of musical development in which Bach lived and worked.
4. Appreciate better the perfection and potential for meaning in Bach's works.

ASSIGNMENTS

BEFORE VIEWING THE PROGRAM:

Read the "Overview" and familiarize yourself with the "Learning Objectives" for this lesson.

In the textbook, Chapter 9, "Music":
    Read pages 285–294 ("Musical Structures"); review pages 308–315 ("Basic Elements").

Look over the "Aids for Study" for this lesson.

VIEW THE TELEVISION PROGRAM *"Music: Meaning through Structure."*

AFTER VIEWING THE PROGRAM:

Review what you have learned, using the "Aids for Study" again.

Evaluate your learning with the "Review Quiz," then check your answers with the "Answer Key" at the back of this study guide.

In accordance with your own interests or your instructor's assignment, complete selected "Additional Activities."

AIDS FOR STUDY

1. What is a theme (consult the definition of "melody" on page 309, if desired). What descriptions does the textbook give for a theme-and-variations structure?

2. How can a modern popular song or a church hymn resemble a rondo form? What is a verbal description of the rondo? How does the textbook describe the rondo using letter notations?

3. How can you describe the fugue form? What mood is associated with the tempo at which a fugue is to be performed?

4. From the descriptions given in the textbook, does the sonata form seem as rigid or rigorous as the fugue? What descriptive term is applied to each section of the sonata? What is the meaning of the notation A-B-A?

5. How does the text compare the fantasia with the sonata? Is the fantasia a less demanding form than the sonata for the composer? Would this mean that the fantasia may be a less demanding, or more demanding, experience for the listener?

6. Recall one or more titles of program music compositions. How does program music differ from other forms discussed in this section? Is it necessary that the listener be informed of the subject matter of program music before hearing it? Would knowledge of the subject matter be necessary if the work were a fantasia?

7. How is the symphony related to the sonata? Why is the symphony the more complex of the two forms? How can tempo, as well as other elements, help to unify the symphony?

8. What is the meaning of each of these tempo notations: *allegro, andante, adagio, vivace, cantabile*?

9. What are the reasons given for Bach's preeminence as a composer? In which period of music did he live and work? (Consult the "Glossary of Styles and Genres" [study guide page 114] if necessary.) In what way does his music bridge the centuries from his era to the present? Which of the instruments played on the program were *not* originally intended by Bach to be used for performance?

10. Did you recognize a similarity to the forms studied in this lesson in any of the compositions played on the program?

43

QUIZ

the best definition or description for each term on the left from the list on the right.

Term	Description/Definition
f 1. fugue	a. slowly
c 2. symphony	b. a free, less demanding form of composition
d 3. sonata	c. a form usually in four movements
b 4. fantasia	d. statement-development-recapitulation or A-B-A
h 5. program music	e. A-B-A-C-A-alternating with a refrain
g 6. allegro	f. a form of counterpoint, statement-answer
a 7. adagio	g. fast
j 8. andante	h. based on events or objects outside of music
	i. very fast
	j. moderately slow

Select the one best answer.

9. The period of history in which Bach composed his music is called the
   a. Renaissance.
   b. Baroque.
   c. Romantic era.
   d. Modern era.

10. Bach's music is enjoyed by many today, largely because he
    a. developed the music of his period to its greatest potential.
    b. was the most popular composer of his time.
    c. wrote for many different instruments.

11. Which of the following was *not* used as a solo or principal instrument on the program "Meaning through Structures"?
    a. harpsichord
    b. violin
    c. harmonica
    d. flute

ADDITIONAL ACTIVITIES

1.   Depending upon your own past experiences with listening to music, select one of the perception keys for further consideration: "Sonata Form" (textbook page 288), "Program Music" (textbook pages 289–290), "The Symphony" (textbook pages 293–294). Listen to a recorded example of the form, if possible, following the music with a copy of the score at the same time (even if you do not read music, the musical notations and this pattern may give you some added insight into the form). Select some of the questions from the perception key and discuss your answers in writing.

2.   Choose one of your own favorite compositions and listen to it carefully. Identify themes, selecting those you consider main themes and those that are secondary themes. Within which of the forms discussed would you classify this work? Describe this listening experience in a brief report.

3.   Select recordings of examples of at least three of the forms described in the reading or mentioned in the program. Describe your response to each of these works. Were you able to identify the important features of each form?

4.   Much of the art of music is abstract, except for program music, which associates its meanings with "external" events and things. Is the art of drama or film equally as abstract as that of music? Discuss your response to music as an abstract art and compare it to what your response would be to abstract film or drama.

MUSIC

LISTENING FOR THE UNEXPECTED

OVERVIEW

Perhaps it is easier to understand "participation" in music than in many of the other arts. Most of us have sung or danced to music and have enjoyed the melody, the harmony, and the beat; some of us have played musical instruments; all of us have snapped our fingers or tapped our feet in time to music. In this lesson, our challenge is the delight of learning how to participate by deeper listening, which can enhance our insight into the composer's purpose. We learn to listen critically and creatively to music in two rather different experiences.

Beethoven has long been recognized as a master composer. His Symphony No. 3 in E^b major, the *Eroica*, or *Heroic* Symphony, received much criticism when it was first performed; even today, it is a challenge to the newly serious student of music. The description and descriptive criticism of this work is, in effect, a comprehensive guide to creative participation in this symphony. Our reading assignments are, by themselves, short. It is hoped that some study time will be devoted to listening to part or all of Beethoven's *Eroica* with the textbook in hand, to guide our perceptions and perhaps lead us to a deeper understanding of the composer's intent.

Beethoven's music was, at one time, "new." Because some elements of his music, particularly its length, its mood, and use of dissonance, were not customary, the work was received unfavorably by many. In music, as in any other art form, we tend to be comfortable with the familiar and to reject the unfamiliar. At the end of this lesson, we reprint the first chapter from *Modern Music,* by John Tasker Howard and James Lyon. The title of the chapter defines the subject: "What Is Modern Music—and Why Have People Never Liked It, at First?" As we read this chapter, we will begin to see that the authors are not suggesting that everyone ought to like new music as soon as they hear it but, rather, that we should listen closely for what is meaningful, what is powerful, and what is different in new and unfamiliar music. Then, on listening to the music a second time, we may find beauty and fullness in it.

LEARNING OBJECTIVES

ON COMPLETING YOUR STUDY OF THIS LESSON, YOU SHOULD BE ABLE TO:

1. Briefly describe Beethoven's Symphony No. 3 in E^b major, the *Eroica.*

2. Identify the form of criticism applied in the textbook to Beethoven's *Eroica.*

3. Apply some of the skills that may be employed to listen creatively to music.

4. State a definition of "modern music."

5. Identify at least one reason new music is often unpopular.

6. Appreciate the need of each age for music that expresses the uniqueness of the age.

ASSIGNMENTS

BEFORE VIEWING THE PROGRAM:

Read the "Overview" and familiarize yourself with the "Learning Objectives" for this lesson.

In the textbook, Chapter 3, "Being a Critic of the Arts":
 •Review pages 49–59 ("Kinds of Criticism").

Consult preceding lessons or a dictionary to acquaint yourself with these terms:

> *adagio*
> *allegro*
> *scherzo*
> sonata form
> theme

Look over the "Aids for Study" for this lesson.

In the textbook, Chapter 9, "Music":
 •Read pages 294–304 ("Beethoven's Symphony No. 3 in E^b major, *Eroica"*). If you wish and if time permits, complete the listening assignment given as the first activity in "After Viewing the Program" section.

VIEW THE TELEVISION PROGRAM *"Music: Listening for the Unexpected."*

AFTER VIEWING THE PROGRAM:

Obtain a recording of Beethoven's Symphony No. 3 in E^b major, the *Eroica*, and listen to the first movement, using the textbook assignment as a guide to creative listening. (You may be able to obtain a recording at your college or local public library, borrow it from a friend, or perhaps purchase a recording for yourself.) If you wish or if assigned to do so by the course facilitator, you may complete the balance of "Additional Activity 1," listening to the remaining movements of this symphony, at this time.

In study guide:
 •Read pages 155–164 ("What Is Modern Music—and Why Have People Never Liked It, at First?").

Review what you have learned, using the "Aids for Study" again.

Evaluate your learning with the "Review Quiz," then check your answers with the "Answer Key" at the back of this study guide.

In accordance with your own interests or your instructor's assignment, complete selected "Additional Activities."

AIDS FOR STUDY

1. What is the form of the first movement of Beethoven's *Eroica* Symphony? In what way does this movement differ from the usual symphonic first movement? How does the textbook describe the emotions brought forth by this movement? Would you add anything to this description from your listening? What are the tempo markings and their meaning for this movement?

2. What are the tempo markings and mood of the second, third, and fourth movements of Beethoven's *Eroica* Symphony? How would you describe the progress of emotions or feelings evoked by the sequence of these movements?

3. In the textbook, the authors comment that one may feel exhausted after such listening as they suggest. What did you feel after your listening experience? Did you find it difficult to identify any of the elements within the music as the text directed your attention?

4. Review the perception key, "Movement I," (textbook pages 298–299). Comment or reflect on the Questions 2, 4, and 5 in particular.

5. How does the article "What Is Modern Music—and Why Have People Never Liked It, at First?" define modern music? How does this definition depart from the usual dictionary definition? Are you acquainted with any music that meets the article's description?

he social setting of earlier ages where "new music"
nand. Describe the influence of the popularization of
ıd the development of a standard repertoire on the
ɔn of "modern" music.

7. From your study of film and drama, what aspects of modern life
can you suggest that should be interpreted by modern music?
What examples does the article give of older music that will
not describe our contemporary life?

8. Of the three types of criticism described in Chapter 3, which
was most evident in the textbook assignment? After reading the
article on modern music, do you agree or disagree with the text
that historical criticism is a secondary, or supporting, kind of
criticism for the other three? Reflect on your answer to this
question, perhaps trying to answer it both ways.

REVIEW QUIZ

Select the one best answer .

1. The first movement of Beethoven's Symphony No. 3 in E^b major, the
   Eroica, differs from first movements of most symphonies in that it is
   a. in sonata form.
   b. brighter and more whimsical.
   c. much more somber.
   d. much longer.

2. The progression of moods through the four movements of
   Beethoven's *Eroica* may best be described as
   a. light-hearted to serious.
   b. consistently serious and depressing.
   c. from grand to somber, then light to stately.
   d. consistently light.

3. The principal type of criticism applied to Beethoven's *Eroica* in the textbook is
   a. interpretive.
   b. descriptive.
   c. historic.
   d. evaluative.

4. Which of the following is *not* essential to creative listening to music?
   a. a copy of the score
   b. awareness of rhythm and dynamics
   c. recognition of theme statements and restatements
   d. sensitivity to mood elicited by the music

5. "Modern music" includes all music
   a. written at the present (or contemporary) time.
   b. composed with modern subject matter in the composer's mind.
   c. enjoyed by modern audiences of serious music.
   d. that departs from traditional material and style.

6. The article on modern music makes it clear that
   a. music that differs from the familiar will usually be resisted at first.
   b. good music is immediately recognized as such by professional critics.
   c. the standards for good music were established in the classic and romantic periods.
   d. all new music should be enjoyable because originality is the chief criterion of good music.

7. The establishment of a "standard repertory" in the nineteenth century
   a. encouraged the development of new music.
   b. taught the new and larger audiences to appreciate modern music.
   c. discouraged the performance of new compositions by encouraging the worship of "old masters."
   d. made the development of newer musical forms unnecessary.

8. In the eighteenth century (the age of Handel and Haydn),
    a. patrons wanted traditional music.
    b. new music was wanted by patrons and was advertised to attract audiences.
    c. people had to accept new music, because recordings were not yet possible.
    d. very little new music was composed compared to the present.

9. According to the article on modern music, new musical forms and styles are needed to
    a. attract larger audiences.
    b. interpret modern science and technology.
    c. break us away from the "old masters."
    d. take advantage of modern musical instruments.

10. The article on modern music, viewed as criticism, may be classified as
    a. interpretive criticism.
    b. evaluative criticism.
    c. historical criticism.
    d. descriptive criticism.

ADDITIONAL ACTIVITIES

1. Complete your listening to Beethoven's *Eroica* Symphony. After each movement, pause and reflect on the perception key for that movement. At the conclusion, or after a short break, listen to the symphony again, this time in its entirety, without stopping and without consulting the textbook. Then write a brief description of your responses to the entire work, using the final perception key on the *Eroica* Symphony (textbook pages 303–304) as a guide.

2. Select a recording of any piece of "classical music" with which you are familiar. While listening to it, write a brief description of the tempo and mood (or moods) you sense in each movement. If possible, describe the major theme or themes of each movement.

3.   Carry out a creative listening experience in modern music.
     Perhaps your local educational television or radio station has a
     program with nontraditional serious music scheduled. Or listen
     to recordings of compositions such as Debussy's *La Mer*,
     Honegger's *Pacific 231*, Stravinsky's *Rite of Spring*, or works by
     Schoenberg or Bartók. Then discuss what effects—feelings or
     emotions—seem to be evoked by this work that might not have
     been achieved by more traditional earlier music.

At the beginning of the twentieth century, music began to evolve into different forms. About 1910, the music of Arnold Schoenberg and Igor Stravinsky was characterized by such features as atonality and 12-tone technique. Over time, these "new" characteristics were modified and incorporated into many musical compositions. In recent years, modern music has begun to incorporate, and rely upon, certain techniques made possible by developments in electronics. Since about 1950, "modern" composers have been taking sounds from a variety of sources—musical instruments, the environment, and machinery—and altering them electronically. These technologically created sounds are then rearranged by the composers to create musical compositions. Although this music, as with all other music, has such features as pitch and intensity, it does not adhere to the rigid principles of organization that characterized earlier music. Some of the most recent music even incorporates mathematics and computers to set the nature of sounds. In "What is Modern Music—and Why Have People Never Like It, at First?" the author describes how the listening public has responded to these "new" musical forms.

WHAT IS MODERN MUSIC— AND WHY HAVE PEOPLE NEVER LIKED IT, AT FIRST?

John Tasker Howard

The word "modern" is a most impermanent adjective. If it means something that belongs exclusively to present or recent times it cannot be used for anything that was modern a few years ago. Long-distance dialing was certainly modern in 1956, but the telephone itself, newfangled in 1900, is hardly considered modern by the younger generation of mid-century, even though some of us who witnessed its introduction still think of it as a modern means of communication.

In the arts modernism is a particularly impermanent term, often inaccurate for what may have been truly modern a quarter-century ago. It does not require much of a memory to recall the days when subscribers who had already paid for their tickets refused to attend concerts at which *Till Eulenspiegel* was to be played.

Also, the degree of modernism in music and painting depends on the experience and taste of those who listen to symphonies and look at pictures. To some, Debussy is still a modernist. To others, Stravinsky's

Firebird and even *The Rites of Spring* are no longer modern and have become "old hat." Thus the significance of the term depends on the point of view of the individual listener, on whether he has become accustomed to more recent patterns or whether he has exposed himself so infrequently to the works of the past half-century that he still considers the composers of the nineteenth century as the norm and standard of all music—past or present.

Apart from the individual listener's conception of modernism, it is essential that the term be defined for purposes of discussion in this volume. If we accept the dictionary definition of the modern as that which originates in the present, we shall become hopelessly confused with what is merely contemporary, for if we consider as modern anything and everything that is written in present times we shall find that we have many works which in style and idiom belong in the past.

Therefore, to be modern, a composition must have other qualities than newness alone; it must deviate in varying degree from tradition in its material and in its style. Furthermore, much of it will have experienced opposition to what Ernest Krenek once called its "conversion into merchandise." It will have been resisted by the public and have found acceptance by concert artists and commercial publishers difficult.

Obviously, this volume will consider as modern only that music which when it was created departed from previous convention and was not readily accepted. We are not concerned with music that is old-fashioned and conventional in style even though it was composed as recently as last month. And since the term is relative we shall have to consider the modern music of various periods in history. Mozart wrote modern music in the latter eighteenth century, so we are concerned with Mozart's music. John Smith in the middle of the twentieth century writes music that Mozart might have written, so we shall not bother our heads with it.

It is interesting to find how the lay public, and musicians too, have reacted to the modern music of their time. Generally they have taken a rather dim view of it, which is not altogether surprising. Our ancestors didn't like it either, even though their modern music was written by Monteverdi, Mozart, Beethoven, and Wagner. Human beings are by nature too complacent to like violent changes, and older generations have always lamented the passing of the "good old days." Even the most adventurous pioneers have taken with them as much of their home environment as they could carry, and as soon as they have made a permanent settlement they have recreated as much of the atmosphere of their former homes as the geography and climate of their new surroundings would permit. Thus, we find New England architecture in Ohio, Spanish buildings in California, and Chinatowns in San Francisco and New York.

If venturesome emigrants demand familiar surroundings, what about those of us who stay at home, among the same neighbors, working at the same jobs, playing the same old games? Fashion designers may create radical changes from season to season to force people to buy new clothes, but most husbands resent the way their wives look in their new hats as much as they are annoyed by the bills. And if anything so trivial as a new set of contract bridge conventions is upsetting to our peace of mind, is it any wonder that new political and sociological ideas give everyone the jitters?

Most of us admit that the world is changing: socially, economically, and politically, so whether we like it or not, we know that our mode of life will have to be adapted to the world about us. Yet, while we are broadminded and practical enough to accomplish this growth in the major matters of life, it seems to some of us a bit futile and unnecessary to disturb ourselves with changes in the less vital things, among them, music.

Music, however, is a living language; or rather, *good* music is. It is composed by human beings, and human beings do have to adapt themselves to shifting conditions, no matter how much they resist them at first. Hence, if music is to remain a living language, that is, if it is to be a sincere and honest expression of the men and women who compose it, it too must grow. Like all languages, it must constantly acquire new words and expressions to convey its meaning in a changing society.

The same principle is true of any language. Greek and Latin are dead languages because they are not used any more for daily conversation; they belonged to past civilizations and have not been adapted to more recent affairs. There are no Greek and Latin words for oil burner, cocktail, movies, television, or jet planes. The dictionaries and grammars of living languages—modern Greek and Italian, English, French, German—are continually revised and brought up to date by the inclusion of new words, and of new phrases and sentence constructions formerly considered bad usage.

It is because music is a living language that we have the so-called modern music. Music is a medium that is constantly increasing its vocabulary and taking into its grammar various devices of harmony, melody, and rhythm that were formerly forbidden by rule. If it failed to accomplish such changes it would soon be as dead as Greek and Latin, and interesting chiefly to historians.

It may be that the music of our day is far more radical, and breaks more sharply with tradition, than did the new music of Mozart, Beethoven, or Mendelssohn, but the conservative music lovers of those days thought their new music shocking enough. Go back even further, to the sixteenth century, and you find Claudio Monteverdi causing as much furor by championing the major-minor tonal system as Schoenberg has caused in our time with his atonality. In the year 1600 a critic wrote of Monteverdi: "Though I am glad of a new manner of composition, it would be more edifying to find in these madrigals reasonable passages, but these kinds of air-castles and chimeras deserve the severest reproof. . . . You hear a medley of sounds, a variety of parts that are intolerable to the ear. . . . With all the best will in the world, how can the mind see light in this chaos?"

Not many of us today would think of Mozart as a disconcerting modernist, but read what an eighteenth-century critic thought of his latest string quartets: "It is a pity that in his truly artistic and beautiful compositions Mozart should carry his effort after originality too far, to the detriment of the sentiment and heart of his works. His new quartets . . . are much too highly spiced to be palatable for any length of time."

A Vienna music patron had several of these quartets performed at his home and was so enraged at finding the dissonances in one of them actually printed in the music that he tore the parts to pieces. Haydn, however, remarked that if Mozart wrote his music with dissonances, he must have had good reasons for doing so.

Beethoven was a shocking radical. He opened his C major symphony, the First, with a chord from the key of F, and passed through the key of G before getting down to business in C, the ruling key of the symphony. At one point in his Third Symphony, the *Eroica*, he had two different chords sounded at the same time. A contemporary critic explained this by saying that "poor Beethoven is so deaf that he cannot hear the discords he writes." One conductor went so far as to correct the "error" at rehearsal.

The composers of the romantic movement—Chopin, Mendelssohn, Schubert, Schumann, Brahms, Wagner—were all resisted by the conservatives and reactionaries of their time. Robert Schumann's teacher never forgave him for admiring Chopin, and when Schumann championed the young Brahms, he was a lone prophet crying in a classic wilderness.

Music is almost always an expression of the age in which it is written. If it isn't, we may be sure that the composer himself belongs spiritually to another age, or that he patterns his work after the music of earlier composers, unconsciously or perhaps deliberately. Then we say that this style is Wagnerian, or Franckian, instead of John Smithian.

This does not mean that originality alone is a sign of greatness, or even a virtue in itself. Progress and change are by no means synonymous. Many things may be wholly original and yet be altogether worthless, and it must be admitted that some composers sacrifice a great deal for what they believe to be originality. It seems as though their chief concern is to keep their music from bearing even the slightest resemblance to anything that has been written before. In such cases, the composer is substituting for sincere expression a conscious style which will inevitably prove artificial and manufactured. If he announces that he never listens to other men's works for fear it will destroy his individuality, he is explaining the limitations of his own music.

The casual listener to music, in the concert hall or on the radio and phonograph, may wonder how he can possibly distinguish between the real article and the work of a charlatan. How, for example, is the man to whom the connecting links of a Beethoven symphony are still a mystery, to know whether Stravinsky's *The Rites of Spring* is an authentic art expression, which he ought to like, or merely a confusion of shocking, ugly sounds? And how is he to acquire the ability to enjoy anything that is at first hearing so highly unpleasant to his ears and his nervous system? Why torture himself by listening to it?

These are the questions this book [*A Popular Guide to Greater Musical Enjoyment*] will try to answer. The music lover must make up his mind that he is going to hear a great deal of modern music if he goes to concerts, or listens to all the numbers of a radio or TV program. If he buys tickets to hear a Beethoven symphony, he may have to listen first to a ballet suite by Stravinsky. Even if he is willing to come late and miss half of what he is paying for, his wife, or whomever he is taking to the concert, may like Stravinsky, and insist that they hear the entire program.

He needn't feel too badly if he thinks the whole business a terrible mess. If the new music is being played for the first time, he will no doubt have plenty of company in his opinion among the professional critics. And he has a distinct advantage over the critics; he may express his opinions to any or all of his friends, and suffer no ill consequences. He has little to lose if the ensuing years prove him wrong. The critic, however, must go on record in print, and allow historians of the future to dig in the files and show him up to posterity.

And how often these unfortunate gentlemen have turned out to be wrong, down through the history of music right to the present day!

Gounod once remarked that César Franck's Symphony in D Minor represented the height of incompetence carried to dogmatic lengths, while in 1905 Richard Aldrich in *The New York Times* described Rimsky-Korsakov's *Scheherazade* as "dull, with an insistence on long drawn oriental chantings and dronings."

"Last night's concert began with a lot of impressionistic daubs of color smeared higgledy-piggledy on a tonal palette, with never a thought of form or purpose except to create new combinations of sounds. . . . One thing only was certain, and that was that the composer's ocean was a frog-pond, and that some of its denizens had got into the throat of every one of the brass instruments."

Those words were written in 1907 for the New York *Tribune*, by Henry E. Krehbiel, one of the soundest and most learned critics who has ever written for a metropolitan journal, and the work he described was Debussy's *La Mer*. Fifteen years later Krehbiel again reviewed a performance of *La Mer*, and called it a "poetic work in which Debussy has so wondrously caught the rhythms and colors of the seas."

The inference to be drawn from these two opinions is clear. When Krehbiel first heard *La Mer*, its strangeness confused him. Fifteen years later he had absorbed the idiom, and became so familiar with it that it had ceased to bother him, and he was able to grasp the true beauty of the work.

Read also what Krehbiel wrote about the Fourth Symphony of Tchaikovsky when he first heard it, in 1890:

"Of the four symphonies of Tchaikovsky which have been heard in New York, it is far and away the least interesting. It is the first of the larger works of the genial Russian, concerning which we feel tempted to say that it ought not to have been performed at all. It would have been treated with manifest kindness if its *Scherzo* had been incorporated in the scheme of some popular concert and the rest of it had been consigned to the limbo of oblivion. The *Scherzo* utilizes strings *pizzicato* throughout and is pretty. Artistically, it stands on the plane, say, of Strauss's *Pizzicato Polka*, though not quite as graceful. As a symphonic movement, it is about as dignified as one of the compositions which delight the souls of college banjo clubs. But in spite of the striving evidenced by Tchaikovsky's recurrence in his last movement to material used in the *Introduction* and the first movement . . . the composition can scarcely be called a *Symphony*, except on the principle of *lucus a non lucendo*. It wants nearly every element which makes the work which opened the concert, for instance [Mozart's G minor], a symphony. There was a great show of effort in the composition, but only a modicum of artistic result."

Again, the critic resisted something new. The first three symphonies of Tchaikovsky were conventional and, incidentally, are rarely if ever heard today. In the Fourth, Tchaikovsky ventured in new fields. He extended the traditional forms, and used a Russian folk song as a motto that tied the work together by recurring in the last movement. Krehbiel didn't like it; its novelty was so offensive to him that he missed entirely the power and dramatic force that have come to thrill thousands, perhaps millions, of music lovers.

Resistance to new music has always existed to a certain degree, particularly on the part of critics, but it is only in the last century and a half that it has become a violent and hostile public reaction. It was in the nineteenth century that the worship of the "old masters" came into being, with its establishment of a standard repertory for symphony orchestras and for individual concert artists. Nowadays new music is played by major organizations largely for general prestige, as a contribution to the advancement of music, not as an immediate box-office attraction. Concert artists look for cash customers for Beethoven, Wagner, or Tchaikovsky; not for the new and untried.

In the 1700s the situation was considerably different. The repertory had not yet come into existence, and new works were performed more often than old ones. Some of this may be explained by the fact that music was still largely the diversion of kings and princes, who maintained their own musicians to perform for the court. It was the duty of the *Kapellmeister* to engage and train the musicians of the court. Music to play was needed, of course, and generally the *Kapellmeister*, in his own handwriting, would arrange and adapt the parts for performance as an incidental part of his duties. He was expected to compose music of his own for all occasions, and even when he played other men's music, it was generally new. Thus, Prince Esterhazy required Haydn to keep his private orchestra supplied with new symphonies, and his quartet with new chamber music.

At the Thomaskirche in Leipzig, Bach was expected to write a new cantata each week, and his large family was kept busy copying out the parts as the father finished each page of the score. During the several years that Bach was *Kapellmeister* for Prince Leopold at Köthen, he wrote the bulk of his orchestral and chamber music. But this was for performance by the Prince's musicians, not for publication. It was not until years later that these works were published and available for performance elsewhere.

When concerts for the public became regular features of European cities, particularly in England, the people apparently wanted new music at first, for the eighteenth-century newspaper announcements invariably featured new works. When Haydn went to London, the contract called for twelve new symphonies to be played at his concerts—six each visit. There was also a demand from the British public for a constant supply of new operas, oratorios, and instrumental works by Handel. In 1742 the Dublin papers announced that "on Monday, the 12th of April, for the benefit of the Prisoners of the several Gaols, and the support of Mercer's Hospital, in Stephen's-street, and of the Charitable Infirmary on the Inn's Quay, will be performed at the Music Hall in Fishambe-street, Mr. Handel's *new Grand Oratorio, called the Messiah,* in which the Gentlemen of the Choirs of both Cathedrals will assist, with some Concertos on the Organ, by Mr. Handel."

It was the same in America. When George Washington visited Boston, a few months after his inauguration as president, a huge concert was planned in his honor. The newspapers announced that the program would contain the "Oratorio of *Jonah,* which has been applauded by the best judges and has never been performed in America." Again in Boston, a Mr. Turner advertised a concert in 1773, and respectfully begged leave "to acquaint his subscribers that his last concert for the season will be on Tuesday eve, at which time will be performed a variety of music received from London by Captain Scott, which never has been performed in this place."

All of this was in the eighteenth century. In the nineteenth century, concerts and opera became the diversion of the people, not alone the luxury of aristocrats. With the public demand for the familiar, there came a resistance to new music that made it difficult for young revolutionary composers to gain a sympathetic hearing. As Ernst Krenek has written: "Theaters and concert halls were thrown open to an enormously increasing number of people, and the operation of music as an institution had thenceforth to depend for its sustenance upon this new audience's desire to buy and its power to buy, a service which formerly was essentially performed by small privileged groups."[1] Thus, in our own time, we find that radical new music generally has its first hearing at nonprofit-making concerts sponsored by groups of composers or subsidized by philanthropists.

---

[1]*Music Here and Now.* New York: W. W. Norton & Co., Inc., 1939.

The inexperienced layman, then, is not alone in his disinclination to bother himself with listening to modern music. Sometimes, however, he is more receptive to it than professionals are, for though he may like best the things he is familiar with, he is often far less hemmed in by traditions than is the veteran concert-goer. Virgil Thomson has gone so far as to claim that modern music is easier for the layman to understand than old music. In an article on "Understanding Modern Music" he wrote:

"There is no reason why anybody in the music world, professional or layman, should find himself in the position of not understanding a piece of twentieth-century music, if he is willing to give himself a little trouble. . . . The art-music of the past, most of all that eighteenth and nineteenth century repertory known as "classical" music, is, on the other hand, about as incomprehensible as anything could be. Its idiom is comprehensible, because it is familiar. But its significant content is as impenetrable as that of the art work of the Middle Ages. It was made by men whose modes of thought and attitudes of passion were as different from ours as those of Voltaire and Goethe and Rousseau . . . were different from those of Bernard Shaw . . . and Gertrude Stein and Mickey Mouse. . . ."[2]

It is surely too much to say that a twentieth-century listener cannot penetrate to the spiritual content of Beethoven, but Mr. Thomson was sound in stating that, aside from the idiom of a contemporary work, no listener can fail to penetrate its meaning, at least partially.

The listener's problem is one of understanding something of the composer's method, and of how his style differs from that of composers in the past. Then he can decide for himself whether or not the twentieth-century message is coherently and effectively expressed; in other words, he will know whether or not he is likely to enjoy a new composition when he has become used to its style and mode of expression.

If he is a lover of the classics, if he likes to listen to his "old favorites," he must realize why music must change its style with the centuries . . . music expresses and reflects the background of the age in which it was composed. Thus, in the twentieth century, when a composer writes descriptive music, he will deal with the sights and sounds that belong to his own era, and instead of painting tone-pictures of sailing vessels he will depict the speedier ocean liners and jet planes; instead of blacksmith shops, he will paint steel mills. In drawing his musical scenes, he finds that the melodic, rhythmic, and harmonic vocabulary of Beethoven will not suffice for the mighty roar of the plunging giant of steel, and like Honegger in *Pacific 231*, he will draw on new combinations

---

[2]New York *Herald Tribune*, January 4, 1942.

of sounds to sing the song of the great locomotive. Nor will the chastely simple pattern of Handel's *Harmonious Blacksmith* serve for describing an iron foundry. The crude dissonances of Mossolov's *Soviet Iron Foundry* are less tuneful, but more faithful to their subject.

Entirely apart from the descriptive functions of music, how can we expect the musical speech of Handel to express the restless, uncertain temper of our age any more effectively than the literary style of *Godey's Lady's Book* would describe an air raid in the pages of *Life* or *Time?* The march of science, the invention of machines, have created an atmosphere wholly unlike the environment that surrounded our fathers.

We need music that expresses the way we feel in our own age. It is not sound to say that we have enough music already, for there must be music to express the voice of every age. If the music lovers of Mozart's day had refused altogether to listen to new music, we wouldn't have any Beethoven. And if the concert-goers of Beethoven's day had decided that they had enough music (which some of them almost did), then there would have been no Schumann, Mendelssohn, Wagner, or Brahms.

For unless we listen to our new music, it will not exist. When music is not performed, it is merely a set of symbols on paper. None of us can tell who the Mozarts or the Beethovens of the future will be, but we must make sure that when they come, if they are not here already, they will have a chance to be heard.

There are just two things that the music lover who wants to enjoy modern music need do. First, he must realize *why* it is, what it is; why the composers of every age have written differently from those who preceded them. Secondly, he must acquaint himself, if only superficially, with a few of the methods used by modern composers to make their music different from eighteenth- and nineteenth-century music. Then he will know whether they have used their tools and materials effectively or inefficiently. And he may come to have a fair idea as to which of them are creative artists and which are mountebanks and fakers.

From *Modern Music: A Popular Guide to Greater Musical Enjoyment,* John Tasker Howard and James Lyons, revised ed.

LESSON 14

LITERATURE

FROM WORDS, TRUTH

Language is the basic coin of literature, but literature uses language for much more than verbal reporting of facts. As this lesson suggests, literature leads to new understanding, new insights—to truth—and it was created when writers and tellers of stories began to use oral and written language toward these ends. Examples are drawn from the writings of selected literary periods to illustrate the following dictionary definition of literature given in the television component of this lesson:

Literature—Literary productions as a whole; the body of writings produced in a particular country or period; or in the world in general. Now also in a more restricted sense, applied to writing which has claim to consideration on the ground of beauty of form or emotional effect.

Although literature has many valid forms, this lesson confines itself largely to literature as poetry and fiction, and great emphasis is placed on the lyric quality implicit in much of our best-loved literature. To illuminate the importance of this lyric quality, the lesson opens with a brief description of the development of language, first as an *oral* tool and then as a *written* tool of communication. Thus, although all the selections for this lesson are part of our written literature, those used in the television program are read aloud to help us appreciate the beauty of their sounds as well as their ideas.

The first historical period visited in this lesson is that of an ancient Greece: the Classic Age. We hear an excerpt from Homer's epic poem, *The Odyssey*, which was written about the eighth or ninth century B.C. A parallel epic from the Medieval period is then introduced with a brief passage from *Beowulf*, which is recited for us in its original Old English tongue, then in a more modern English translation. Generally considered to mark the beginning of English literature, *Beowulf* was probably composed in the eighth century after Christ.

The Middle English period is represented with a few lines from Chaucer's richly humorous *Canterbury Tales.* It is in this period that the English language began to be accepted as a literary medium. In addition, the influence of the Renaissance was beginning to be felt; men and women came to sense the joys of life and the importance of human values in fuller degree than they had in the Medieval era.

Elizabethan literature, which followed Chaucer by some 200 years, is represented by one of Shakespeare's sonnets and by a famous passage from the King James translation of the Bible, the *Song of Solomon,* Chapter 2. Note the imagery and lyricism in these works, which sing the praises of human love.

This romantic Elizabethan age was followed by the Age of Reason, mentioned in this lesson especially for the development of the literary form called the novel. The novel brought to literature a sense of "oneness," or wholeness.

The Romantic period of the eighteenth and nineteenth centuries is illustrated with selections that vividly portray the source of their writers' inspiration and spiritual quest: nature in its beauty and perfection. Two poems, Wordsworth's "The Tables Turned" and Keat's "Cold Philosophy," praise nature above science, art, and philosophy.

Tension between material and spiritual values is a major characteristic of the nineteenth-century Victorian age. The uncertainty growing out of this period, which was a time of radical change and extreme social criticism, is evident in Matthew Arnold's "Dover Beach." The flavor of this period in the United States can be felt in the selection from Herman Melville's *Moby Dick,* and from Whitman's poem, "When I Heard the Learned Astronomer," which reflects a more romantic influence.

Modern American literature is represented with examples of the two related but distinct schools of Realism and Naturalism. We hear selections from Hemingway's *A Farewell to Arms*, Edna St. Vincent Millay's "My Candle Burns at Both Its Ends," F. Scott Fitzgerald's *The Great Gatsby*, and Steinbeck's *The Grapes of Wrath*. We should perhaps be quite conscious that it is, in part, left to us to determine which examples are unadorned Realism and which are the more negative perceptions of the Naturalist school, which sees humans as controlled by blind forces.

We should also hear a slightly different tone in the last selection read by Maya Angelou in the television portion of the lesson. Distinctively modern and certainly neither optimistic nor romantic, these lines excerpted from Robert Frost's "The Star Splitter" seem to seek for an eternal truth—a timeless answer to the questions that trouble humankind.

LEARNING OBJECTIVES

ON COMPLETING YOUR STUDY OF THIS LESSON, YOU SHOULD BE ABLE TO:

1. Understand the origins of literature from spoken language.
2. Identify at least three distinctive qualities of literature that are more evident when read aloud than when read silently.
3. Recognize five historical literary periods and associate an author or work with each period.
4. Identify an attitude or value important to each of the four of the literary periods discussed in this lesson.
5. Appreciate the role of literature in questioning or clarifying the values held by a society.

ASSIGNMENTS

BEFORE VIEWING THE PROGRAM:

Read the "Overview" and familiarize yourself with the "Learning Objectives" for this lesson.

In the textbook, Chapter 1, "The Humanities: An Introduction":
- •Review pages 10–14 ("Perception" and "Abstract Ideas and Concrete Images").

Consult a dictionary, an encyclopedia, or the textbook to acquaint yourself with these terms:

> epic
> literature
> lyric
> Middle English
> Naturalism (literary school)
> novel (literary form)
> Old English
> sonnet

Look over the "Aids for Study" for this lesson.

VIEW THE TELEVISION PROGRAM *Literature: From Words, Truth.*

AFTER VIEWING THE PROGRAM:

In the textbook, Chapter 7, "Literature":
- •Read pages 207–211 (introductory material).

Select a poem or passage from the reading assignment or the television program for this lesson (or from a source of your own choosing) and read it aloud, preferably recording it for your later consideration. After listening to your recording, do you feel that any beauty or value in the work is highlighted by reading it aloud?

Review what you have learned, using the "Aids for Study" again.

Evaluate your learning with the "Review Quiz," then check your answers with the "Answer Key" at the back of this study guide.

In accordance with your own interests or your instructor's assignment, complete selected "Additional Activities."

1. Give two reasons for the emphasis in this lesson upon recitation of literature rather than on silent reading.

2. What are some of the parallel elements in *Beowulf* and *The Odyssey*? Can you suggest a reason for including an example of the original language of the former poem?

3. Compare and contrast the romantic interests of the Elizabethans with those of the eighteenth- and nineteenth-century Romantic movement, basing your answers on the examples presented in the television program.

4. The literary importance of the Age of Reason includes the fact that the novel as a distinct literary form was perfected in this period. What were some of the other characteristics of this period that are mentioned in the program?

5. Conflicts during the Victorian era resulted in radical social changes. Mention at least two important areas or ideas in which such conflict and changes occurred.

6. Walt Whitman, an American poet of the Victorian era, reflects the values of the Romantic period as well as the Victorian. How is this especially well illustrated by his poem, "When I Heard the Learned Astronomer," which is read in the television program?

7. Mention a few characteristics of the Jazz Age literature.

8. Name two writers associated with the Naturalistic school. Summarize the beliefs they held about humankind and nature.

QUIZ
_____

Select the one best answer, or write the correct answer in the space provided.

1. Which one of the following is *least* likely to be overlooked if a work is read silently rather than aloud?
   a. the rhythm of consecutive phrases.
   b. the sequence of words and ideas.
   c. the emotional tone of the work.
   d. the sound of the words themselves.

2. *The Odyssey* is associated with which literary period?
   a. Neoclassic
   b. Romantic
   c. Classic
   d. Age of Reason

3. Shakespeare is considered the preeminent writer of which period?
   a. Neoclassic
   b. Elizabethan
   c. Romantic
   d. Victorian

4. Steinbeck is associated with the
   a. Neoclassic period.
   b. Victorian period.
   c. Age of Reason.
   d. Modern period.

5. Edna St. Vincent Millay is associated with the
   a. Neoclassic period.
   b. Victorian period.
   c. Age of Reason.
   d. Modern period.

6. Wordsworth and Keats are associated with the
   a. Neoclassic period.
   b. Romantic period.
   c. Victorian period.
   d. Modern period.

7. *The Odyssey* and *Beowulf* reflect the value placed on
   a. heroic struggle and adventure.
   b. love and nature as ideals.
   c. conflict over economic and social change.
   d. science and reason.

8. *The Canterbury Tales* and its author are described as an example of new awareness of
   a. epic adventure.
   b. love and nature.
   c. joy in present life.
   d. reason and science.

9. Wordworth's poem "On His Books" places the highest value on
   a. knowledge and reason.
   b. the inspiration of nature.
   c. epic adventure.
   d. realism.

10. Hemingway's writing, as described in the program, provides an example of the beliefs held by the
    a. Naturalistic school.
    b. Romantic school.
    c. Realistic school.
    d. Victorian school.

11. Name one work or selection read in the program "Literature: From Words, Truth" that seems to question the values of the society.

    Farewell to Arms
    Great Gatsby
    Grapes of Wrath

ADDITIONAL ACTIVITIES

1. Select one of the historical periods mentioned in this lesson and gather further information through an encyclopedia, annotated literature anthology, or other reference. What social patterns or social changes made themselves felt in the literature of the period? What literature most influenced the period?

2. Select one of the writers included in this lesson (such as Hemingway or Fitzgerald) and read other selections by him. Do these works harmonize with the generalizations concerning the historical period presented in the program?

3. As the essential values of each period are highlighted in this program, do you sense an increased pessimism from the Middle English through the Modern period? Are literary writers (to quote Matthew Arnold) increasingly aware of being "as on a darkling plain/swept with confused alarms of struggle and flight"? Consider your answer (or answers) to this question and, if possible, discuss them with others.

4. Earlier lessons in this course may tend to emphasize the separateness of arts such as films, drama, and literature. Discuss some similarities you perceive among these three art forms in the Modern era.

LITERATURE

THE SYNTHESIS OF POETRY

In this lesson, we learn how a particular literary form, in this case, poetry, is especially suited to developing certain kinds of meaning. Both the textbook and the television program acquaint us with the various elements composing the poetic form, and the television program presents examples of both lyric and epic poetry, along with numerous selections from the poems of Robert Frost.

The lyric poem—a poem that seems to be written to be sung rather than spoken or read—is perhaps the form of poetry most familiar to us. In contrast to narrative poems, which relate a story, lyric poems create a setting and elicit feelings and emotions from audience. A lyric poem, quite frequently, is an intensely personal statement by the poet, and the feelings the poet communicates through the poem may help us to better understand our own feelings.

Early in the television program for this lesson, we hear quoted the words of several noted poets: Wordsworth, Shelley, Coleridge, Voltaire, Dickinson, Pound, and Sandburg. In these poet's words (sometimes with tongue in cheek), we hear their definitions of what poetry is.

Throughout their definitions is one common theme: Poetry is a form designed to evoke an emotional response. Many of the poets quoted also refer to the economy and precision of language that characterize poetry and to the ability of poetry to convey insights not expressible in simple prose.

The subject matter of poetry is defined for us by Maya Angelou as, first, "that which has tangible existence in time and space," such as people, places, things, and events; and, second, subjective material such as ideas, thoughts, feelings, emotions, beliefs, pains, ecstasies, fears, and desires. Most poems, like those we hear or read in this lesson, have elements of both categories of subjects.

Many elements used in the development of poetry are identified in this lesson: rhythm (meter), division (feet), and rhymes and stanzas. Each of these terms implies a pattern, and poetry is made of such patterns. Blank verse (no rhyme) and free verse (no consistent pattern) may be more complicated to analyze than more traditional forms, yet a pattern or structure unique to the poem is usually discernable. Poets also use devices based on sounds: alliteration, consonance, and assonance. The poet usually employs some type of imagery or symbolism, usually through the use of the metaphor (speaking as if one thing were actually something else) or if the simile (a direct comparison, using such words as "like" or "as if").

The last third of the television program provides an intimate look at Robert Frost. We learn something of his background, personal life, and his activities as a noted artist in America. This background helps us to understand the individuality and uniqueness of Frost as a poet. It illustrates the importance of understanding the individual poet if we seek fully to appreciate his or her poetry. Biographies, personal writings, and even brief articles can assist us to understand other poets just as we are given this insight into Frost.

LEARNING OBJECTIVES

ON COMPLETING YOUR STUDY OF THIS LESSON, YOU SHOULD BE ABLE TO:

1. List three characteristics of poetry.
2. Identify three elements used in most poetry.
3. Differentiate the two levels of subject matter that poets employ.
4. Define the term "lyric poem."
5. Appreciate the aspect of feelings and emotions present in a lyric poem.
6. Relate several significant aspects of Frost's thought and life.

ASSIGNMENTS

BEFORE VIEWING THE PROGRAM:

Read the "Overview" and familiarize yourself with the "Learning Objectives" for this lesson.

Consult a dictionary for definitions of these terms:

> alliteration
> assonance
> consonance
> metaphor
> meter (poetry)
> simile

Look over the "Aids for Study" for this lesson.

VIEW THE TELEVISION PROGRAM *"Literature: The Synthesis of Poetry."*

AFTER VIEWING THE PROGRAM:

In the textbook, Chapter 7, "Literature":
  • Read pages 218–232 ("The Lyric," "The Image," "The Metaphor," and "The Symbol").

Review what you have learned, using the "Aids for Study" again.

Review Chapter 2, "What Is a Work of Art?" in the textbook, which deals with unity and organization in a work of art.

Evaluate your learning with the "Review Quiz," then check your answers with the "Answer Key" at the back of this study guide.

In accordance with your own interests or your instructor's assignment, complete selected "Additional Activities."

AIDS FOR STUDY

1. Did one or more of the definitions of poetry given in the program seem especially memorable? How would you paraphrase Carl Sandburg's definition that "Poetry is the achievement of the synthesis of hyacinths and biscuits"? What were the three characteristics of poetry summarized in the "Overview" of this lesson? Would you add others? Which characteristic, to you, is the most significant?

2. Two levels of subject matter for lyric poetry were identified in the program. Select one poem heard or read and identify which subject matter predominates (or is used exclusively). Look at Blake's "The Tygre" (textbook page 221). What is the "outward" subject of the poem? What may be the inward meaning—an idea, emotion, or concept?

3. The word "lyric" implies a song. In what sense are most of the lyric poems studied in this lesson similar to a song? What three other characteristics attributed to lyric poetry are discussed in the textbook? With what type of poetry is lyric poetry contrasted in the discussion in the program?

4. Recall the meter (rhythm) of the following lines by Frost:
   "The living come with grassy tread
   to read the gravestones on the hill"
   Identify the accented syllables. How many accents (or "feet")
   are there in each line?

5. What is the rhyming pattern of the first four lines of Keat's
   sonnet on textbook page 218? What is one characteristic of this
   poem that identifies it as a sonnet? What is the type of poetry
   that has neither rhyme nor meter?

6. In the poem "Pied Beauty" by Hopkins (textbook page 219),
   what types of sounds are most frequently repeated? What is the
   term for this type of repetition? What are the other types of
   sound repetition?

7. Two types of symbolic comparisons were discussed in the
   program. Which type of comparison is found in lines 17 and 18 of
   Arnold's "Dover Beach" (textbook pages 221–222)? Both types of
   comparison are used in lines 21 through 23. Can you identify
   them?

8. Thinking back over the poetry read in the television program,
   which one work best represents, for you, the description of lyric
   poetry given in the text?

9. In what part of the United States did Frost live? How did he
   describe the influence of his geographical background? Why did
   it help understanding of the poem "Once by the Pacific" to know
   that Frost's thinking was shaped by naturalistic philosophy of
   the nineteenth century, that "blind, invincible forces apparently
   rule an unwitting universe"?

10. Consider again Frost's words quoted at the end of the program,
    "Giving anything form gives you confidence in the universe—
    that it has form . . . poetry begins in delight and ends in a
    clarification of life—a momentary stay against confusion." How
    does this relate to the definition of art given in Chapter 2 of the
    textbook?

√ QUIZ

Select the one best answer.

1. Which of the following is a characteristic of poetry mentioned in several definitions in the program?
   a. poetry is usually written to be set in songs
   b. poetry is usually written as a story
   c. poetry usually brings forth emotions
   d. poetry usually refers to nature

2. Language chosen for use in poetry tends to be
   a. carefully selected for its effect.
   b. formal and impersonal.
   c. literary, in classic style.
   d. similar to everyday language.

3. The two levels of subject matter used by poets might be described as
   a. people and events.
   b. ideas and emotions.
   c. tangible or "outward" objects or events and inward experiences.
   d. everyday occurrences and rare or imaginary occurrences.

4. The subject matter of Blake's "The Tyger" is most probably
   a. love and human affection.
   b. the natural animal living in the wild.
   c. fear of nature.
   d. the nature of evil or of nature itself.

5. Lyric poetry is defined in the text as
   a. any poetry that can be set to song.
   b. a personal statement, revealing a deep feeling.
   c. a poem that relates a story as a series of significant events.
   d. any short poem dealing with serious subject matter.

6. How many stressed syllables are in each of the following lines?
   That time of year thou mayst in me behold
   When yellow leaves, or none, or few, do hang
   a. three
   b. five
   c. four
   d. six

7. Which type of sound repetition is illustrated in the following lines?
   Whatever is fickle, freckled (who know how?)
   With swift, flow; sweet, sour; adazzle, dim;
   a. alliteration
   b. assonance
   c. consonance
   d. none of the above

8. A metaphor is a type of symbolic comparison that
   a. compares something in nature to an inward feeling.
   b. compares an inward feeling with a specific event.
   c. uses the word "like" or "as" to compare two apparently
      dissimilar things.
   d. compares two apparently dissimilar things but uses neither
      "like" nor "as."

9. Walt Whitman's poems quoted in the program and printed in the
   text were in the form called
   a. rhymed verse.
   b. narrative.
   c. sonnet.
   d. free verse.

10. Robert Frost had strong ties to
    a. England.
    b. New England.
    c. the Midwest.
    d. the Pacific coast.

ADDITIONAL ACTIVITIES

1. Select another type of poetry, such as the narrative poem or epic
    poem. (Tennyson's "Charge of the Light Brigade" or "Casey at
    the Bat" might be examples.) Discuss the poetic elements you
    find in your example. Compare those elements with the ones of
    the lyric poems studied in this lesson.

2. Describe how Frost's poem, "Once by the Pacific," reflects a
    naturalistic acceptance of nature's "blind, invincible forces." In
    the study of tragedy in the drama unit, the importance of fate in
    classical tragedy was discussed. What similarity and difference
    do you see in the view of the universe reflected in this poem, as
    opposed to the view held by Sophocles as reflected in *Oedipus
    Rex?*

3. If possible, tape record one of the poems studied in this lesson,
    and then listen to it as you have read it. Determine for yourself
    what the *content* of this poem is (remembering Frost's comment
    that one listens a second time for meaning, a third time for
    another meaning). Briefly state your understanding of this
    meaning, and discuss whether or not this poem's content
    illustrates Frost's comment, "Poetry begins in delight and ends in
    a clarification of life."

LITERATURE

THE STORY BEYOND

OVERVIEW

In our study of drama, we considered the importance of esthetic or psychic distance: the necessity of maintaining a certain detachment from the artistic event and of not identifying too closely with the protagonist. The goal of our participation in the arts should not be purely "escape" through the vicarious experiencing of a character's pains and pleasures, even though our emotional responses are an important part of our participation.

The television program for this lesson provides us with an opportunity to practice our participation in literature through the detailed examination of a single short story, "The Lottery," by Shirley Jackson. In our study of this story, we will not only learn about some of the elements of fiction so skillfully used by the author to convey her meaning, we will also learn how to go beyond our emotional reaction to the story to see how it contributes to our understanding of what the author wanted to say.

In addition to the detailed presentation of "The Lottery," the television program also contains a discussion of traditional elements of all literature, such as point of view, characterization, atmosphere, tone and style, and plot of theme.

The textbook describes different forms of literature, examples of which can be found in both poetry and prose: the narrative, the episodic narrative, and the quest narrative. The study of symbolic devices in literature, which was begun in the preceding lesson with explanations of images and metaphors, is completed in this lesson with a discussion of the symbol itself—"a further use of metaphor."

Those who have not read "The Lottery" before they hear the story in the lesson may well remember the story long after they have consciously forgotten some of the other topics presented in this lesson. "The Lottery" is, in one sense, a modern horror story, a compelling tale with a bizarre twist that may strike "close to home" for many. Regardless of our responses to the story, our analysis of the techniques used by the author to construct this story will improve our skills in analyzing other pieces of literature we will encounter in the future.

LEARNING OBJECTIVES

ON COMPLETING YOUR STUDY OF THIS LESSON, YOU SHOULD BE ABLE TO:

1. State a simple definition of "literature."
2. Define "point of view" and identify an example of each basic type.
3. List four basic techniques of characterization.
4. Define atmosphere, tone, and style.
5. Describe narrative forms of literature.
6. Define symbolism and be sensitive to the tentative quality of literary symbols.
7. Appreciate and be more sensitive to the complexity that may be found within even a straightforward, short work of fiction.

ASSIGNMENTS

BEFORE VIEWING THE PROGRAM:

Read the "Overview" and familiarize yourself with the "Learning Objectives" for this lesson.

Consult a dictionary to acquaint yourself with the following terms:

> exposition
> fiction
> first person
> narrative
> second person
> symbol
> third person

Look over the "Aids for Study" for this lesson.

In the textbook, Chapter 7, "Literature":
  • Read pages 212–217 ("Literary Structures").
  • Review pages 228–232 ("The Symbol").

VIEW THE TELEVISION PROGRAM *"Literature: The Story Beyond.*

AFTER VIEWING THE PROGRAM:

Review what you have learned, using the "Aids for Study" again.

Select and read a short story by another author such as Ernest Hemingway, John Dos Passos, Dorothy Parker, or any twentieth-century writer. Read the story for enjoyment, then list the elements discussed in this lesson and summarize how they are employed within the story.

Evaluate your learning with the "Review Quiz," then check your answers with the "Answer Key" at the back of this study guide.

In accordance with your own interests or your instructor's assignment, complete selected "Additional Activities."

AIDS FOR STUDY

1. What are two implications of narrative style? If both a narrator and an audience must seem to exist, in which examples given in the text is the specific identity of the narrator most significant? Can you think of other examples studied in this unit in which the narrator is less important or the audience is more important?

2. What examples of episodic narrative have been presented in this unit? Are you familiar with any modern novels that might be classified as episodic narratives or quest narratives? How would you classify most detective stories?

3. How does the use of symbolism differ from the use of metaphor that was studied in the previous lesson? Why can there be no single, final answer to the meaning of a symbol in such a work as Blake's poem "The Sick Rose" (textbook page 229)? What cautions does the textbook suggest before you begin to examine symbolic meanings in a poem or story? Would these same precautions be useful in studying the symbolism in other arts, such as film, drama, or music?

4. Do you agree with the definition of literature implied in the quotation read by Maya Angelou: "Writers of literature have as their quest the discovery of truth beyond fact, and when they succeed in poetry or prose they've created literature"? Is "truth beyond fact" evident in the examples in the reading assignments for this lesson?

5. What is meant by "point of view," and why is it an important element in the craft of fiction? What freedom does the author (or narrator) have when the "author omniscient" point of view is employed? How does "third person limited" differ from "third person objective"? What example of first person was read in this lesson? Which point of view was employed by Shirley Jackson in "The Lottery"?

6. What four types of characterization are defined in the television program? Which type of characterization is developed by Jackson in "The Lottery"? Which type is used in

the excerpt from "My Oedipus Complex" in the text? Which
type is used in the poem "Paralytic"?

7.   How does the atmosphere of a story differ from its tone? Which
element is related to the author's attitude toward his or her
subject matter? Which one is related to the emotional
environment of the story? What is the name given to that
element of literature that concerns the author's selection and use
of words?

8.   How would you describe the plot of "The Lottery"? How would
you describe its theme? Of these two terms—plot and theme—
which one has to do with the *meaning* of the story, the author's
intention?

9.   What symbolism in "The Lottery" is suggested in the program?
If a symbol is one part of a comparison, an outward and visible
part, and the thing symbolized is intentionally vague and more
difficult to define, will everyone agree on the symbolic meaning
of this story? Do other meanings suggest themselves to you?

10.   Although not stressed in this lesson, some critics view a short
story as any work that has only one plot and one character
development, whereas a novel is seen as any work that
incorporates subplots and has numerous characterizations. Yet,
as Maya Angelou pointed out in the program, "The Lottery"
contained lesser themes, related to the primary content of the
story. Can you identify a subplot or story element in "The
Lottery," as well as the primary story? Does this additional
complexity of the story make it more or less enjoyable for you?

IZ _____

: best answer, or write the correct answer in the space provided.

1. Literature may be defined as
    a. any work of fiction.
    b. published writing that tells a story or has narrative or lyric qualities.
    c. any work in which the author expresses meanings that go beyond facts.
    d. any work of fiction that contains plot, theme, and characterization.

2. In a story in which the author or narrator describes not only what can be seen and heard but the thoughts and emotions experienced by any character, the point of the view of the story is called
    a. author omniscient.
    b. first person.
    c. third person (limited).
    d. third person (objective).

3. In a story in which only the thoughts and feelings of a single character are expressed, although the single character is not telling the story, the point of view of the story is called
    a. author omniscient.
    b. first person.
    c. third person (limited).
    d. third person (objective).

4. What type of characterization is employed in "The Lottery"?

    author exposition

5. What type of characterization is employed in the poem "Paralytic"?

    presented from within

6. The general emotional mood within a story is called its
   a. tone.
   b. atmosphere.
   c. style.
   d. characterization.

7. The term used to describe the words selected by the author and the manner in which these words are used is
   a. tone.
   b. atmosphere.
   c. style.
   d. characterization.

8. The story in which the events are related as a series of events not closely connected is called the
   a. epic.
   b. episodic narrative.
   c. quest narrative.
   d. novel.

9. Which of the following is most likely to be most difficult to define?
   a. a literary symbol
   b. the thing symbolized
   c. the things compared by metaphor
   d. the plot

10. The meaning or writer's intention in a work of fiction is called
   a. plot.
   b. characterization.
   c. theme.
   d. point of view.

ADDITIONAL ACTIVITIES

1. Discuss the symbolism within the story you read as part of your postviewing assignment. Be certain to identify the persons, objects, or events (or combinations) that were used symbolically and then express your view about what the author is symbolizing. In your opinion, how does this symbolism reflect the author's intention in writing the story?

2. Discuss how each type of characterization used in a written story might be employed in a dramatic work. For the most part, what type of characterization was employed in *Pygmalion*? In *The Misanthrope*? Which type of characterization would be most difficult to employ in drama?

3. Select a novel according to your own interest and read it, being especially sensitive to subplots and secondary themes. Discuss whether the author could have fully developed his or her themes in a short story or even in a series of short stories as effectively as in the novel.

LITERATURE

BEHIND THE WORDS

Most of us have probably experienced an "afterglow" on finishing reading a particular poem, short story, or an especially moving novel. The piece of literature producing this effect has left us with a certain "feeling" even though we may not be able to pinpoint the exact image, dialogue, scene, or character that evoked the feeling. Yet, the meaning intended by the poet or the author persists, and we might say that the experience has enhanced our perception of human values.

Of all the literary forms, poetry is perhaps the one form that is most subject to varying interpretations and critical responses. You may recall from an earlier lesson Robert Frost's comment to the effect that the first reading of a poem provides the story; the second reading, a meaning; and the third reading, another meaning. Because poetry can be interpreted in different ways, it is a natural form to use as a subject for developing our critical skills in literature.

This lesson provides three experiences that may be helpful for us in analyzing our responses to a specific poem. In the first, we learn what a poet thought as he wrote the poem and about the emotions and desires he experienced as he developed the images in the poem to convey his intended meaning. A second part of this lesson is a poem about poetry: the poem itself is an analytical description of one poet's concept of what a poem is. The third part of this lesson is based on a poem that is part of the text read for an earlier lesson. In this lesson, we are given the opportunity for studying and analyzing the poem in more detail.

The "Additional Activities" for this lesson are designed to direct us toward applying critical skills to short stories and other prose forms. In sum, the purpose of this lesson is to increase our enjoyment of poetry and other forms of literature by helping us to acquire skills that will enable us to more accurately perceive the author's intent.

LEARNING OBJECTIVES

ON COMPLETING YOUR STUDY OF THIS LESSON, YOU SHOULD BE ABLE TO:

1. Differentiate the subject matter and content of three poems.
2. Identify examples of imagery, symbolism, and other poetic elements in the poems and describe how their uses support the poet's meaning.
3. Demonstrate participation in a poem and identify the emotional content or theme of the work.
4. Appreciate more fully an author's intent in a given piece of literature.

ASSIGNMENTS

BEFORE VIEWING THE PROGRAM:

Read the "Overview" and familiarize yourself with the "Learning Objectives" for this lesson.

Review Chapter 3, "Being a Critic of the Arts" (textbook pages 47–67).

Review the sections in Chapter 7, "The Image," "The Metaphor," and "The Symbol").

Look over the "Aids for Study" for this lesson.

Review the meaning of the following terms:

> lyric poem
> metaphor
> meter
> simile
> sonnet
> symbol

VIEW THE PROGRAM *"Literature: Behind the Words."*

AFTER VIEWING THE PROGRAM:

In the study guide:
- Read the article "How a Poem Is Made" by C. Day Lewis and the poem "Ars Poetica" by Archibald MacLeish.

In the textbook:
- Read "Polo Grounds" by Rolfe Humphries (pages 222–223).

Review what you have learned, using the "Aids for Study" again.

Evaluate your learning with the "Review Quiz," then check your answers with the "Answer Key" at the back of this study guide.

In accordance with your own interests or your instructor's assignment, complete selected "Additional Activities."

AIDS FOR STUDY

1. How many lines does the poem by C. Day Lewis contain? What type of poetry form is suggested by the number of lines? What is the rhyme pattern for this poem? Is the rhyming freer than that of the poetry of Shakespeare or Keats?

2. Which type of comparison is contained in the second line of the poem by C. Day Lewis? Which line of this poem indicates

strongly that the "mist" the poet speaks of is a symbol and not a literal one? What does the mist symbolize in this poem? How does the poet, in his comments on the poem, describe line 12? Does the phrase "quicksand and a wreck" seem to you to mean only "hurts"?

3. According to C. Day Lewis, what are the two themes contained in his poem? What does he mean by the closing words "like time that has flagged out their course"? To what kind of flags is he referring? Where did he obtain the images he used to symbolize his meanings in this poem? How would you summarize the meaning this poem has for you?

4. What is the primary subject matter of "Ars Poetica"? Is there a rhyme *pattern* in this poem? Is there a rigid rhythm or meter? Are there many rhymes? Is there a rhythm? (Note the "almost rhymes" of wordless—birds; releases—tree.)

5. In "Ars Poetica," MacLeish has directed our attention to the three separate stanzas of his poem. What statement about the characteristics is made in each stanza? Can a spoken poem convey these characteristics? Recall the thoughts of Ingmar Bergman in the lesson "Film: Seeing All There Is," in which he stated that the important part of the film was not the dialogue or script but the emotions, feelings, and mood he wished to convey. Is MacLeish making a similar statement about poetry?

6. Identify the rhythm and pattern of "Polo Grounds." Is the rhythm more settled and repetitive in this poem than in "Ars Poetica"? (Note especially that each line of "Polo Grounds" seems divided into two phrases of approximately equal weight.) Does this rhythm seem suitable for description of a baseball game (as in the stanza beginning "Hubbell takes the sign")? What is the subject matter of the next stanza? Is the rhythm better suited to this topic? What new clue about the subject matter of the poem is in the last two lines of this stanza?

7. In the next to last stanza of "Polo Grounds," who or what is the "shadow"? If "time is the essence" means the most important time is *now*, why is so much attention paid to memory in this poem? What fact of life does the poet seem to accept in the last

stanza? Is this said bitterly, with resignation, or with some
other emotion?

REVIEW QUIZ

Select the best answer.

1. The poem by C. Day Lewis is in the form of
    a. an epic or narrative.
    b. a sonnet.
    c. free verse.
    d. a quatrain.

2. The themes within the C. Day Lewis poem are best summarized as
    a. an experience of children walking out of doors early in the
       morning.
    b. children's desire for adulthood and a parent's desire to protect
       them.
    c. the dangers and wrecks of life as perceived by an older person.
    d. a parent's need to have love from his children.

3. What type of comparison is contained in the line "tissue of mist
    that veils a valley's lap"?
    a. simile
    b. metaphor
    c. alliteration
    d. metrical

4. C. Day Lewis states that most of the images used in this poem came
    from
    a. actual experiences of his children.
    b. a careful selection of natural occurrences that could symbolize
       his emotions.
    c. inspiration spontaneously arising from his subconscious.
    d. actual experiences from his own childhood.

5. The poem "Ars Poetica" is in a form best described as
   a. free verse.
   b. sonnet.
   c. narrative.
   d. prose.

6. The requirements implied in "Ars Poetica" for a poem, if taken literally,
   a. would require a poet to write in traditional forms.
   b. could only be followed by master poets.
   c. would be impossible to achieve.
   d. could apply only to poems of limited strength.

7. One interpretation of "Ars Poetica" is that the poet is referring to
   a. life or love rather than to poetry or writing.
   b. the emotions, feelings, and mood created by a poem.
   c. arts other than poetry.
   d. the actual poems he enjoyed in childhood.

8. The subject matter of "Polo Grounds" can best be described as
   a. a narration of an actual baseball game.
   b. the response of crowds to the players and the game.
   c. a person's thoughts during a baseball game.
   d. memories of past glories as a baseball player.

9. The "left-handed catcher named Jack Humphries" is important because he
   a. has the same last name as the poet.
   b. was an outstanding player in the game.
   c. played most often in the outfield.
   d. is the first player mentioned by name.

10. When the poet says "the crowd and players are the same age always, but the man in the crowd is older every season" he is
   a. making an observation about people in the stands.
   b. showing acceptance of his own advancing age.
   c. bitter because he is not on the team.
   d. referring to the players he remembers from earlier years.

ADDITIONAL ACTIVITIES

1. Select a modern short story and write a brief descriptive criticism of the work. Be certain to include description of elements other than the plot and character development. In particular, comment on the point of view of the story. If the story is told in first person, for example, discuss the type of story development made possible by this particular point of view and how other points of view might not be as effective. Also, identify any literary elements such as imagery that are used. How does the author lead you to sympathetic understanding (or the reverse) of the leading character in this story?

2. From your own reading, try to recall a short story or poem that you believe has a symbolic meaning underlying the apparent subject matter. Reread the work and write a brief interpretation of it. Check your interpretation by assuring yourself that it can apply to the entire story or poem, not just to a portion of it.

3. Discuss each of the images employed by MacLeish in the poem studied in this lesson, suggesting how each image applies to the subject matter and meaning of the poem. (In this and other activities, be assured there is no single "correct" interpretation or understanding of a work of art. Your own interpretation is bound to be subjective. The purpose of this activity is to encourage you to try to determine what the poet meant when he compared a poem to the sensations an old medallion gives when touched by a thumb or to a moon slowly climbing behind the branches of a tree in winter.)

In the 1930s, the poetry of Cecil Day Lewis, along with that of W. H. Auden, Louis MacNeice, and Stephen Spender, reflected the poet's left-wing political involvement. Later, however, his poetry evolved into traditional lyric forms and his style became more contemplative and rambling. Day Lewis's position as a leading contemporary poet was formally acknowledged when he was appointed poet laureate of England in 1968, a post he held until his death in 1972.

Archibald MacLeish, (1892–1982), a second poet whose work is presented in this lesson, was born in Illinois. Much of his work reflects his concern with the principles of liberal democracy, and during the presidency of Franklin Delano Roosevelt, MacLeish was sometimes referred to as "the poet laureate of the New Deal." Although much of his poetry reflects his political orientation, the poems for which he is most admired generally express his more private and personal feelings. Interestingly, the "art for art's sake" philosophy that he expresses in the poem reprinted in this lesson was later discarded by MacLeish.

HOW A POEM IS MADE

C. Day Lewis (1905–1972)

Children look down upon the morning-gray
Tissue of mist that veils a valley's lap:
Their fingers itch to tear it and unwrap
The flags, the roundabouts, the gala day.
They watch the spring rise inexhaustibly
A breathing thread out of the eddied sand,
Sufficient to their day: but half their mind
Is on the sailed and glittering estuary.
Fondly we wish their mist might never break,
Knowing it hides so much that best were hidden:
We'd chain them by the spring, lest it should broaden
For them into a quicksand and a wreck.
But they slip through our fingers like the source,
Like mist, like time that has flagged out their course.

The seed of this poem was a strong feeling I had about my own two
children. It is a feeling most parents have, at one time or another—a
feeling of sadness that their children must grow up, must leave their

protection and go out into the dangerous and difficult world. When you are young, you sometimes resent your parents having that feeling: you *want* to grow up and be independent.

Now, if you look at the poem again, you'll see there are two themes, or subjects, in it—the original one, my *own* feeling, which comes out in the last six lines; and the *children's* feeling of impatience and expectation, which comes out in the first eight. These two themes are intended to balance and contrast with each other.

Before I actually start writing a poem, I often find a line of verse comes into my head—a line which gives me a clue to the theme and pattern which the poem will develop: a sort of key-line. When I sat down to begin this sonnet, such a line of verse at once came into my head. That line (it is the only one I didn't have to work for) was "The flags, the roundabouts, the gala day." I thought about this line, and saw that it was an image of a fête or a fair, the sort of thing a child looks forward to; obviously, it symbolized (that is, "stood for") the grown-up world which a child is so impatient to enter. The idea of *impatience* then added some more lines—the first three. Here, the early-morning mist covering the valley represents the veil which the children wish to tear away, as they would tear the tissue paper off a birthday present—the veil which shuts them off from the grown-up world. The image came out of my memory, recalled from a day several years ago when I was taking my children to school in Devonshire, and we paused at the top of a hill and saw the whole of the valley below covered with mist; I remembered thinking at the time that it looked like tissue paper, but I'd forgotten all about the incident until I began to write this poem.

Next, I wanted a second image-sequence, as a variation on the theme expressed in the first four lines. You'll find it in line 5 to 8—the picture of a spring bubbling up out of the earth, and the children bending down to watch its "breathing thread." The word "breathing" gives you a clue to the meaning of this passage: The spring represents life near its source, *young* life; and the children are only half satisfied with it; "half their mind" is looking forward to the time when their life will have broadened out, as a stream broadens into an estuary, and becomes more important and exciting. The image of the spring, like that of the mist, came out of my memory: it was a particular spring, near a country house in Ireland, which used to fascinate me as a child; I remember spending hours watching it, wondering how such a tiny thread of water managed to force its way out of the earth.

Next, the other theme had to be started—the *parent's* feeling about the children going out into the world. Notice that, although this theme was the original seed of the poem, it now occupies a relatively small space (lines 9 to 12): it often happens, when you are writing a poem, that you find the poem turning out quite differently from what you expected — in other words, you don't know what a poem is going to be like till you have gone some way with the composing of it; indeed, to a certain extent, a poem *composes itself.* Lines 9–12 say, quite simply, "We grown-ups wish the mist of childhood might never break for our children, because, when it does, they'll see the world is not such a pleasant place as they imagined. We'd like to chain them to their childhood, to save them from being hurt ('a quicksand and a wreck') as everyone must sometimes be hurt by life when he grows up." But the poem couldn't end like that, could it? After all, a parent can't really prevent his children growing up, even if it was right for him to try and do so—which it isn't. So, in the last two lines, I describe how children grow independent of their parents, slipping away from them like mist or water ("the source") slips through one's fingers: they must fend for themselves, run their own race—and time has already "flagged out their course."

I wonder whether you have noticed something about those last six lines. Except for the quicksand and the wreck there are no new images in them. Even the phrase "flagged out their course" (which, by the way, is another memory-image of mine, derived from a two-mile steeplechase I ran in as a boy of fourteen)—even this phrase echoes "the flags" of line 4. Instead of using new images, I have repeated those of the first eight lines—mist, the spring, the estuary ("lest it should *broaden* / For them into a quicksand and a wreck"), the flags. . . [An] important part is played in poetry by repetition. It is not only words and phrases, but also images, which can be repeated. And they are repeated in this poem, so that you can see the two main themes from a number of different angles, just as you can see many different reflections of yourself if you walk down a corridor of mirrors.

Lastly, what I have told you about the sources of these particular images will help you to understand how a poem grows. The seed of this poem took root in my mind. Then, without my being aware of it, it somehow attracted to itself several experiences I had had at quite different periods of my life and forgotten about. It got hold of a Devonshire mist, an Irish spring, and a steeplechase course in Dorset; it added an estuary with yachts sailing on it (I still don't know where that last picture came from): and, when I began to write the poem, these four images rose out of my mind all ready to illustrate the theme . . .

ARS POETICA

Archibald MacLeish (1892–1982)

A poem should be palpable and mute
As a globed fruit,

Dumb
As old medallions to the thumb,

Silent as the sleeve-worn stone
Of casement ledges where the moss has grown—

A poem should be wordless
As the flight of birds.

* * * * *

A poem should be motionless in time
As the moon climbs,

Leaving, as the moon releases
Twig by twig the night-entangled tree,

Leaving, as the moon behind the winter leaves
Memory by memory the mind—

A poem should be motionless in time
As the moon climbs.

* * * * *

A poem should be equal to:
Not true.

For all the history of grief
An empty doorway and a maple leaf.

For Love
The leaning grasses and two lights about the sea—

A poem should not mean
But be.

From *Collected Poems*, by Archibald MacLeish,
Houghton-Mifflin Co., Boston.

LESSON 18

PAINTING

VISIONS THROUGH THE AGES

OVERVIEW

In every age, those who paint or draw have sought to reveal truth through their art. The great Renaissance artist Leonardo da Vinci characterized his work as "sight with insight." In this lesson, we will study how artists throughout the ages have achieved "sight with insight" and will consider the importance of our visual sense to appreciating and comprehending a painting.

This lesson's television program begins with humankind's earliest examples of art: prehistoric cave paintings that probably were drawn as part of a magic spell to ensure success in hunting. The program then moves on to ancient Egypt, where many paintings were done on the walls of tombs for the enjoyment of the spirits of the dead rather than of the living. The next paintings presented are those of the Greeks and Romans. The Greek and Roman art we see on pottery and in temples, homes, and public places depicts more lifelike forms, which display far more vitality and movement than did the forms of Egyptian art.

With the advent of the Christian Era in Western civilization, the realistic human figure as an element in painting was diminished, as most paintings emphasized religious themes. In one striking example of how paintings of the time reflected the relative values of religious and worldly matters, we see a painting in which a human figure has been deliberately miniaturized.

Although religious themes continued to dominate many paintings of the next historical era—the Renaissance—there was renewed interest in the human form and emphasis on all the arts and sciences. The values of the Renaissance facilitated the painting of many realistic portraits of persons of that era, and all subjects are painted with a sense of beauty, harmony, and humanity. Among the many paintings by Renaissance painters shown in the program are the Sistene Chapel frescoes by Michelangelo, the *Mona Lisa* by Leonardo da Vinci, and *St. George and the Dragon* and *Madonna* by Raphael.

Paintings of the Baroque—the next major era—were characterized by meticulous attention to detail. At this time, landscapes, portraits, and still lifes developed into distinct art forms. Artists of the Baroque whose works are shown in the program include Velázquez, Vandyke, Vermeer, and Rembrandt.

In breaking away from the rigid structures and forms of earlier periods, the artists of the Baroque provided the foundation for the eventual evolution of modern art. Some modern artists may strive to strip away externals and "portray the raw nerve of essential quality," whereas others attempt to portray their feelings through representations of objects and people in the real world. Modern art has taken many forms: Impressionism, Cubism, Expressionism, Futurism, Surrealism, and Abstractionism. The wide variety of modern art forms is illustrated by the works of Renoir, Monet, Pissarro, Degas, Cassatt, Toulouse-Lautrec, and Van Gogh. Abstractionism is, perhaps, the ultimate "language" in which an individual artist can express his or her inner vision. In abstract paintings, "the colors and shapes themselves make their own statements." In the program, we see the first abstract art by Kandinski as well as a later example by Jackson Pollock.

Regardless of the art or of the age, new forms are seldom received kindly or quickly. Those who were comfortable with Renaissance art no doubt were uncomfortable with Baroque art. Today, many of us may not be comfortable with abstract art or some of the other contemporary art forms. Yet, as our narrator reminds us, all painters seek new values and new perceptions to interpret the world around themselves. In providing a historical perspective of artists and their works, this lesson may help us to view all works of art with fewer preconceived ideas about what is "good" and what is "bad."

LEARNING OBJECTIVES

ON COMPLETING YOUR STUDY OF THIS LESSON, YOU SHOULD BE ABLE TO:

1. Appreciate the value of applying visual skills to enjoyment of an object in and of itself.
2. State the purpose of painted frescoes in Egyptian tombs
3. Identify some characteristics of Greek and Roman painting.
4. Contrast the subject matter and treatment of painters of the early Christian church with those of the Renaissance.
5. Recall names of some significant painters from the Renaissance, Baroque, and Modern periods.
6. Appreciate more fully the realities that painters of each age have attempted to reveal.

ASSIGNMENTS

BEFORE VIEWING THE PROGRAM:

Read the "Overview" and familiarize yourself with the "Learning Objectives" for this lesson.

Look over the "Aids for Study" for this lesson.

In the textbook, Chapter 4, "Painting":
- Read pages 69–74 (Introductory material, "The Clarity of Painting," and "The 'All-at-Onceness' of Painting").
- Scan pages 74–84 ("Representational and Abstract Painting") to familiarize yourself with the terms "abstract art" and "representational art."

VIEW THE TELEVISION PROGRAM *"Painting: Visions through the Ages."*

AFTER VIEWING THE PROGRAM:

Review what you have learned, using the "Aids for Study" again.

Evaluate your learning with the "Review Quiz," then check your answers with the "Answer Key" at the back of this study guide.

In accordance with your own interests or your instructor's assignment, complete selected "Additional Activities."

AIDS FOR STUDY

1. Do you respond positively or negatively to the questions and challenges posed by the perception key, "Your Visual Powers" (textbook pages 70–71)? Do you feel there would be value to you in "enjoying things as they show themselves"? The authors of the textbook seem to feel our workaday vision is not "whole." Do you agree with them that "with their [the artists'] aid, our vision can be made whole again"?

2. What was the purpose of frescoes inside Egyptian tombs? What kind of changes in art technique and portrayal are evident in the Greek and Roman art seen in the program? How did the Greeks and Romans use their paintings differently than did the Egyptians?

3. What was the purpose of art in the early Christian churches? Suggest how the portrayal of individual people as subject matter changed from these years to the Renaissance.

4. Works of which Renaissance artists were shown in the program? What subject matter did Renaissance artists frequently use in their paintings? What new elements of realism did they introduce into their works?

5. Works of which Baroque painters were presented in the program? What subject matter predominated in the examples shown?

6. Of the artists whose works were shown representative of the Modern period, which were painters of representational art and which of abstract art?

7. What reality was revealed in the paintings of the artists of the Renaissance? Of the Baroque? Of the Modern era?

e best answer when choices are given or write a correct name in the space provided.

1. According to the textbook, an appreciation of art should begin with
    a. knowledge of the use of materials and of techniques for light, form, and structure.
    b. sensitivity to the qualities of objects and colors in themselves.
    c. using vision to classify objects quickly into groups or categories.
    d. the development of actual painting skills.

2. Egyptian artists decorated the walls of tombs to
    a. create a pleasant environment for the families of the departed.
    b. promote their religious beliefs.
    c. provide pleasant scenes for the spirit of the dead person.
    d. cast a magic spell.

3. The paintings of Greece and Rome were different from those of the Egyptians because
    a. portrayal of the human body was more lifelike and realistic.
    b. the paintings were used to promote religious devotion.
    c. the paintings were meant to invoke protection from gods and spirits.
    d. many were portraits of individuals.

4. Early Christian art emphasized
    a. important figures in the church, such as those who made large donations.
    b. the central beliefs of the religion: the incarnation and the redemption.
    c. scenes of contemporary worship.
    d. figures from the traditions of Greece and Rome.

5. Which of the following was *not* a characteristic of painting of the Renaissance?
    a. realism of the human body combined with reverence for humanity
    b. emphasis upon religious subjects
    c. individuality of style in the treatment of subjects
    d. portrayal of contemporary social conditions

6. List the names of three painters of the Renaissance.

da Vinci
Tintaretto
Michelangelo
Raphael

7. The Baroque period is characterized by its
   a. preoccupation with religious subject matter.
   b. extreme simplicity of detail.
   c. preoccupation with earlier themes of Greece and Rome.
   d. landscapes, portraits, and still lifes.

8. List the names of three important painters of the Baroque era.

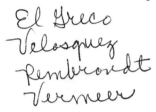

El Greco
Velosquez
Rembrandt
Vermeer

9. Two trends of modern art mentioned in this lesson are
   a. a return to portrait paintings, abstract art.
   b. attention to the essential qualities of a subject, abstract art.
   c. attention to the essential qualities of a subject, religious subjects.
   d. abstract art, myths and legends of the Renaissance.

10. List the name of one modern painter of representational art
    (including Impressionistic) and the name of one painter of abstract
    art mentioned in the program.

Representational:

Monet

Abstract:

Pollock

ADDITIONAL ACTIVITIES

1. Perform Experiment 5 in the preception key, "Your Visual
    Powers" (textbook page 70). Then discuss your feelings concerning
    this experiment, considering such questions as:
    a. Do you find you can heighten your enjoyment of a single color
        by shifting or arranging other components in your field of
        vision?
    b. Do you find a similarity between your experiment and the
        painting *Earth Greens* in Color Plate 16.
    c. Would you find it easier to enjoy an object, such as the one in
        Experiment 7 (textbook page 70), than a color? Why or why
        not?

2. Select two painters discussed in the program, one from the
    Renaissance or Baroque and one from the Modern period. Look at
    reproductions of several of their paintings. Then comment on
    how, in each painting, the artist reflects the artistic trend of his
    or her time, as discussed in the program.

3. Discuss similarities and differences of Baroque composers and
    painters. If possible (consulting other sources if you wish), use
    specific artists as examples, such as Bach and Rembrandt.

PAINTING

CREATING A POINT OF VIEW

Because the visual impact of this lesson is especially significant, the visual portion of the lesson should be viewed on a color television set that has good picture quality. You may wish to review Chapter 2, "What Is a Work of Art?" before proceeding with the lesson, even though at this point in your study you may already be able to "participate" readily in a work of art. Note, too, that readings from the Martin and Jacobus textbook are carefully selected especially to complement the television presentation.

Artists use certain visible elements to express subject matter and translate it into a visual image of some reality perceived by the artist. This lesson begins with an introduction to the primary elements artists employ in painting: color, space, and line. Color, it is noted in the lesson, dominates most paintings, and its sensory impact is more important than the identity of the objects in the painting. Color and line create shapes, and substance is a blend of shape and color. Shapes hold color and lend themselves to arrangements that define space. Lines are used for clarification and expressive force, and the artist is free to distort lines as he or she chooses in presenting a personal view of reality.

The elements of painting are also called *sensa* because they function to stimulate the sense organs of the person perceiving the painting. Sensa are the cause of visual, tactile, aural, and olfactory sensations; they may or may not be associated with specific objects or events. In this lesson, we are asked to attend to these sensation-producing elements (sensa) themselves rather than to the form, shape, or object they represent.

The importance of color is illustrated by Josef Alber's painting, *Homage to the Square*, a work that has but a single color; by Mark Rothko's *Earth Greens*, a contrast between two strong colors framed by a softer color; and by Hans Hoffman's *The Golden Wall*, which extols the vitality and moods of many colors.

The artist modifies, intensifies, and subdues color through the use of light and shadow. Works by Cézanne, Rubens, Rembrandt, and Manfredi show how light and dark may dramatize a scene, emphasize what the artist judges most important, and, in many cases, help the artist convey an emotional or psychological facet of the subject. Some of Monet's works are displayed to show how light and color were, for him, not just elements but the very essence of painting.

The use of line in art is introduced through several examples. Lines are hinted in Monet's work; they are distinct and visible in Cézanne and dominant and expressive in Picasso. Lines may give force to a painting and create movement (or lack of movement), mood, and expectation. A contrast of the effect of line is drawn between Eugene Delacroix's *The Lion Hunt* and Edward Hopper's *The Nighthawks*. In one, we see how the lines create tension, action, and expectation of surging movement. In the other, we sense a depression or ennui; stiff, angular objects suggest resignation or defeat. Other elements, of course, support the mood and tone of each picture. But take particular note of the predominating effect of line in each of these.

The third element, space, is presented first as an arrangement of shapes—objects "in a satisfying, overall relationship to each other and the picture space." A Claez still life shows an obvious but purposeful placement of one subject in relation to others. Other uses of this element reveal that picture space is not to be confused with "real" or "everyday" space. Artists manipulate space as they do color and line. El Greco's *Feast in the House of Simon* and Braque's still life show deliberate distortion of space and objects, which aid the artists in achieving their purposes.

In abstract painting there is no true space as such. Abstract painting deals not with specific objects and events but with the *qualities* of these objects and events, revealing the sensa for their own sake. In an abstract painting such as Rothko's *Earth Greens*, or Mondrian's *Composition in Black, White and Red*, there is nothing to attend to but sensa. The perceiver thus experiences a sense of presentational immediacy and timelessness—or here-now sensation, as it is described by Martin and Jacobus.

Representational painting, too, has much to say about sensa, but it has specific objects and events as its subject matter. The sensuous is "situated" in events that imply a future and a past: sensa are fused with objects and events. Still, the representational painting is always interpreted differently, just as is the abstract painting.

In the concluding moments of the television program, a series of examples summarizes an important principle of this art: Whether a painting is representational or abstract, the artist selects what it is he or she wishes to present and eliminates details that are unimportant in order to communicate insight into a deeper reality. Although artists all employ these same elements, each has different insights to express. Thus, each artist—and each painting—is a new experience.

The narrator ends the televised lesson saying, "The urge to create a visual image of true reality is probably the most common element among artists." As we learn, the artist's "true reality" may not be what we would perceive as reality.

LEARNING OBJECTIVES

ON COMPLETING YOUR STUDY OF THIS LESSON, YOU SHOULD BE ABLE TO:

1. Name three primary elements of the art of painting.
2. Understand to what extent an artist's point of view is a decisive factor in use of elements to create art.
3. State two means by which the artist may modify color.
4. Name two artists whose use of the line element differ markedly.
5. Identify what is meant by "space" in painting.
6. Appreciate the principle that painting is never solely representational.
7. Recognize the differences and similarities between abstract and representational painting.

ASSIGNMENTS

BEFORE VIEWING THE PROGRAM:

Read the "Overview" and familiarize yourself with the "Learning Objectives" for this lesson.

Consult a dictionary, an encyclopedia, or the textbook to acquaint yourself with these terms:

    abstract art
    representational art
    sensa
    Surrealism

Look over the "Aids for Study" for this lesson.

VIEW THE TELEVISION PROGRAM *"Painting: Creating a Point of View."*

AFTER VIEWING THE PROGRAM:

In the textbook, Chapter 4, "Painting":
- Read pages 74–84 ("Representational and Abstract Painting") and pages 88–90 ("Parmigianino").
- Review pages 69–74.

Review what you have learned, using the "Aids for Study" again.

Evaluate your learning with the "Review Quiz," then check your answers with the "Answer Key" at the back of this study guide.

In accordance with your own interests or your instructor's assignment, complete selected "Additional Activities."

AIDS FOR STUDY

1. In Alber's *Homage to the Square* and Rothko's *Earth Greens*, color predominates. How is color used differently in each?

2. A series of pictures by Cézanne is used to show some uses of color. How important is color to the artist? Why?

3. Explain briefly how Rembrandt revealed more about his subjects through use of shadow and light. What do you think Rembrandt revealed in his painting of a group of local businessmen?

4. In the television program, the narrator said that the artist is free to distort a line if it clarifies his or her presentation or reality. List an example from the program and an example from your reading in which the artist distorts a line. Explain how the artist used distortion to help convey his or her view of reality.

5. When you view the program for this lesson, take special note of the segment that contrasts the composition of Delacroix's *Lion Hunt* with Hopper's *Nighthawks*. Contrast the two works by
   a. describing the lines in *Lion Hunt*, then describing the lines in *Nighthawks*.
   b. describing the colors in *Lion Hunt*, then those in *Nighthawks*.
   c. describing the apparent tones or shading of each if you view the program in black and white rather than on a color television.

6. What "reality" or "truth" do you feel is communicated by the *Lion Hunt*? By *Nighthawks*?

7. Did you find the distortion of normal space relationships in El Grego's and Braque's still life compositions disturbing or did the "picture space" seem "real" to you? Is there a similarity between such distortion of space in these paintings and the use of light and shadow by Rembrandt, Rubens, and Manfredi? Explain your answer.

8. Study Color Plate 17 in your textbook. Comment on Matisse's color, tone, and space in his painting *Pineapple and Anemones*. What is changed from the everyday, normal appearance of the objects? The narrator for this lesson said, "Artists are less interested in naturalistic detail than in letting imagination and creative force give new insights into reality." Could you suggest such an insight in Matisse's still life?

9. Review the perception key, *"Mont Sainte Victoire"* (textbook pages 71–72). Describe some of Cézanne's uses of color, line, and space in *Mont Sainte Victoire*. Summarize the textbook's explanation for the changes that the author made from reality.

10. Look again at Color Plate 18, Parmigianino's *Madonna with the Long Neck*, and the comments on textbook pages 89–90. Identify within the painting each of the descriptions given at the bottom of the textbook page 89, beginning "The design of this delicate work . . . "

11. Parmigianino's Madonna is technically a representational painting. But in what ways could it also be said to be an abstract work?

12. What is meant by the statement, "A new set of lenses begins to grow in your eyes, and with it a way of seeing such things as mountains with extraordinary clarity and satisfaction"?

Select the one best answer, or write in the word or phrase best completing the thought.

1. The three elements identified as central to the art of painting are
   a. color, light, and shadow.
   b. color, line, and form.
   c. color, form, and space.
   d. color, line, and space.

2. The *sensa*, as used in the text, refers to
   a. scenes.
   b. materials.
   c. qualities such as colors, lines, and space.
   d. all of these.

3. Color is modified by
   a. light.
   b. shadow.
   c. light and shadow.
   d. neither light nor shadow.

4. Through use of color and modification, the artist can
   a. more closely approximate nature.
   b. emphasize color and shape.
   c. probe into or reveal the character of the subject.
   d. show movement.

5. Lines are used with other elements to portray movement, tension, and action in
   a. Eugene Delacroix's painting of a lion hunt.
   b. Edward Hopper's painting of an all-night restaurant.
   c. Albers's *Homage to a Square.*
   d. Claez's still life.

6. Lines are also used with other elements to create an effect of isolation, stiffness, and resignation in
   a. Eugene Delacroix's painting of a lion hunt.
   b. Edward Hopper's painting of an all-night restaurant.
   c. Alber's *Homage to a Square*.
   d. Claez's still life.

7. The lines in *Madonna with the Long Neck* are described as
   a. sensuous.
   b. tension-building.
   c. depressing.
   d. rhythmic.

8. Placement of objects in Claez's still life is
   a. a function of use of lines.
   b. an arrangement of space.
   c. balanced by the use of colors.
   d. a means for using light and shadow.

9. Two examples of distortion of space in a painting were shown in this lesson to illustrate that the artist
   a. modifies space to achieve the proper overall composition.
   b. seeks to deceive the eye.
   c. does not need to understand real relationships of space.
   d. made an error.

10. Which of the following was emphasized as a common thrust or motive among artists?
    a. to distort space in order to emphasize the most important detail
    b. to create a visual image of a true reality
    c. to emphasize a single most important detail in a painting
    d. to develop a mood as the central meaning

11. Name one painting discussed in the text that illustrates the answer given for question 10.

    Cézanne
    Mont Saint Victoire

ADDITIONAL ACTIVITIES

1. Select one representational painting from the color plates, other illustrations in the text, or another source. Describe the artist's use of the elements presented in this lesson. If you prefer, write your own perception key as an outline. Be certain to identify elements that the artist may have changed from "reality."

2. Select one abstract painting from the text or any source. Describe the artist's use of each element and its effect on your perception. Is there an emotional mood or tone suggested to you by the painting? Is there any suggestion of a "real" object or event?

3. Depending upon resources available to you, visit a gallery or obtain a book from your library containing examples of other works by one of the principal artists studied in this lesson: Rembrandt, Matisse, Monet, El Grego, or Delacroix. Write a description of at least three other paintings by this artist, with particular attention to how his use of the elements varies from or corresponds with those presented in the lesson.

4. If a gallery or museum is available to you, find a Cézanne landscape painted after 1855 or locate a color reproduction of one in a book. Compare the painting with the *Mont Sainte Victoire* painting reproduced in the textbook. How does Cézanne use colors, line, and space in each of the two? Does he "distort" in order to achieve "reality?"

5. From a gallery or from reproductions in a book, select paintings in which the artist seems to have made particular use of *one* of the elements to achieve an effect. Try to find one painting for each element. Describe the artist's use of color, line, or space, and suggest the effect that, for you, the artist has achieved.

6. It is sometimes argued that abstract painting is totally disconnected from reality. Do you agree? Why?

PAINTING

ROUSSEAU—THE LOVELY DREAM

OVERVIEW

By now it is becoming apparent that we live in an age of experimentation in the arts, in which artists seek to break free of the traditions, structures, even the materials of the past. They attempt new forms to convey new meanings. To gain an insight into the forms and meanings of the arts in our present age, it helps to look back, just a little, at the times and the figures who were the harbingers of our current styles. Such a figure is Henri Rousseau, who, during his artistic years, sought new forms through which he could express new visions.

In this lesson, the television program presents a montage of facts, dates, and moments to suggest the influences that stirred Rousseau to his level of artistic expression. The facts of his life do not appear to meld together smoothly. For example, at the height of his artistic development, he was convicted of embezzlement. We will learn, too, that although he never visited the tropics, he painted numerous jungle scenes that were, and are, considered by many to be his most significant works. As with many artists who break from the traditional forms, Rousseau's works were initially scorned by the critics. However, the critics became tolerant of his styles after they became familiar with them.

From this sketch of his life and the glimpses of a sequence of his paintings, we will gain insight into the meanings one artist sought to capture through the visual medium of painting.

As you view the program, watch carefully and note the following highlights:

- Rousseau's early life before beginning to paint seriously and the experiences that may have influenced some of his works
- the years and subjects of his first efforts
- the response to his painting of his wife in the New Salon of the Independents
- the period in which he began to devote his total effort to painting
- the influence of his life style and his neighborhood on his painting
- his paintings *War*, *Sleeping Gypsy*, and the *Paean*
- the elements and inspiration for his jungle paintings
- his final entry in the Salon of the Independents, *The Dream*.

Some of the text reviewed for this lesson, "The 'All-at-Onceness' of Painting," stresses an important characteristic of paintings: they can be experienced as a whole in an instant's time. All the other arts studied in this course must be experienced from different perspectives or over a lengthy period of time. Sculpture and architecture, for example, are three-dimensional arts that can, and should, be viewed from all angles. Painting is two-dimensional, and the entirety of the painting can be encompassed in a single glance. Film, drama, music, and literature are all art forms that demand considerable attention over a protracted time before the work of art can be experienced in its entirety. Such is not the case with a painting. We can experience a painting quickly, although we may well want to linger at it and even examine small sections of it to heighten our perception of it.

LEARNING OBJECTIVES

ON COMPLETING YOUR STUDY OF THIS LESSON, YOU SHOULD BE ABLE TO:

1. Identify the productive years of Rousseau as an artist.
2. Name and describe some of his more notable paintings.
3. Select from a list significant influenced upon Rousseau's subject matter.
4. Appreciate better the style and content of Rousseau's later works.
5. Appreciate the influence of Rousseau upon later Surrealist and Modern painters.

ASSIGNMENTS

BEFORE VIEWING THE PROGRAM:

Read the "Overview" and familiarize yourself with the "Learning Objectives" for this lesson.

In the textbook, Chapter 4, "Painting":
    • Review pages 71–73 ("The Clarity of Painting"), pages 73–74 ("The 'All-at-Onceness' of Painting"), and pages 83–84 ("Representational Painting").

Consult a dictionary or encyclopedia for definition of these terms:

    petit bourgeoisie
    Academie
    paean

Look over the "Aids for Study" for this lesson.

VIEW THE TELEVISION PROGRAM *"Painting: Rousseau—The Lovely Dream."*

AFTER VIEWING THE PROGRAM:

Review what you have learned, using the "Aids for Study" again.

Evaluate your learning with the "Review Quiz," then check your answers with the "Answer Key" at the back of this sudy guide.

In accordance with your own interests or your instructor's assignment, complete selected "Additional Activities."

AIDS FOR STUDY

1. What were the influences on the older, academic art styles?
    What was the influence of the Barbizon school?

2. What were Rousseau's occupations before he turned to painting?
    Which one of these may have influenced some of his paintings?
    In what way?

3. When did Rousseau paint his first works? What was the subject
    matter? What was the subject of the first work shown in the
    program that was in his first salon exhibition? What was the
    response of critics?

4. In what year did Rousseau begin to devote full time to his
    painting? In what ways did the neighborhood in which he
    lived influence the subjects of his works?

5. In what way did Rousseau treat the subject of war? Do you recall
    what was said about his actual war experiences? How did he
    portray the "fear, tears, and ruins," which were used by the
    narrator in describing the picture? The painting *Sleeping Gypsy*
    is described as dream picture—how does it depart from reality?

6. What elements did Rousseau apparently employ to create the
    uniqueness of his jungle paintings? Was the fact that he did not
    use actual tropical jungles as a model influential in his work? If

ʼr actually saw the jungles, yet painted them, what type
ˈ is he portraying in his paintings?

ʼ. What painting did Rousseau show at the 22d Salon of the
Independents that attracted favorable attention? Although the
superficial appearance of the painting is in the traditional
manner, how did Rousseau make it appear distinctively
original?

8. What were the subjects of Rousseau's first commissioned
painting?

9. What was most outstanding about *The Hungry Lion* or *The
Dream*? How does *The Dream* relate to the poem that
accompanied the picture: "Yadivigha, peacefully asleep, enjoys
the lovely dream; she hears a kindly snake charmer playing
upon his reed. On stream and foliage glisten the silvery beams of
the moon, and savage beasts listen to the gay, entrancing tune."
Are there contradictions within the painting that match the
contradictions of the poetry?

10. From earlier reading in this unit or from your own experiences in
viewing paintings, do you see similarities between Rousseau's
work and that of twentieth-century Surrealist and Modern
painters? Do you detect any influences of Rousseau's work upon
these painters?

REVIEW QUIZ

Select the one best answer.

1. The academic style of painting was
    a. traditional and aristocratic.
    b. revolutionary.
    c. abstract.
    d. experimental.

2. Rousseau's earlier years were marked by a period
    a. painting portraits.
    b. in music.
    c. in the military service.
    d. in the sciences.

3. Rousseau's main efforts in painting began after
    a. 1880.
    b. 1890.
    c. 1900.
    d. 1910.

4. The first paintings exhibited by Rousseau
    a. were responded to warmly by critics.
    b. became widely popular in Paris.
    c. were judged harshly by art critics.
    d. were ignored by critics.

5. The subject matter of Rousseau's earlier paintings
    a. was abstract.
    b. was surrealistic.
    c. included landscapes and city scenes.
    d. included family outings and activities.

6. A painting that marks the period at which Rousseau retired to
    devote full time to painting was a
    a. portrait of his wife.
    b. self-portrait.
    c. jungle scene.
    d. sleeping gypsy.

7. His painting *War* was
    a. a recollection of his military years.
    b. an attack upon the values of the city.
    c. a study of family conflict.
    d. a condemnation of war.

8. Rousseau obtained "models" for his jungle paintings from
   a. a brief trip into the tropics.
   b. northern European forests.
   c. hothouse plants and similar sources.
   d. photographs and drawings.

9. Critics are felt to have become "gentler" in comments on Rousseau's work at the time of
   a. Rousseau's first exhibition.
   b. the 22d Salon of the Independents.
   c. the Universal Exhibition of 1889.
   d. his retirement.

10. *The Dream* is noted as
    a. the first of Rousseau's jungle paintings.
    b. the culmination of Rousseau's jungle paintings.
    c. Rousseau's most accomplished portrait.
    d. a nonrepresentational work.

ADDITIONAL ACTIVITIES

1. From your local library, select two or more reproductions of Rousseau's paintings and describe them in a few paragraphs. Comment on the elements and subject matter they present, relating these to the periods discussed in the program. Also discuss your reactions to his uses of color, line, and light and shadow.

2. Read a biographical sketch of one other painter of this period, such as Monet, Cassatt, Gauguin, or Matisse. Discuss the critical responses to the works of this artist. Are influences upon his or her life mentioned that suggest the reality the artist sought to express?

LESSON 21

PAINTING

"... THINGS WE HAVE PASSED ..."

When we first considered criticism in this course, we learned that historical criticism is considered a secondary or subordinate approach to critical participation in the arts. We described three basic kinds of criticism: descriptive, or focusing on the form; interpretive, or focusing on the content; and evaluative, which reveals the relative merits of a work of art. We noted that historically oriented criticism enriches the other three.

Yet, how illuminating it is to consider an artist and his or her art in relation to the times and environment; often, for example, it is difficult or even impossible to correctly interpret and evaluate a work unless one considers the context from which it came. In the preceding lesson, we experienced a deeper understanding of the work of Henry Rousseau by exploring the external forces that influenced him. Historical facts cannot, of course, replace a knowledge of how a painter uses color, light, and shadow, nor an appreciation of manipulation of line and form; yet, knowing about his or her environment and the atmosphere of those times will help us perceive the content as the painter expresses it. And we can more easily seek a balance between descriptive, interpretive, and evaluative criticism on the one hand and historical approach on the other.

Such a balance is presented to us in this lesson as the textbook asks us to consider three famous paintings from the thirteenth and fourteenth centuries that each have similar subject matter but whose meaning and content differ quite widely, both because of the painters' perceptions of reality and as a response to the changing values of the times in which they were created.

The earliest of the paintings, Coppo di Marcovaldo's *Madonna and Child* (ca. 1275), allows the sacred to dominate the secular decisively. This is expressed in the size of the Madonna and Child, their obliviousness to space surrounding them, and the remote, impersonal air of the figures that seem to say that they are not of the world around them. The work is a distinct reflection of the dominant place of religion in art and society of the time.

In contrast, Cimabue's *Madonna and Child* (ca. 1290) does not separate the sacred from the secular so rigidly, but the sacred is still transcendant. The facial features of Madonna and Child are still stiffly unnatural, but there is more warmth and liveliness apparent than in the earlier *Madonna and Child*.

Giotto's *Madonna Enthroned* (ca. 1310) is a stolid, forthright mother figure, who suggests more of a sense of being "here" rather than in the "hereafter." Her facial expressions and the space in front of her make her seem more approachable; and the saints and angels surrounding her are placed on the same ground as her earthly throne. The painting is still Christian, of course, but the religious feeling is not so strong, and there is a hint of challenge to the sacred.

The changes visible to the discerning eye in these paintings can be understood as a reflection of changing Florentine society in which there was a resurgence of confidence in nature and in the power of humans, and a lessening of the dominance of the church over all aspects of life.

In learning to interpret content and meaning, we will, in this lesson, also learn how to distinguish whether a work is truly representational or whether it is abstract. We are asked if a work is representational if it merely "shows" but does not "interpret" (reveal) objects and events of its title. Frankenthaler's *Flood* is offered as an example. Does this painting reveal and interpret flooding with movement, rhythm, light, and color? If so, then it can be said to be representational for the beholder. If not—if perception of flooding merely helps one attend to the sensa—then it is abstract. The sensa *are* the content and meaning.

It is, of course, easier to apply historical knowledge to art of the past rather than to the work of contemporary artists because of the strong trend toward rapid change and experimentation occurring in painting within the last hundred years. These new styles (some of which were discussed in earlier lessons) include Impressionism, Post-Impressionism, Cubism, Surrealism, Suprematism, Constructivism, Expressionism and Abstract Expressionism, and Op Art. Even without the use of a historical yardstick, we can—if we understand the differences among these new art forms—still have a firm base from which to participate with such works if we can use the three standards for critical analysis: description, interpretation, and evaluation.

As the textbook notes, never in history has there been so much help available to those of us who would become more keenly aware of the fullness of the visually perceptible.

LEARNING OBJECTIVES

ON COMPLETING YOUR STUDY OF THIS LESSON, YOU SHOULD BE ABLE TO:

1. Identify distinctive features of three Medieval-Renaissance paintings, indicating features that show increased attention to human values.

2. State a criterion for differentiating between representational and nonrepresentational art.

3. Identify simple descriptions of several modern styles of painting, such as Expressionism, Cubism, Dada, Constructivism, and Abstract Expressionism.

4. Appreciate how small details may significantly reveal content of a painting.

5. Respond to significant style characteristics of a modern painting with increased understanding of the artist's purpose.

ASSIGNMENTS

BEFORE VIEWING THE PROGRAM:

Read the "Overview" and familiarize yourself with the "Learning Objectives" for this lesson.

Consult previous lessons for the meaning of the term *sensa*.

Consult a dictionary or comprehensive text on art history to familiarize yourself with these terms:

> Impressionism
> Expressionism
> Cubism
> Surrealism
> Suprematism
> Dada
> Constructivism

Look over the "Aids for Study" for this lesson.

In the textbook, Chapter 4, "Painting":
- Read pages 84–88 and 90–91 ("Comparisons of Paintings with Similar Subject Matter"); review pages 88–90 ("Parmagianino").
- Read pages 91–93 (Determining the Subject Matter," "Recent Painting," and "Summary").

VIEW THE TELEVISON PROGRAM *"Painting: ' . . . Things We Have Passed . . .'"*

AFTER VIEWING THE PROGRAM:

Review what you have learned, using the "Aids for Study" again.

List three of four questions based upon the televison program presentation that you could employ to critically describe or interpret a painting.

Evaluate your learning with the "Review Quiz," then check your answers with the "Answer Key" at the back of this study guide.

In accordance with your own interests or with your instructor's assignment, complete selected "Additional Activities."

1. Identify details in the work of Coppo di Marcovaldo (Color
    Plate 11) that lead the authors of the textbook to state that
    "the human qualities . . . are barely recognizable." What was
    the purpose of this nonlifelike interpretation of human figures?

2. Did Cimabue's work (Color Plate 9) appear less stylized and
    rigid after you compared it with Coppo di Marcovaldo's work?
    What historical forces do the authors of the textbook see
    influencing this painting? What features of the Madonna's face
    contrast sharply with that in the earlier work?

3. What contrast is suggested between the "point of beginning" used
    by Cimabue and Giotto in their respective treatment of the
    Madonna?

4. What features of the painting make Giotto's Madonna more
    lifelike? What details are suggested to support the feeling that
    he reflects "a rocklike kind of endurance"? In what way does
    this Madonna seem more approachable than Cimabue's?

5. In the view of the authors, which of the two works, *Flood* and
    Mountain, Table, Anchors, Navel is abstract? Which is
    representational? What is the criterion employed to determine
    this classification? Would you suggest another definition of
    representational and abstract? Do you disagree with the
    authors' judgment on either of the paintings?

6. For several of the styles of painting listed in the section "Recent
    Painting" there are examples cited in the textbook. Study the
    examples for a further understanding of these brief descriptions.
    Then contrast some seemingly related styles—Impressionism
    with Post-Impressionism, Cubism with Suprematism,
    Expressionism with Abstract Expressionism. If time permits,
    consult a book containing prints of works by the other artists
    mentioned.

one best answer.

1. The portrayal of the Madonna and Child by Coppo di Marcovaldo
    was probably intended to
    a. emphasize the human qualities of the figures.
    b. represent sculpture rather than living figures.
    c. imitate earlier styles of Egyptian or Greek art.
    d. emphasize the divine qualities of the figures.

2. Cimabue's painting of the Madonna, in the opinion of the textbook
    authors,
    a. reflects a social change toward a more secular view of life.
    b. reflects a social climate turning more religious.
    c. reflects a decreasing interest in human form and emotion.
    d. reflects unchanged continuation of the style of earlier painters
        in that era.

3. Features in Giotto's Madonna that tend to support the textbook's
    contention that the artist started his work by reference to natural
    figures include
    a. the eyes.
    b. the mouth.
    c. the hands.
    d. all of these.

4. Of the three considered, Giotto's painting might be described as
    a. most lifelike and most religious in content.
    b. most lifelike and least religious in content.
    c. most lifelike but equally religious in content.
    d. no more lifelike but least religious in content.

5. Two works were selected to illustrate the discussion of subject matter
    of paintings. Of these
    a. *Flood* was considered abstract, and *Mountain, Table, Anchors,
        Navel* representational.
    b. *Flood* was considered representational, and *Mountain, Table,
        Anchors, Navel* abstract.
    c. both were considered representational.
    d. both were considered abstract.

6. For a painting to be representational there should be
    a. little or no distortion of the subjects.
    b. a clearly stated title.
    c. intensified perception of sensa.
    d. interpretation of objects or events.

7. The painting *Mont Sainte Victoire* is cited as an example of
    a. Impressionism.
    b. Expressionism.
    c. Post-Impressionism.
    d. Futurism.

8. Suprematism or Constructivism is described as a style
    a. revealing play of sunlight on colors.
    b. revealing permanent properties and three-dimensional qualities of things in closed space.
    c. portraying sensa in movement.
    d. portraying sensa in sharp geometric patterns.

9. "The portrayal of sensa in movement with the expression of powerful emotion or energy" is a description of
    a. Abstract Expressionism.
    b. Cubism.
    c. Impressionism.
    d. Suprematism or Constructivism.

10. Dada is described as
    a. expression of the subconsious.
    b. poking fun at the absurdity of everything.
    c. portrayal of sensa and things in motion.
    d. revelation of scenes portraying strong emotion.

ADDITIONAL ACTIVITIES

1. You may find it interesting to experiment with the concepts of more than one field of art. For example, select the various elements of art that may apply to music (even by stretching meanings a little) and attempt a description or descriptive criticism of one work of music. Does this exercise suggest to you the artist's intent or purpose in treating his or her subject matter? Is any content suggested that is new to you? You may prefer to employ elements of music that (again, with some liberalization of meaning) could apply to art and perform a similar description. Perhaps the terms themselves—melody, harmony, theme, rhythm, meter, forte and piano, color, light, shadow, form, line—may have added meanings for you.

2. Select three or four works (other than those in the textbook) by any of the painters listed in the section "Recent Paintings" and write a brief description of each, relating your description to the comments on the style given in the textbook. Select one of the paintings for more extensive participation and express its content and meaning as you perceive it.

3. Visit a gallery or public display on original paintings. Select one or more for participative viewing. Take notes for a fairly extensive description as you are viewing it. If the work is representational, relate how the artist's treatment of the subject matter interprets the object-event in a new way for you. If it is abstract, tell how the artist's treatment of the sensa changes your awareness of them.

SCULPTURE

MIRROR OF MAN'S BEING

A new awareness of sculpture as an art separate from painting may be experienced during this lesson on the historical development of sculpture. Like painting, sculpture is a visual art, but it is something more than merely visual. Sculpture appeals to the tactile sense, the sense of touch. It is not only intended to be seen; it is also to be touched, or, if it cannot be touched, at least the participant feels an implicit *invitation* to touch. The Perception Keys in the reading assignments for this lesson will challenge us to experiment with the tactile sense, using it to perceive and experience some aspects of this art.

The human body has historically been a primary subject of sculpture for several reasons, one of which is related to the tactile sense. The human body is beautiful and sensuous, and it is complex and challenging in structure. But the body in sculpture, especially in sculpture in the round, may also help us interpret our inward-outward tactile sensations and provide for us something of an objective image of our own internal bodily awareness.

Sculpture is known to have existed since 30,000 B.C.—long, long before the written word—and each succeeding age has brought its own creativity and innovation to this art. During these centuries, sculpture has served many purposes: religious expression, magic, decoration, aesthetic pleasure, patriotic and social inspiration, and as a historical record of human beings' changing concepts of themselves. In the television program for this lesson, we see some interesting examples of prehistoric and primitive sculpture, most of which were probably created by skilled artists to cast a magic spell, promote fertility, ensure a good hunt, or to protect the dead. Egyptian sculpture, with its emphasis on the life of the royal pharaohs, provides fascinating examples of artistic beauty from an early recorded historical period.

Life preoccupied the artist of classic Greece, and Greek sculpture gloried in the beauty of humanity. Later, Roman artists, copying not only Greek styles but often copying the actual work of Greek sculptors, added a dimension of realism by revealing emotional and psychological aspects of the human subjects. Where the Greeks tended toward idealism, Roman sculptors were more realistic. Roman artists also created the great triumphal arches that remain as a monument to their own creativity and innovative spirit.

Religion dominated the thought and art of the Middle Ages. In this lesson, we will become acquainted with art that served the church by communicating messages to people who could not read. Thus, sculpture graphically portrayed human virtues and vices, the agonies of hell, and the religious ideals of the church. During the Renaissance, however, sculpture began to reflect the interests of powerful and wealthy families who replaced the church as patrons of art. This period of "reawakening" is reflected in the works of Donatello and Michelangelo.

Following the reawakening, art—especially music—became more emotional, dynamic, ornate; and it often happened that sculpture, painting, and architecture were confined in a single work meant to convey a total environmental experience. This period in the history of art is known as the Baroque period.

With the advent of the nineteenth century, the Baroque period waned, and art became more realistic and impressionistic under the influence of advances in communication and transportation, social and technological changes, and a new spirit of experimentalism. Auguste Rodin, whose life spanned the late nineteenth and early twentieth centuries, bridged the gap between the unified artistic heritage of the past and the modern period, in which art seems to be "fractured" into special interests. This achievement is seen in glimpses of such Rodin works as *Age of Bronze, The Kiss, The Shadow*, the *Head of Dalou*, and *Balzac*.

Modern sculpture appears to be experiencing a period of innovation and experiment, and it is suggested that the twentieth century might well have produced more innovation and artistic variety than any other century in history. "Found objects" (*The Ice Bag*) are used in new ways to declare that beauty can be found anywhere. Artists create "mobiles" and add motorized movement to their works. Others use rocks, earth, structures made of manufactured materials such as Mylar, sound, light, and even cliffs to express their points of view.

The visual presentation of this lesson ends on a questioning note about modern sculpture: Does it reflect a loss of individuality, a return to idealism, or a search for the abstract ideal?

LEARNING OBJECTIVES

ON COMPLETING YOUR STUDY OF THIS LESSON, YOU SHOULD BE ABLE TO:

1. Appreciate the importance of the tactile sense in the perception of sculpture.
2. Compare the different experiences involved with perceiving, or "participating with," a sculpture and perceiving a painting.
3. Contrast the subject matter of Egyptian, Greek, and Roman sculpture.
4. Identify a significant difference in the subject matter of sculpture in the Middle Ages and the Renaissance.
5. Suggest two reasons for the sculptor's preference for the human body as a subject.
6. List at least four modern innovations or experimental directions taken in the art of sculpture.
7. Name one important sculptor from the Renaissance, Baroque, Nineteenth-Century, and Modern periods; and identify at least one work by each sculptor.

ASSIGNMENTS

BEFORE VIEWING THE PROGRAM:

Read the "Overview" and familiarize yourself with the "Learning Objectives" of this lesson.

Familiarize yourself with the following terms:

> sculpture in the round: sculpture that has no background
>   plane; contrasted with relief sculpture
> tactility: capable of affecting the sense of touch
> found object: any object, usually manufactured, that is
>   incorporated into a sculpture by the artist, without change

Look over the "Study Aids" for this lesson.

Look at the frontispiece of the text and all illustrations for Chapter 5. It is not necessary to read the captions at this time, but it is necessary to remember that you are looking at two-dimensional photographs of three-dimensional objects.

In the textbook, Chapter 5, "Sculpture":
  • Read pages 95–98 ("Sculpture and Touch," "Sculpture and Density," "Sensory Interconnections," "Sculpture and Painting Compared") and pages 112–126 ("Sensory Space," "Sculpture and the Human Body," "Tactility: Inward and Outward Sensations," and "Sculpture in the Round and the Human Body").

VIEW THE TELEVISION PROGRAM *"Sculpture: Mirror of Man's Being."*

AFTER VIEWING THE PROGRAM:

Review what you have learned, using the "Aids for Study" again.

Evaluate your learning with the "Review Quiz," then check your answers with the "Answer Key" at the back of this study guide.

In accordance with your own interests or with your instructor's assignment, complete selected "Additional Activities."

1. Refer to the perception key, "Experiment with Touch," textbook page 95, in the section "Sculpture and Touch" and do the exercise suggested. If someone else does not participate with you, carry out both parts, modeling and drawing from the sense of touch yourself. Then answer the following questions:
    a. Can you perceive what an object would look like from touching it? Can you tell from looking at it how an object might feel?
    b. What different sensations might you experience by touching an object?

2. Prehistoric sculpture and primitive sculpture apparently were often employed as magic spells to ensure a good hunt or to guard the dead, for instance. How was this different from the way Egyptian artists used sculpture?

3. Review the comments on *Aphrodite* (*Venus Anadyomene*) in the textbook and note the comments on Grecian sculpture made in the television program. In the program, Greek sculpture is described as becoming naturalistic, but the text describes this copy of a Greek sculpture as idealized. Can both statements be true? How?

4. Two characteristics of Roman sculpture are noted (in addition to their tendency to copy Greek styles.) Describe each of these.

5. Sculpture was related to the religious quality of the Middle Ages in what two ways?

6. What two works by Michelangelo are depicted in the textbook illustrations?

7. Summarize the reasons given in the text section "Sculpture in the Round and the Human body" for the use of the body as a subject for sculpture.

8. Who is the Baroque sculptor mentioned in the television program? What were some of the characteristics of his style?

?odin's nineteenth century sculpture related to Baroque
.. Name at least one way in which it varies.

10. The modern sculptor Marcel Duchamp is mentioned for an
    innovation and for an experiment in sculpture. Identify the
    innovation and the experiment.

11. List at least four of the experimental types of sculpture
    described in the last few minutes of the television program.
    Describe one of them in some detail. (If you wish, you might
    refer to parts of the textbook that describe some of these new
    approaches to sculpture.)

REVIEW QUIZ

Select the one best answer or add words to complete the statement.

1. Something that appeals to our tactile senses makes us wish to
   a. taste it.
   b. see it.
   c. touch it.
   d. hear it.

2. Tactile senses are aroused when something has
   a. a variety of colors.
   b. depth and dimension.
   c. a flat surface.
   d. a pleasing appearance.

3. Egyptian sculpture deals largely with

   life of pharaohs

4. Greek sculpture is especially noted for

   beauty of humanity, idealism

5. Roman sculpture tended to show the human body and face

realistically

6. Sculpture in the Middle Ages centered on subjects revolving around
   a. death.
   b. Christianity.
   c. human activity and achievement.
   d. fertility symbols.

7. Sculpture in the Renaissance tended to focus on subjects revolving around
   a. death.
   b. religion.
   c. patrons.
   d. fertility symbols.

8. The body has been a favorite subject for sculpture in
   a. the Greek era.
   b. the Middle ages.
   c. the Baroque era.
   d. every period.

9. Which of the following reasons was not given by the authors of the textbook for the popularity of the human body as a subject for sculpture?
   a. It is a sensuous object.
   b. It causes response of outward and inward sensations.
   c. Its shape and structure are complex and challenging.
   d. Artists are preoccupied with themselves.

10. From the following list select two that are not modern innovations in sculpture:
   a. sound and light sculpture
   b. low-relief sculpture
   c. mobile sculpture
   d. motorized sculpture
   e. environment (responsive) sculpture
   f. sculpture in the round
   g. earth sculpture
   h. found objects

11. Which of the following was a Renaissance sculptor?
    a. Michelangelo
    b. Bernini
    c. Rodin
    d. Duchamp

12. Which of the following was a sculptor of the Baroque period?
    a. Michelangelo
    b. Bernini
    c. Rodin
    d. Duchamp

13. Which of the following was a sculptor of the Modern period?
    a. Michelangelo
    b. Bernini
    c. Rodin
    d. Duchamp

ADDITIONAL ACTIVITIES

1. Visit an art gallery or display and compare a work of sculpture and a work of painting that are related by themes or subject. Record your responses to each work separately. How did you participate in each work? After noting your responses, feelings, and perceptions, compare your experiences with that described in the text section "Sculpture and Painting Compared" (textbook pages 97–98). In a brief paragraph or two, comment on any differences in your experience from those of the text authors. Do you feel that your perceptions of these art works were influenced by having earlier read this section?

2. Visit an art gallery and select sculptures from two different major periods of history, preferably two of the periods that were discussed in the lesson. Compare and contrast the sculptures as to materials, theme, appearance, and treatment. Then, compare your descriptions with the generalizations concerning the period given in the television program. Comment on any

significant differences. (If necessary, use good reproductions from an art book for this exercise.)

3. Study and discuss a work by Rodin, preferably one that has as its subject the human body. Compare your perceptions of this work with the quotation from Rodin in the section "Sculpture in the Round and the Human Body."

4. Discuss the similarities of two periods, for example, the Renaissance and Modern, that you find in the art of music and the art of sculpture. Substantiate your views by selecting a representative artist for each of these arts and periods.

SCULPTURE

ELEMENTS OF DIMENSION

OVERVIEW

The preceding lesson emphasized that sculpture, unlike painting, is an art form that appeals to the tactile sense, as well as to the visual sense. In this lesson, we will trace the various elements of sculpture that artists have mastered in order to communicate to us through three-dimensional solid forms.

This lesson provides us with definitions and examples of the basic types of sculptural forms: sunken (incised) relief, surface (flat) relief, low (bas) relief, high relief, and sculpture in the round (monolithic sculpture).

The earliest examples of sculpture shown in the program are Egyptian incised reliefs. In a manner reminiscent of drawing, the figures in the sculpture are outlined with grooves. Although some may feel that these examples are not truly sculpture because of their minimum degree of three-dimensionality, the authors of the textbook feel that these Egyptian examples are sculpture because they invite a tactile response. In other words, one wishes to participate in this art not only by looking but also by touching.

Numerous examples of other relief sculpture—from low to high—are also presented in this lesson. Low relief and high relief are somewhat relative terms, identifying the degree to which a sculptured image projects from the background plane. In all relief works, the sculptor strives to model the figures to create the illusion of roundness and depth. Among the representative relief sculptures studied in this lesson are reliefs sculpted by the Greeks for the Parthenon and Temple of Zeus and the reliefs done by Lorenzo Ghiberti for the doors of the Baptistry of Florence in the fifteenth century. The bronze doors of the Baptistry are especially notable examples of relief sculpture. The east doors of the Baptistry are quite impressive, for in these doors, Ghiberti brought the art of relief sculpture to new levels of dimension and depth.

The evolution of sculpture in the round is also traced in this lesson. This type of sculpture exhibits striking changes over the centuries. Both the ancient Egyptians and Greeks created monolithic sculptures, but there were important differences in their uses of sculptural elements. Much of the Egyptian sculpture, with the notable exception of that done during the brief Amarna period, was rigid and not naturalistic. In comparison, the Greek sculpture that developed from Egyptian sculpture was far more relaxed and portrayed subjects in softer and more lifelike forms. Ultimately, Greek sculpture achieved new heights of perfection in presenting the fullness of the human body. The Greeks were able to create such free-standing human forms because they developed and used certain sculptural devices—such as a piece of drapery or a tree trunk—to provide support for the human figure and solve the problem of the weakness of the carved stone.

After the "technical virtuosity" achieved by the Greeks, sculpture returned to its earlier role as an adjunct to architecture. In the Middle Ages and even in the early Renaissance, most sculpture was designed to be placed in niches in the walls of buildings. With the Renaissance, however, sculptors again turned to the more natural, free-standing form. Among the examples of Renaissance sculpture shown in the program are Donatello's *Gattamelata* and Vernocchio's *Colleoni*, two superficially similar equestrian statues. Michelangelo was, perhaps, the greatest of the Renaissance artists, and his sculpture is especially interesting. In the program, we will see examples of how Michelangelo achieved perfection through his "sculptural consciousness": an ability to see the subject within the stone before he began carving. Interestingly, unlike most other sculptors of the Renaissance, whose sculptured figures were entirely free-standing, Michelangelo frequently carved figures only partially free of their stone. These figures—known as captive figures—enabled

Michelangelo to overcome the limitations inherent in the weakness of the stone as well as to express his personal belief about "the divine spirit of man struggling to free himself from the bonds of earthly existence."

The modern era in sculpture is represented by the work of Auguste Rodin. Rodin's figures are definitely not of the classical tradition; they twist and distort in ways that are never seen in the sculpture of the earlier ages. Rodin manipulated the elements of his sculpture to convey his insights into the psychology of his subjects.

This lesson also considers the use of artisans and technicians to execute the actual work of the sculptor. This practice—which has been followed by sculptors from Michelangelo to the present—raises questions about how important "touch" really is to the actual creation of a piece of sculpture. With some sculptures, it is most important for the sculptor to retain complete control in order to communicate clearly his or her intention; with other sculptures, impersonal , efficient industrial production techniques may be most appropriate for conveying the sculptor's intention.

The program concludes with a comparison of abstract sculpture and representational, or "figurative," art. Much contemporary abstract sculpture has reached the point of being "nonobjective"; that is, it does not have any relationship to any other object. Nonobjective sculpture, which may be baffling to some, can provide interesting insights into the artist's feelings about the subject by identification of the elements and the way in which they have been abstracted. Contemporary sculptors of nonobjective art are the first in the history of sculpture to create nonobjective art as an end in itself, rather than as a form of decoration. We can participate in the work of nonrepresentational sculptors, as well as in that of more traditional artists, if, as our host says, we "decide which answers work and which don't work. In making the choice, [we] join the artist in the final step of making art."

LEARNING OBJECTIVES

ON COMPLETING YOUR STUDY OF THIS LESSON, YOU SHOULD BE ABLE TO:

1. Recognize and describe the following types of sculpture: sunken (incised) relief, surface (flat) relief, low (bas) relief, high relief, sculpture in the round (monolithic or free-standing sculpture).

2. Identify a basic point of separation between the arts of sculpture, painting, and architecture.

3. Appreciate, as a participant, the importance of "sculptural consciousness" in the creation of sculpture in the round.

4. Identify a limitation of materials used by sculptors and identify at least one method by which the limitation can be overcome.

5. Identify several examples of sculpture with their creators.

6. Appreciate the fact that meaning may be derived from abstractions of representational or figurative subjects.

ASSIGNMENTS

BEFORE VIEWING THE PROGRAM:

Read the "Overview" and familiarize yourself with the "Learning Objectives" for this lesson.

Consult a dictionary or encyclopedia to familiarize yourself with the following terms:

   sunken (incised) relief
   low (bas) relief
   surface (flat) relief
   high relief
   sculpture in the round (monolithic)

Note that the following terms may have somewhat varying meanings:

representational art: art that uses a concrete object or event as its
subject matter

figurative art: approximately the same meaning as above; may be
used in the sense of "nonobjective."

abstract art: may be used in the sense of "nonobjective" below; or
may be used to mean art that is representational, yet selects
from the "realistic" figure only certain elements for emphasis.

nonobjective art: art forms not based on concrete objects or events.

Look over the "Aids for Study" for this lesson.

In the textbook, Chapter 5, "Sculpture":
  • Read pages 98–112 ("Sunken Relief Sculpture," "Surface-Relief
    Sculpture," "Sculpture and Architecture Compared," "Low-Relief
    Sculpture," "High-Relief Sculpture," and "Sculpture in the Round").
  • Review pages 95–98 ("Sculpture and Touch," "Sculpture and
    Density," "Sensory Interconnections," "Sculpture and Painting
    Compared").

VIEW THE TELEVISION PROGRAM *"Sculpture: Elements of Dimension."*

AFTER VIEWING THE PROGRAM:

Experiment with simple sculpture techniques : Use any reasonably soft
substance, such as clay, wood, or plastic foam, to form a simple
representational or abstract (nonobjective) shape using incised relief
outline. Then (perhaps testing your own "sculptural consciousness"), try to
see a shape within another block of the substance. Carve and shape down
to this form. If possible, take an instant-printing photograph of each of
your efforts for later reference. (One of the "Additional Activities" refers
to this assignment.)

Review what you have learned, using the "Aids for Study" again.

Evaluate your learning with the "Review Quiz," then check your answers
with the "Answer Key" at the back of this study guide.

In accordance with your own interests or with your instructor's
assignment, complete selected "Additional Activities."

1. What is incised relief? Surface relief? Low relief? Give an example of each from the program or the textbook. What are the reasons given by the textbook for classifying these forms as sculpture rather than painting? Do you have other reasons for considering reliefs to be sculpture rather than some other art form?

2. What distinguishes low relief from incised relief or surface relief?

3. What are the characteristics of low- and high-relief sculpture? Give an example of each from the program or the text.

4. Look at Rodin's *Danaïde* (Figure 5-18). Would you classify this as sculpture in the round or high-relief sculpture? What distinguishes free-standing sculpture or sculpture in the round from other forms discussed in this lesson?

5. Why are the panels of Ghiberti's doors of the Baptistry at Florence (Figure 5-3) sculptures rather than paintings? Why is Goertitz's *Five Towers of the Satellite City* (Figure 5-4) termed sculpture rather than architecture? Review the textbook's differentiation of each. Are these rigid definitions or merely guidelines useful in classifying equivocal forms of art?

6. What does the term "sculptural consciousness" mean? Select two or three examples in which, in your opinion, the sculptor clearly exhibits this quality.

7. Stone has strength and stress limits that could be exceeded if a heavy figure (the standing human, for example) is set upon extremely thin or extended pillars. How did Greek artists overcome this limitation? How did Michelangelo?

8. What may we learn from the abstraction or stylization of representational subjects?

9. Review the textbook and the program and identify the sculptors of the following:

Gattamelata   Can-Can Dancers
Walking Man   The Five Towers of the Satellite City
Ghost   Times Square Sky
Pietà

REVIEW QUIZ

Match the technique or style on the left with the description on the right. A description may be used more than once.

_____ 1. Surface relief
_____ 2. High relief
_____ 3. Monolith
_____ 4. Sunken relief
_____ 5. Low relief
_____ 6. Sculpture in the round
_____ 7. Incised relief
_____ 8. Bas relief

a. Outlines of objects are cut in grooves of varying depth in the surface of the material.
b. The surfaces are not raised, but background scenes are composed, using such devices from painting as foreshortening for perspective.
c. The subjects stand out, relatively slightly, from background planes.
d. The sculptured objects stand out, almost free from the background planes.
e. The sculptured object is free from any background.

Write the answer in the space provided.

9. According to the textbook, what is the difference between painting and sculpture?

10. According to the textbook, what is the difference between sculpture
     and architecture?

Select the one best answer.

11. "Sculptural consciousness" is a term used to signify the ability to
     a. classify an object as either painting, sculpture, or architecture.
     b. perceive the object desired within the block before beginning to
         shape it.
     c. carve an object in flat, low, or medium relief.
     d. understand the meaning of abstract or nonobjective sculpture.

12. Late Greek sculptors overcame the inherent weakness of stone by
     carving sculpture in the round
     a. from bronze.
     b. with figures supported by such objects as tree trunks or drapery
         at the weakest points.
     c. leaving much of the figure within the stone.
     d. carving thin or extended portions of the body, such as ankles,
         much thicker than they would realistically be.

Name the artist who carved each of the following:

13. North and east doors of the Baptistry of Florence

14. *Walking Man*

15. *Pietà*

ADDITIONAL ACTIVITIES

1. Write a brief summary of your sculpturing assignment. Comment on the similarities and differences of incising sculpture and drawing a picture. Also, comment on your own "sculptural consciousness" as you attempted to perceive a form within the material before sculpting. Finally, comment on the differences between the two objects you created and their representations in the photographs. Does a photograph tend to emphasize any elements of sculpture? Does a photograph subdue certain elements?

2. Using illustrations from the textbook or illustrations from any other book, select two or three modern nonobjective sculptures. Describe them briefly, then identify elements of the works that reflect techniques discussed in this lesson. For example, are there any techniques derived from the relief forms? Do you see any points at which the artist may have reinforced his or her materials to add strength?

3. With a camera, visit a cemetery and perform Activities 1 and 2 in the perception key, "Cemetery Sculpture, Heuler, and Nicholson" (textbook page 100). Report on your findings and discuss the following questions:
    Did you find any examples of nonobjective sculpture?
    Did you find examples that were representational, yet abstracted from the subjects so that they were not truly "realistic"?

SCULPTURE

MEANING THROUGH THE BODY'S FORM

The content of a work of art is more than the subject matter of that work; more accurately, it is how the artist has chosen to reveal the subject and express his or her particular insight. In this way, an artist expresses a truth beyond facts. In this lesson, we will explore the specific ways in which meaning is expressed in sculptural forms. Our search for a sculptor's meaning will be facilitated if we have knowledge of the elements and styles that have been employed to express an idea in three dimensions. Again, in this lesson, we will sharpen our perceptual skills through the close study of one particular sculptor: Auguste Rodin.

In many respects, Rodin's creative life parallels that of Rousseau. The early works of both artists were rejected by critics of the time. It was only after lengthy periods, during which the critics gradually became familiar with their works, that Rodin and Rousseau were accorded attention and respect. With both artists, it was as if they had to wait for the rest of the world to catch up with their visions.

The television component of this lesson emphasizes Rodin's fascination and absorption with the human figure and its capacity to express emotion. We see the full range of Rodin's sculptural forms, from his first important work, *The Man with the Broken Nose*, to his final work, a simple sculpture, molded from his own hand. Among the major works by Rodin shown in the program are *The Age of Bronze, St. John the Baptist Preaching, The Burghers of Calais, Balzac,* and *The Gates of Hell. The Gates of Hell* is an extensive work, containing numerous individual pieces of sculpture, many of which are examined in close detail. Particular attention is given to one part of the work, *The Thinker,* perhaps Rodin's most famous sculpture. In all of Rodin's work, we can see how the artist was able to skillfully communicate strong emotions through his sculpture.

Rodin was especially intrigued by the relationship between men and women, and this interest was expressed in a number of notable works: *The Kiss, Eternal Spring,* and *Eternal Idol.*

In viewing Rodin's works or those of any sculptor on a television screen or in looking at them in a photograph, our experiencing of them is hampered because they are three-dimensional objects presented in a two-dimensional medium. However, the television program for this lesson attempts to overcome this limitation by showing Rodin's work from all sides, as the camera slowly rotates around the sculpture. Although nothing can completely substitute for the personal experience of being able to walk around a work, to touch it, and to be able to sense the dimensions and textures of the work, the film of Rodin's sculpture provides as close an approximation as possible.

The text assignment for this lesson provides information on the three different techniques sculptors use in creating forms and conveying their meanings: modeling, carving, and assembling. Of the three techniques, Rodin employed both modeling and carving, and it is intriguing to think about how Rodin employed these different techniques to achieve desired effects in his various works.

LEARNING OBJECTIVES

ON COMPLETING YOUR STUDY OF THIS LESSON, YOU SHOULD BE ABLE TO:

1. Describe the emotional background and content of *The Burghers of Calais*.

2. Relate examples of critical rejection of Rodin during his career, suggesting some of the features that made his contemporaries uncomfortable with his sculpture.

3. Briefly describe the plan for *The Gates of Hell* and one or more of the figures designed for this work.

4. Name at least two major emotions Rodin portrayed in his works.

5. Cite examples of subject matter Rodin employed to express his concepts of beauty.

6. Appreciate some of the qualities of Rodin's works that were considered excesses by his contemporary critics.

7. Describe two sculpting techniques.

ASSIGNMENTS

BEFORE VIEWING THE PROGRAM:

Read the "Overview" and familiarize yourself with the "Learning Objectives" for this lesson.

In the textbook, Chapter 5, "Sculpture":
  • Review pages 112–120 ("Sensory Space" and "Sculpture and the Human Body").

Consult previous lessons and the textbook to refresh your memory concerning relief sculpture and sculpture in the round.

If you are not familiar with Dante's *Inferno*, you may wish to read an encyclopedia entry on this work or consult the introduction and some illustrations in an annotated edition.

Look over the "Aids for Study" for this lesson.

VIEW THE TELEVISION PROGRAM *"Sculpture: Meaning through the Body's Form."*

AFTER VIEWING THE PROGRAM:

In the textbook, Chapter 5, "Sculpture":
    •Read pages 127–130 ("Techniques of Sculpture").

Review what you have learned, using the "Aids for Study" again.

Evaluate your learning with the "Review Quiz," then check your answers with the "Answer Key" at the back of this study guide.

In accordance with your own interests or with your instructor's assignment, complete selected "Additional Activities."

AIDS FOR STUDY

1. *The Man with the Broken Nose* seems to symbolize the period of Rodin's rejection by the Salon. How does his tenacity in saving the face of a disintegrating model, and his later reconstruction if it, illustrate the triumph of Rodin's entire life?

2. On what was the critical rejection of *The Age of Bronze* based? How did Rodin try to counteract this criticism? How did he counteract this criticism with *St. John the Baptist Preaching*?

3. Are the works for whom Rose Beuret, Camille Claudel, and other women modeled related more to Rodin's *The Gates of Hell* or to his interest in the man-woman relationship? It is implied that his sculptures based on the two women named, were inspired by the intimacy of his relationship with each. Do the sculptures reflect this intimacy?

4. What is the historical background for *The Burghers of Calais*? What type of emotion is reflected in these figures? Which style of painting was described in the previous unit as interpreting strong emotion and feeling? How is much of Rodin's work akin to this painting style?

5. What was the overall plan of *The Gates of Hell* as described in the program? Which of the works within this overall scheme has become Rodin's best-known figure? What two figures are combined to form the work entitled *I Am Beautiful*? How do these figures relate to Dante's work? What emotions can you relate to such figures as *Eve*, *I Am Beautiful*, and *She Who Was the Helmet Maker's Beautiful Wife*?

6. What features can you detect that may account, in part, for the critical derision directed at *Balzac*?

7. What is the thematic basis for *The Kiss, Eternal Spring*, and *Eternal Idol*?

8. Note the variation in subject matter for *Pas de Deux* (can-can dancers), *The Cry* (the anguish of life), and *Victor Hugo* and describe the differences in the emotions expressed in each of these.

9. The program closes with reference to the artist's attention to details of hands. Can you recall examples of precise attention to small detail in other art forms? Is this attention to hands and, as the program suggests, creativity another separate theme of Rodin's work, or is it related to the theme emphasized throughout this program?

10. Outline the basic steps of modeling and carving. What are the limitations of each, and which of these limitations are caused by the materials?

REVIEW QUIZ

Select the one best answer.

1. Rodin's early major work, *The Age of Bronze*, was rejected by a Salon jury because it appeared too
   a. grotesque.
   b. abstract.
   c. accurate in form.
   d. incorrectly proportioned.

2. In his work *St. John the Baptist Preaching*, Rodin sought to counteract the criticism of his earlier work by deliberately
   a. creating a form that followed a physically attractive, classic style.
   b. shaping the body out of normal proportion.
   c. forming the body of the work much larger than life.
   d. forming the work by molding the body of the model.

3. The emotional scene or content of *The Burghers of Calais* might be described as
   a. pomposity and grandeur.
   b. despair and torment.
   c. stalwart heroism.
   d. fortitude in facing disaster.

4. Rodin's work, expressive of strong emotion and feeling, is closely related to
   a. Expressionism.
   b. Impressionism.
   c. Surrealism.
   d. Cubism.

5. Rodin's most famous work is probably
   a. *Mignon*.
   b. *The Thinker*.
   c. *Balzac*.
   d. *The Kiss*.

6. *The Gates of Hell* is best described as
   a. a massive single figure, sitting in frozen contemplation.
   b. two figures intertwined, expressing an agony of torment.
   c. a massive collection of many figures.
   d. a single expression of a figure in torment.

7. *Balzac* was probably rejected, in part, because
   a. it appeared to be an exact physical replica of the model.
   b. it bore no physical resemblance to the supposed subject.
   c. the interpretation of emotion and feelings made the work appear grotesque to the critics.
   d. most of the figure was still embedded in the block of original substance from which it was carved.

8. The theme of *The Kiss* and *Eternal Idol* was the
   a. torment of earthly life.
   b. relationship of man to woman.
   c. the creativity of the human mind.
   d. power of the lonely prophet.

9. Of the following sculpturing techniques, the one that is most limited by the strength of materials used is
   a. modeling.
   b. carving.
   c. assemblage.
   d. space drawings.

10. Some of the later steps in the creation of a piece of sculpture are often performed by specialized workers other than the artist in
   a. modeling.
   b. carving.
   c. assemblage.
   d. space drawings.

ADDITIONAL ACTIVITIES

1. If possible, consult an illustrated text on Rodin, reviewing some of the works presented in this lesson while discussing Question 9 in "Aids for Study."

2. Discuss the revelation concerning the human form that you perceive in the works of Rodin. Do you perceive other revelations concerning suffering, love, and other overwhelming human emotions? Is there still other content, for you, in his works?

3. Select another sculptor of the nineteenth or twentieth century and summarize descriptive or interpretive criticism of at least three of his or her other works, using a comprehensive illustrated text on the artist. Using this same book or another reference, outline some important influences in the sculptor's life, such as place of residence, education and training, and critical acceptance.

SCULPTURE

MOST DIFFICULT OF ARTS

Throughout this unit, we have been encouraged to perceive how sculpture differs from a purely visual art, and our perception has been assisted by a skilled critic's descriptive contrast of his experiences in viewing a painting and a sculpture. We were further helped to participate in specific sculptures by the movement of the camera as we viewed the artistry of Rodin.

In this lesson, we share the thoughts of noted sculptor Henry Moore, who tells us how he consciously expresses three-dimensional feeling in his work. We will also briefly interpret some contemporary forms of sculpture appearing on the scene today as artists experiment with new materials and grapple with the realities of technology.

Moore notes that sculpture may be the most difficult of all arts for both the artist and the participant, for the ability to respond in three dimensions is crucial to both artist and beholder. Both sculptor and sensitive observer must visualize the complex form "all around itself," must feel shape apart from any idea of what it might become. Moore suggests that the possibilities for such shapes are infinite—from shells and pebbles to the human form. Holes in and through the material can also be as suggestive and significant as the shape of the solid material itself.

But shape and form are not ends in themselves; associational and psychological factors play a large part in the work. Rounded forms, for example, may suggest fruitfulness and maturity. Moore also insists that size is connected with vision, not the actual material. A carving several times life-size can be "petty," whereas a small carving can convey a feeling of grandeur.

Space sculpture, which depends upon assemblage as its particular technique, differs from other kinds of sculpture in its technique, its density, and its relationships with space. It never loses its ties to materials from which it is formed, but it adds space perception to the perception of mass, enriching the expression of mass. Rivera's *Brussels Construction* is a space sculpture because its relationships with space are as interesting as the steel material of which it is made. We are warned not to let ourselves be led away from the space sculpture rather than into it by absorption with the production process, since that would destroy useful criticism; yet we are asked if conjecturing about the production process does not enrich the participatory experience.

In sculpture, more than in most arts, the artist can use some of the most sophisticated advances of technology. Every medium is subject to its own rules, and the artist must remain true to the materials. But the artist can use his or her materials to protest the dominance of technology or to reflect a positive notion about technology. For example, Ernest Trova's *Study: Falling Man (Wheelman)*, a faceless robot with spiked wheels for arms is a protest against loss of free will in a mechanical society. George Segal's *Bus Driver* speaks of loneliness and decay. Both have much to say about the dehumanization of man. On the other hand, Smith's *Cubi X* is true to its technological materials of steel and cylinders, but these are wed to nature in pleasing tribute to technology.

Pop sculpture respects products as well as materials. Kurt Schwitter puts together cast-off cardboard, wire mesh, paper, and nails, in such a way that we experience them for the first time. Machine sculpture tries to reveal the machine and some of its powers. Tinguely's *Homage to New York* self-destructed in what is interpreted as an effort to humanize the machine.

Sadly, many of the new experimental sculptures are rarely exhibited (partly because of expense), and thus they are not available for interpretation and participation.

LEARNING OBJECTIVE

ON COMPLETING YOUR STUDY OF THIS LESSON, YOU SHOULD BE ABLE TO:

1. Identify the two sources of shapes listed by Moore.
2. List two possible functions of holes in sculpture.
3. Differentiate between the terms "size" and "scale" as used by Moore.
4. Appreciate the significance of shapes in abstract or surrealistic sculpture.
5. Relate characteristics of a work to styles that exemplify truth to materials or protest against technology.
6. Feel greater sensitivity to the purpose of the modern sculptor, particularly in abstract work.

ASSIGNMENTS

BEFORE VIEWING THE PROGRAM:

Read the "Overview" and familiarize yourself with the "Learning Objectives" for this lesson.

Consult a dictionary for technical meaning of the terms:

mass
volume

Look over the "Aids for Study" for this lesson.

VIEW THE TELEVISION PROGRAM *Sculpture: Most Difficult of Arts.*

AFTER VIEWING THE PROGRAM:

In textbook Chapter 5, "Sculpture":
- •Read pages 126–127 ("Space Sculpture") and pages 130–156 ("Tactility, Mass, and Space," "Contemporary Sculpture," "Sculpture and Architecture," and "Summary").
- •Review pages 95–98.

Read the essay "Notes on Sculpture" by Henry Moore, printed with this lesson. Be certain to note photographs of Moore's works in the textbook (Figures 5–22, 5–29, and 5–30).

Review what you have learned, using the "Aids for Study" again.

Evaluate your learning with the "Review Quiz," then check your answers with the "Answer Key" at the back of this study guide.

In accordance with your own interests or with your instructor's assignment, complete selected "Additional Activities."

AIDS FOR STUDY

1. What is the difference between the style described as "space sculpture" and other forms of the arts? Is some of the appeal of space sculpture similar to what Moore describes for holes through a work? Why do the text authors not classify Moore's works in Figures 5–22 and 5–29 as space sculpture? Do you agree?

2. Based on the definitions you have previously read in your text, would you classify Calder's *Gates of Spoleto* (Figure 5–24) as abstract, or surrealist? How would you classify Hepworth's *Pelagos* (Figure 5–26)?

3. What does Moore mean by "form-blind"? Do most people tend to view objects as flat forms? What might a person do to attempt to increase sensitivity to the "all-aroundness" of objects?

4. Are Moore's comments on the shapes themselves (in the section "Three Dimensions") related to what we have learned about the sensa in painting? Is it possible to appreciate a shape, such as a seashell, without some related associations coming to mind?

5. What might be some of the "universal shapes" that Moore speaks of? Is a sphere one such shape? Could these comments ("Shells and Pebbles") be related to his other comments on the human form?

6.   Use Moore's comments on holes in sculpture as a basis for studying his works in the three text photographs. In which ones are holes "revelations"? Even though we are restricted by the flat dimensions of photography, do we sense the three-dimensional qualities of any of these works differently because of the hole? Which figure seems to you most influenced by a hole entirely through the figure? Would the absence of the hole materially change your perception of the work?

7.   What might Moore mean by his phrase "the mystery of the hole"? Could he deliberately be asking you to continue this thought by his phrasing (he wrote what would be termed an "incomplete sentence")? There may be cave-type holes in *Reclining Figure* shown in Figure 5–22. Do these suggest mystery? Fascination?

8.   Figure 5–30, another of Moore's *Reclining Figures*, is less than one meter in length, yet to some it may give a feeling of huge size, at least in the photograph. Is there a feeling of "massiveness" in this work for you? Is this the "scale" that Moore speaks of—the size to scale connected with vision? Do you agree that physical size will affect your emotional response? Would *The Gates of Spoleto* appear different to you if reduced in size to a few inches? Two or three feet?

9.   In discussing Abstraction and Surrealism, Moore contrasts various aspects of the artist's inspiration—such as "order and surprise." Which of the styles of the various styles we have studied emphasized each of these kinds of input? What is Moore saying about them?

     Do his comments on the associational factors related to shapes contradict what he said earlier about regarding shapes for themselves? In part, Moore seems to be saying that most shapes have psychological meanings for us, often conditioned responses in the subconscious. See if you can apply this perception to the various works photographed for the textbook chapter.

10. What are the characteristics of Moore's work in Figure 5–22 that are cited as "truth to materials"? Do you find evidence of this tendency in Rodin's *Danaïde*?

11. What are the elements of protest seen in the sculpture in Figure 5–34? In your other reading on contemporary sculpture, what other trends did you find that are partially applied in this work? The works in Figures 5–35 and 5–36 are classified as "protests against technology" in the belief that technology dehumanizes people. Are there other forces in our culture that enhance the conditions symbolized in these works?

REVIEW QUIZ

Select the one best answer.

1. Surrealist sculpture would portray subject matter obtained from
   a. the shapes in themselves.
   b. subconscious contents.
   c. natural objects or events.
   d. the raw materials themselves.

2. The perception of "all-aroundness" mentioned by Moore means
   a. the artist perceives a complex shape from every direction.
   b. all forms with inherent meaning are rounded or spherical.
   c. the artist should be familiar with Representational, Abstract, and Surrealist schools of art.
   d. the shape should relate to a natural shape.

3. Our perception of shape in sculpture should be similar to our perception of
   a. line and form in painting.
   b. plot and character in drama.
   c. imagery in poetry.
   d. sensa in painting.

4. An example given of an activity that may expand one's awareness of shapes is
   a. a closer study of elements of a sculpture.
   b. experiments with drawing various designs.
   c. form shapes with a plastic material.
   d. examine randomly gathered pebbles individually.

5. A hole is likely to be worked into a sculpture to
    a. weaken the basic material.
    b. reveal its three-dimensional quality.
    c. make the material appear lighter.
    d. reduce the viewer's attention to materials.

6. Moore compared the mysterious quality of holes in sculpture to
    a. the shape of the hole itself.
    b. the mystery of shadows in painting.
    c. caves in hillsides and cliffs.
    d. natural shapes in nature.

7. Moore states that a work small in actual physical size
    a. may give a feeling of huge size.
    b. will always cause an emotional response to smallness.
    c. will appear petty and insignificant.
    d. should be delicately carved or modeled.

8. Moore's own inspiration in most of his carvings, if not all of them, comes from his perception of
    a. the shapes and character of inanimate objects.
    b. the shapes and character of the human body.
    c. sharp geometric figures.
    d. shapes and character of plant life.

9. "Truth to materials" refers to a style or tendency that seeks to
    a. retain the natural shape of materials.
    b. present shape without regard to the type of materials used.
    c. create forms and shapes primarily to show the underlying structure of the raw material.
    d. produce a shape in harmony with the type of material used.

10. *The Demonstrators II* reflects a view of humans as
    a. individuals seeking their own identity.
    b. individuals isolated from the group.
    c. part of a dehumanized group.
    d. noble beings with dignity of their own.

ADDITIONAL ACTIVITIES

1. Discuss your own responses to the size and scale of a particular sculpture. For example, do you feel it sustains your attention better in a larger size than if it were smaller? Also speculate on the relationship of our response to larger size in sculpture and the close-up of film.

2. Locate and describe a sculpture that exemplifies the trend called "truth to materials." Discuss your response to this work. In particular, discuss whether or not your response would have been the same had the form been executed in other materials and whether or not you can appreciate the original raw material differently because of its treatment in this work.

3. Perform an experiment with pebbles, seed pods, shells, or any small natural object, similar to Moore's description of his search among a handful of pebbles for new shapes. Try to identify two or three significantly different shapes among these objects. If possible, photograph them and describe your responses to them.

4. Visit a display of sculpture. Develop your own "perception key" based on Moore's article and describe one work, commenting on your responses to such features as three-dimensional quality, open areas or holes within the work, the human characteristics of shapes.

5. Find one work of sculpture that follows one of the lines suggested in the "Contemporary Sculpture" section of the textbook chapter. Discuss what perceptions you have of this work that would have escaped you before reading this lesson. Then give a brief description of the overall work.

Henry Moore (1898-1986) was for many years a teacher at the Royal College of Art in London and then at the Chelsea School of Art. He organized his writing like a teacher, systematically; one can almost see the term's work taking shape in these "notes," putting general ideas next to special applications and setting all in the frame of the history of modern culture. He composed his sculpture with the same systematic precision. Everything is in the service of a full three dimensions. Flatness is out. To make these dimensions clear, he developed a style characterized by piercings of his figures and by rounding of their edges that carries the viewer's eye well beyond the surfaces first presented. Moore was a sculptor in depth and a thinker about sculpture in the same dimension.

NOTES ON SCULPTURE

Henry Moore

It is a mistake for a sculptor or a painter to speak or write very often about his job. It releases tension needed for his work. By trying to express his aims with rounded-off logical exactness, he can easily become a theorist whose actual work is only a caged-in exposition of conceptions evolved in terms of logic and words.

It is likely, then, that a sculptor can give, from his own conscious experience, *clues* which will help others in their approach to sculpture, and this article tries to do this, and no more. It is not a general survey of sculpture, or of my own development, but a few notes on some of the problems that have concerned me from time to time.

THREE DIMENSIONS

Appreciation of sculpture depends upon the ability to respond to form in three dimensions. That is, perhaps, why sculpture has been described as the most difficult of all arts; certainly it is more difficult than the arts which involve appreciation of flat forms, shape in only two dimensions. Many more people are "form-blind" than colour-blind. The child learning to see first distinguishes only two-dimensional shape; it cannot judge distances, depths. Later, for its personal safety and practical needs, it has to develop (partly by means of touch) the ability to judge roughly three dimensional distances. But having satisfied the requirements of practical necessity most people go no further. Though they may attain considerable accuracy in the perception of flat form, they do not make the further intellectual and emotional effort needed to comprehend form in its full spatial existence.

This is what the sculptor must do. He must strive continually to think of and use form in its full spatial completeness. He gets the solid shape, as it were, inside his head—he thinks of it, whatever its size, as if he were holding it completely enclosed in the hollow of his hand. He mentally visualizes a complex form *from all round itself*: he knows while he looks at one side what the other side is like; he identifies himself with its centre of gravity, its mass, its weight; he realizes its volume, as the space that the shape displaces in the air.

And the sensitive observer of sculpture must also learn to feel shape simply as shape, not as description or reminiscence. He must, for example, perceive an egg as a simple single solid shape, quite apart from its significance as food, or from the literary idea that it will become a bird. And so with solids such as a shell, a nut, a plum, a pear, a tadpole, a mushroom, a mountain peak, a kidney, a carrot, a tree-trunk, a bird, a bud, a lark, a ladybird, a bullrush, a bone. From these he can go on to appreciate more complex forms or combinations of several forms.

BRANCUSI

Since Gothic, European sculpture has become overgrown with moss, weeds— all sorts of surface excrescences which completely concealed shape. It has been Brancusi's special mission to get rid of this overgrowth, and to make us once more shape-conscious. To do this he has had to concentrate on very simple direct shapes, to keep his sculpture, as it were, one-cylindered, to refine and polish a single shape to a degree almost too precious. Brancusi's work apart from its individual value has been of great historical importance in the development of contemporary sculpture. But it may now be no longer necessary to close down and restrict sculpture to the single (static) form unit. We can now begin to open out. To relate and combine together several forms of varied sizes, section, and direction, into one organic whole.

SHELLS AND PEBBLES—
BEING CONDITIONED TO RESPOND TO SHAPES

Although it is the human figure which interests me most deeply, I have always paid great attention to natural forms, such as bones, shells, pebbles, etc. Sometimes, for several years running, I have been to the same part of the seashore—but each year a new shape of pebble has caught my eye, which the year before, though it was there in hundreds, I never saw. Out of the millions of pebbles passed in walking along the shore, I choose out to see with excitement only those which fit in with my existing form interest at the time. A different thing happens if I sit down and examine a handful one by one. I may then extend my form experience more by giving my mind time to become conditioned to a new shape.

There are universal shapes to which everybody is subconsciously conditioned and to which they can respond if their conscious control does not shut them off.

HOLES IN SCULPTURE

Pebbles show Nature's way of working stone. Some of the pebbles I pick up have holes right through them.

When first working direct in a hard and brittle material like stone, the lack of experience and great respect for the material, the fear of ill-treating it, too often result in relief surface carving with no sculptural power.

But with more experience the completed work in stone can be kept within the limitations of its material, that is, not be weakened beyond its natural constructive build, and yet be ruined from an inert mass into a composition which has a full form existence, with masses of varied sizes and sections working together in spatial relationship.

A piece of stone can have a hole through it and not be weakened—if the hole is of a studied size, shape, and direction. On the principle of the arch it can remain just as strong.

The first hole made through a piece of stone is a revelation.

The hole connects one side to the other, making it immediately more three-dimensional.

A hole can itself have as much shape-meaning as a solid mass.

Sculpture in air is possible, where the stone contains only the hole, which is the intended and considered form.

The mystery of the hole—the mysterious fascination of caves in hillsides and cliffs.

SIZES AND SCALE

There is a right physical size for every idea.

Pieces of good stone have stood about my studio for long periods, because, though I've had ideas which would fit their proportions and materials perfectly, their size was wrong.

There is a side to scale not to do with its actual physical size, its measurement in feet and inches—but connected with vision.

A carving might be several times over life size and yet be petty and small in feeling—and a small carving only a few inches in height can give the feeling of huge size and monumental grandeur, because the vision behind it is big. Example: Michelangelo's drawings or a Masaccio madonna—and the Albert Memorial.

Yet actual physical size has an emotional meaning. We relate everything to our own size, and our emotional response to size is controlled by the fact that men on the average are between five and six feet high.

An exact model to one-tenth scale of Stonehenge, where the stones would be less than us, would lose all its impressiveness.

Sculpture is more affected by actual size considerations than painting. A painting is isolated by a frame from its surroundings (unless it serves just a decorative purpose), and so retains more easily its own imaginary scale.

If practical considerations allowed me (cost of material, of transport, etc.) I should like to work on large carvings more often than I do. The average in-between sizes do not disconnect an idea enough from prosaic everyday life. The very small or the very large take on an added size emotion.

DRAWING AND SCULPTURE

My drawings are done mainly as a help towards making sculpture—as a means of generating ideas for sculpture, tapping oneself for the initial idea; and as a way of sorting out ideas and developing them.

Also, sculpture compared with a drawing is a slow means of expression, and I find drawing a useful outlet for ideas which there is not time enough to realize as sculpture. And I use drawings from life (drawings of bones, shells, etc.)

And I sometimes draw just for its own enjoyment.

Experience, though, has taught me that the difference there is between drawing and sculpture should not be forgotten. A sculptural idea which may be satisfactory as a drawing always needs some alteration when translated into sculpture.

At one time whenever I made drawings for sculpture I tried to give them as much the illusion of real sculpture as I could—that is, I drew by the method of illusion, of light falling on a solid object. But now I find that carrying a drawing so far that it becomes a substitute for the sculpture either weakens the desire to do the sculpture, or is likely to make the sculpture only a dead realization of the drawing.

I now leave a wider latitude in the interpretation of the drawings I make for sculpture, and draw often in line and flat tones without the light and shade illusion of three dimensions; but this does not mean that the vision behind the drawing is only two-dimensional.

ABSTRACTION AND SURREALISM

The violent quarrel between the abstractionists and the surrealists seems to me quite unnecessary. All good art has contained both abstract and surrealist elements, just as it has contained both classical and romantic elements— order and surprise, intellect and imagination, conscious and unconscious. Both sides of the artist's personality must play their part. And I think the first inception of a painting or a sculpture may begin from either end. As far as my own experience is concerned, I sometimes begin a drawing with no preconceived problem to solve, with only the desire to use pencil on paper, and make lines, tones, and shapes with no conscious aim; but as my mind takes in what is so produced a point arrives where some idea becomes conscious and crystallizes, and then a control and ordering begin to take place.

Or sometimes I start with a set subject, or to solve, in a block of stone of known dimensions, a sculptural problem I've given myself, and then consciously attempt to build an ordered relationship of forms, which shall express my idea. But if the work is to be more than just a sculptural exercise, unexplainable jumps in the process of thought occur; and the imagination plays its part.

It might seem from what I've said of shape and form that I regard them as ends in themselves. Far from it. I am very much aware that associational, psychological factors play a large part in sculpture. The meaning and significance of form itself probably depends on the countless associations of man's history. For example, rounded forms convey an idea of fruitfulness, maturity, probably because the earth, women's breasts, and most fruits are rounded, and these shapes are important because they have this background in our habits of perception. I think the humanist organic element will always be for me of fundamental importance in sculpture, giving sculpture its vitality. Each particular carving I make takes on in my mind a human, or occasionally animal, character, and personality, and this personality controls its design and formal qualities, and makes me satisfied or dissatisfied with the work as it develops.

My own aim and direction seems to be consistent with these beliefs, though it does not depend upon them. My sculpture is becoming less representational, less an outward visual copy, and so what some people would call more abstract; but only because I believe that in this way I can present the human psychological content of my work with the greatest directness and intensity.

LESSON 26

ARCHITECTURE

THE EVOLVING SKYLINE

OVERVIEW

Early in this course, we considered the question: What is art?
Architecture is an art form, but, in this lesson, we must consider the
question: What is architecture? Surely not all structures placed upon the
earth are architecture, just as not all words printed on a page are
"literature," nor all sounds "music," nor all daubs of paint "painting."
Structures are usually erected to serve some function, but a structure that
is architecture is more than something that serves a purpose; it is,
instead, a structure that is a *meaningful* design of an area—a region of
space—for human activity. As with the other art forms, a structure that
is architecture communicates the artist's (architect's) unique perception
of the world. It is important to note that architecture is, of all the arts,
perhaps the most severely constrained by limitations, not only those of
the materials used to construct buildings but also those of the functions
the buildings must serve. In spite of those constraints, however, the
expressions of artistic visions throughout human history have been most
remarkable and fascinating.

Through the ages, humankind has erected a diverse array of structures. At first, the structures were built mainly to provide shelter for people and their possessions. Once basic needs were satisfied, structures could be, and were, built to serve other purposes, such as religion, commerce, government, and recreation.

The varied purposes of architecture, along with the diversity of architectural styles found throughout the world are encapsulated in the history of architecture of America. The television program for this lesson begins with the simple shelters constructed by the pioneers out of the materials at hand. Once the immigrants to this country had established themselves, they developed more decorative types of architecture, much of which echoed the architecture of their native lands. Other sources of ideas for the design of buildings were in the classical forms of ancient Greece and Rome, along with the Gothic, Romanesque, Renaissance, and neo-Baroque. We see many examples of New World architecture inspired by Old World structures: a Georgian colonial mansion; a Chinese pagoda; Gothic towers; Spanish missions; state capitals with Renaissance domes and Greek-temple façades; the Washington Arch, fashioned after the triumphal arches of the Roman Empire; the New York Public Library, modeled after the square temples of ancient Rome.

Influences from earlier styles of architecture persisted in American architecture well into this century. Even when new materials and technologies made possible the construction of skyscrapers, the façades of the structure were often decorated with neo-Classical designs and forms. Perhaps the single most important technological advance in shaping modern American architecture was the development of the steel frame. This solid structure is free standing; that is, it does not need heavy walls for support. The steel frame enabled buildings to rise to new heights and permitted walls to be made of such previously impractical materials as glass. Two striking examples of buildings made possible by the free-standing steel frame are Lever house, from the early 1950s, and the Seagram Building, designed by Mies van der Rohe in 1957. Such slab skyscrapers, as exemplified by the Lever house and Seagram Building, became common on our skyline, their simple streamlined appearance accurately mirroring our twentieth-century technological culture.

From the linearity and geometry characteristic of the first modern architecture, we are now beginning to incorporate curves to balance straightness, not unlike many painters, such as Cézanne, have done in their paintings.

The program concludes with a consideration of how modern architecture, along with all other architectural styles, reflects the culture of which it is a part. The sculpture that was such an integral part of the Baroque architecture often glorified the absolute monarchs of the day. The façades of our buildings, even though they appear decorative, may be designed to regulate the amount of light and heat and thus conserve energy. Yet, we have found ways to make functional façades as decorative as those of the Baroque. Finally, the architects of today do not reject the past. Rather, they feel free to draw upon it, modify it, and adapt it in wondrously imaginative ways to meet the needs of our times.

The text assignment for this lesson considers that most important of all features defined by architecture: space. It is a primary function of architecture to order the position of parts within space. The architect, unlike the sculptor who generally works in three dimensions to mold out into space, works in three dimensions to enclose space.

It is through space, more specifically centered space, that people move to experience architecture. In essence, a building can be considered architecture if it clarifies, rather than muddles or ignores, the elements of the scene and stimulates us to participate with the art by being sensitive to the space defined by the structure.

LEARNING OBJECTIVES

ON COMPLETING YOUR STUDY OF THIS LESSON, YOU SHOULD BE ABLE TO:

1. Identify examples of architecture representative of other cultures.
2. Identify examples of architecture representative of the artistic styles of other times.
3. List several features of modern skyscraper construction.
4. Define the concepts "centered space" and "configurational center."
5. Appreciate the importance of a structure that reveals something about the space it contains and the activities within and about it.

ASSIGNMENTS

BEFORE VIEWING THE PROGRAM:

Read the "Overview" and familiarize yourself with the "Learning Objectives" for this lesson.

Consult a dictionary or encyclopedia for definitions of the following terms as they relate to architecture:

>   basilica
>   column (Greek: Dorian, Ionian, Corinthian)
>   federalist
>   Gothic
>   Renaissance
>   Romanesque

Look over the "Aids for Study" for this lesson.

VIEW THE TELEVISION PROGRAM *"Architecture: The Evolving Skyline."*

AFTER VIEWING THE PROGRAM:

In the textbook, Chapter 6, "Architecture":
  • Read pages 157–164 ("Space in General," "Centered Space," "Space and Architecture," "Chartres," and "Living Space").

Review what you have learned, using the "Aids for Study" again.

Evaluate your learning with the "Review Quiz," then check your answers with the "Answer Key" at the back of this study guide.

In accordance with your own interests or with your instructor's assignment, complete selected "Additional Activities."

AIDS FOR STUDY

1. Why did immigrants to America copy building styles from their former countries? In addition to copying their native styles, what styles are reminiscent of more ancient heritages?

2. What were some of the features of Roman architecture copied in the Washington Arch? For what kinds of buildings did the architecture of Rome serve as models?

3. How did the introduction of stainless steel construction make possible "walls of glass"? What new effects could such buildings have on the surrounding? What effect did the "square geometry" lines of the first examples of slab skyscrapers shown have on you?

4. According to the program, Rome's Colosseum may have inspired some modern circular buildings. Can you suggest differences in the circularity and the effect on Roman and modern buildings? Could such differences be due to the availability of materials and technology?

5. According to the program, "latest inventions regulate the amount of light and heat to be admitted to the interiors. Functional façades are at the same time decorative. Beauty is discovered in the natural pattern of materials. Color and texture are emphasized instead of ornate Victorian decoration. Complexity is transformed into simplicity." Do you know of examples of these trends in recent American architecture? How would you summarize these trends? What aspects, if any, of our contemporary culture do they reflect?

6. The program noted at the same time that some elements of design continue to be employed. For example, columns and arches are still designed as a part of walkways and entryways. How do these differ in design from the columns and arches of earlier ages?

7. The definition of space given in the text is contrasted with the generally used scientific description. What is space in this artistic sense?

8. What is "centered space"? What is the "power of space" that
    the text speaks of? Why do we so often ignore it and not feel its
    effect? Is it more because we do not have things positioned
    properly in our space, or is it that we are too busy to pause and
    appreciate the arrangement?

9. How does the text define architecture? What is a
    "configurational center"? What is a "nonarchitectural"
    building? Does the example of Trinity Church in New York, as
    related in the text, seem to indicate that a building that was at
    one time significant may become "nonarchitectural"?

REVIEW QUIZ

Select the one best answer.

1. Most of the examples of older American architecture shown in the
    program are based on
    a. styles of European or Asian cultures.
    b. the style developed for the nation's capital.
    c. the availability of local materials.
    d. Victorian and Georgian architecture.

2. American public buildings were frequently based on
    a. English Gothic styles.
    b. Oriental styles.
    c. Roman styles.
    d. none of these.

3. The "sheer walls of glass" of modern skyscrapers do not
    a. reflect the surroundings.
    b. reflect light.
    c. have highly decorated exteriors.
    d. appear slender and sheer from a distance.

4. The designs of the Lever house and the Seagram Building were indirectly compared to
   a. abstract painting.
   b. Cubism.
   c. Impressionism.
   d. all of these.

5. One significant difference between the Roman Colosseum and modern circular buildings is that
   a. the modern buildings are larger.
   b. the Colosseum was more architectural.
   c. architects of modern circular buildings have greater freedom of design.
   d. the architects of the Colosseum were not hampered by tradition.

6. Among the characteristics *not* usually found in modern skyscraper architecture is
   a. use of functional façades as decoration.
   b. enhancement of the natural beauty of materials.
   c. presence of intricate ornamentation.
   d. use of color and texture.

7. Arches and columns found in present-day buildings, which are reminiscent of Greek and Roman architectural traditions,
   a. tend to be exact copies of older styles.
   b. tend to be slimmer and smoother than their predecessors.
   c. are criticized because they mix modern and classical architectural styles.
   d. are designed so that they have no function, such as support for a roof.

8. The positioned interrelationships of structures around a major location or activity is termed
   a. space.
   b. centered space.
   c. living space.
   d. organized space.

9. The text describes Chartres as an example of architecture because
    a. it provided the author with a consciousness of its conservation of space.
    b. it is now obtrusive in its surroundings.
    c. the art and stained glass windows are beautiful elements.
    d. its style is no longer meaningful.

10. Which of the following is *not* an example of a configurational center?
    a. one's home
    b. one's work
    c. the location of an organization or society
    d. a highway or roadway traveled frequently

ADDITIONAL ACTIVITIES

1. Write a description of your community, based on the latter half of the perception key "Space as the Positioned Interrelationships of Things" (textbook pages 157–158). Try to identify, then describe, at least one meaningful "center of activity" in your community that seems to draw one to it by its architecture.

2. Discuss the author's definition of architectural and nonarchitectural buildings. If you wish, do the perception key on "Nonarchitectural Buildings" (textbook page 163). If you prefer, select and describe a building in your community that is architectural in the sense of the text. If you can, take photographs of your example, from more than one angle. See if you can learn more from the photographs, after studying the buildings in actuality.

3. Select a building or other structure that has for you the power of centeredness. If possible, go to the building and write a description of this centeredness while actually experiencing it. If you are not able to go to the building, describe the design of the building and how the architect emphasized its center or centrality.

ARCHITECTURE

FROM EARTH TO SKY

OVERVIEW

In the preceding lesson on architecture, we learned that architecture is the meaningful conservation—the ordering—of space. The structures within which we live and work can be so designed that the spaces they contain are meaningful, not only with respect to the functional positioning of elements but also by whether—and how—they encourage one to be conscious of the space itself: its beauty, function, and security.

Architecture is unique among the art forms in that the exterior that encloses the interior space is placed within the larger environment of earth and sky. This relationship between a structure and its environment is perhaps the most crucial element in the design of a particular piece of architecture, for it is one that the architect cannot ignore. At some point, a structure is always placed upon the earth, and rises—however minimally—into the sky. How a particular structure relates to earth and sky has substantial influence on our perception of, and response to, that structure.

The lesson for this program considers three principal types of structures in their relationship to earth and sky: earth-rooted architecture, sky-oriented architecture, and earth-resting architecture.

Architecture characterized as earth-rooted emphasizes the strength, fertility, and security associated with the earth itself. Such architecture does not appear to sit upon the earth; instead, it gives the impression that it is an organic extension of the earth. The Parthenon is a notable example of earth-rooted architecture: this temple seems to rise naturally out of the rocky cliff on which it is situated. Other elements that characterize earth-rooted architecture are gravity—such buildings accept, rather than oppose, that force; raw materials—earth-rooted buildings frequently achieve their oneness with the earth through the use of native, natural materials; and centrality—a structure with strongly centered inner space and outer space emphasizes the relationship between the structure and the earth in which it is rooted.

Sky-oriented architecture pulls our attention upward, away from the earth. In comparison to earth-rooted buildings, sky-oriented buildings not only oppose gravity, they defy that force. In keeping with their lack of oneness with the earth, sky-oriented structures are often constructed of nonnatural materials.

Axis mundi is a concept important to understanding the impact of sky-oriented architecture. Briefly, this concept refers to the apparent need of humans to center themselves in relation to the sky through an upward-thrusting structure. Many obvious examples of *axis mundi* can be found in primitive cultures, and the authors of the text feel that more recent architecture, such as Chartres and Mont Saint Michel, may also serve as an *axis mundi.* A final characteristic of sky-oriented architecture is the integration of outside light into the inside of the structure.

The third type of architecture—earth-resting architecture—is by far the most common. This architecture is neither planted in the earth nor reaching toward the sky. In earth-resting architecture, the earth is a stage; the sky, a backdrop. This type of architecture has the potential for being most dramatic because it must make its statement independent of the support from, and interaction with, earth and sky. Two interesting examples of earth-resting architecture are the Farnsworth house, designed by Mies van der Rohe, and the Palazzo Farnese, designed by Antonio da Sangallo and Michelangelo.

One can rather quickly learn to identify the three principal types of architecture described in this lesson. Each type comprises certain distinctive elements, elements that, in themselves, are often dictated by the function and site of the structure. For instance, churches serve an other-worldy function, so their orientation is usually skyward. Modern society, with its concentrated population and limited supply of land, has also resulted in the construction of sky-oriented apartment and office buildings to serve the function of adequately meeting the needs of people. In analyzing the elements of a structure, we must also evaluate how effectively and truthfully they reveal the content or purpose of the structure. This lesson should provide you with knowledge to use in making that evaluation.

LEARNING OBJECTIVES

ON COMPLETING YOUR STUDY OF THIS LESSON, YOU SHOULD BE ABLE TO:

1. Define earth-rooted architecture and explain how site, gravity, and centrality are essential elements of earth-rooted architecture.

2. List the characteristics of sky-oriented architecture.

3. Define earth-resting architecture.

4. Appreciate the integrating possibilities of architecture, particularly for the area beyond the building itself.

5. Make a preliminary evaluation of a building to determine if its elements combine to reveal its contents or purpose.

ASSIGNMENTS

BEFORE VIEWING THE PROGRAM:

Read the "Overview" and familiarize yourself with the "Learning Objectives" for this lesson.

Consult an encyclopedia or other reference texts for illustrations of the following structures:

Cathedral of Florence, Italy
Palace of Versailles, France
The Pantheon, Rome
The Parthenon, Greece
Rockefeller Center, New York City

Look over the "Aids for Study" for this lesson.

VIEW THE TELEVISION PROGRAM *"Architecture: From Earth to Sky."*

AFTER VIEWING THE PROGRAM:

In the textbook, Chapter 6, "Architecture":
  •Read pages 176–198 ("Earth-Rooted Architecture," "Sky-Oriented Architecture," and "Earth-Resting Architecture").

Review what you have learned, using the "Aids for Study" again.

Evaluate your learning with the "Review Quiz," then check your answers with the "Answer Key" at the back of this study guide.

In accordance with your own interests or with your instructor's assignment, complete selected "Additional Activities."

AIDS FOR STUDY

1. What example is given to illustrate that an earth-rooted structure will draw our attention to its environment? Does the Kaufman house ("Falling Water") also draw attention to the surroundings? How?

2. In what way does the Parthenon "accept" gravity more revealingly than does, for example, Mont Saint Michel? What sense of security do the authors feel derives from the Parthenon's "surrender to gravity"?

3. Describe how the Kaufman house uses both native materials and manufactured materials to emphasize its rootedness to its environment. Does the actual shape of this building emphasize some natural features surrounding it?

4. The authors of the text seem to speak of centrality in two senses: outward and inward. Why is the inner space of the Parthenon weaker in centrality? How is the inner space of Chartres stronger in this respect?

5. What are the three elements that may make a building "sky-oriented"? Give an example of a building with each type of element.

6. What does the term *axis mundi* mean? Do all tall buildings serve to organize the space around them this way? Why can Trinity Church (Figure 6–5) no longer organize the sky?

7. In discussing the "defiance of gravity" that some buildings seek, why does the text feel that many skyscrapers fail to appear beyond gravitational pull? Is it a question of elements such as lines? Is it the apparent massiveness of the lower part of the Woolworth Building? If a building is tall, yet fails to be sky-oriented, how would you classify it?

8. Does sky-oriented architecture seem to ignore the world, or does it accent and reveal the world? Perhaps it would be easiest to consider this question in terms of specific examples.

9. The textbook suggests that light-integrating buildings are also sky-oriented. Does a building need to be large, or tall, to be sky-oriented?

10. How does earth-resting architecture relate to earth and sky? What are three characteristics of earth-resting architecture? In what way does the Wiley house seem to test the limits of earth-resting architecture? Under what circumstances, according to the textbook, is the earth-resting style preferred over the earth-rooted style?

11. What elements of line did the textbook feel are superior in the Mies van der Rohe complex (Figure 6–33, Lafayette Park) as compared to the Reston complex (Figure 6–32)? Do you sense, looking at the photographs, a better balance in one than in the other?

12. What is the primary criticism in the textbok of the National Gallery of Art? According to the textbook definition, is this building truly architecture? What do the authors of the textbook feel a building should reveal?

REVIEW QUIZ

Select the one best answer.

1. The Kaufman house
    a. draws attention to its surroundings by mimicking natural shapes.
    b. does not particularly draw attention to its surroundings.
    c. draws attention to its surroundings by use of natural materials and reflecting glass.
    d. draws attention to its surroundings by projecting above the earth.

2. As an example of a structure exhibiting "surrender to gravity," the text described
    a. the Parthenon.
    b. Mont Saint Michel.
    c. Chartres.
    d. the Woolworth Building.

3. The inner centrality of the Parthenon was considered weak because
    a. its outer centrality is strong.
    b. it is entirely open.
    c. it is too divided inside.
    d. it drew one into the center of the building.

4. Sky-oriented architecture may do all of the following *except*
    a. emphasize or accent the earth around it.
    b. appear to defy gravity.
    c. stand high and centered.
    d. integrate inner and outer light.

5. A building that appears tall and centered and stands comparatively alone suggest the characteristic called
    a. defiance of gravity.
    b. *axis mundi.*
    c. surrender to gravity.
    d. isolation.

6. A building will appear to defy gravity if it
    a. is tall enough to make a person appear insignificant.
    b. draws our eyes upward.
    c. is not designed to appear "earth-rooted."
    d. is built of reflective materials.

7. Sky-oriented architecture tends to
    a. make the world seem unimportant by calling attention to itself.
    b. reveal the world by calling attention to the sky, horizon, or light.
    c. reveal its surroundings by calling attention to nearby elements.
    d. any of these.

8. One type of sky-oriented structure that may not have to be built on a large scale is
    a. gravity-defying architecture.
    b. skyscraper architecture.
    c. light-integrating architecture.
    d. any of these.

9. Earth-resting architecture usually includes all the following structures *except* those that
    a. are integrated into the surrounding earth.
    b. are only a few stories high, at most.
    c. have flat roofs.
    d. have no vertical projections such as spires.

10. The authors of the textbook think that the Mies van der Rohe
    complex at Lafayette Park is more successful than the complex in
    Reston, Virginia because
    a. all important lines are vertical.
    b. vertical and horizontal lines are balanced.
    c. the tall building causes the viewer to ignore the shorter,
        townhouse units.
    d. the tall building is masked by the many smaller dwelling units
        around it.

ADDITIONAL ACTIVITIES

1. Select a museum, art gallery, or library in your community and
    compare its architecture with that of the National Gallery of
    Art in Washington, D.C. Do you find the example you have
    picked inviting? Does it reveal its function? Does it reveal its
    surroundings or its presence in some way?

2. Study photographs (and commentary if available) on one of the
    architects named in the reading assignment. Do you find certain
    elements or styles appearing repeatedly? How would you
    describe these styles?

3. Select a home or building in your community that, in your
    opinion, is especially attractive. Describe this building in terms
    of its orientation. What elements of the building, if any, cause it
    to be related to its surroundings? What type of centrality do you
    find within the building? If you can, learn who designed it and
    something of the building's history. Does the building reveal its
    function?

ARCHITECTURE

MEANING IN A POET'S VISION

OVERVIEW

Above all artists, the architect must keep his or her public in mind, for
architecture is a peculiarly public art, and quite often the building of the
architect's creation must be financed with funds from either public or
major private sources. Because of its public nature, architecture must—if
it is to be considered art—interpret the essential values of its society. In a
very direct way, then, the common or shared values of contemporary
society are an integral part of the architect's subject matter.

To participate with a work of architecture fully, we as observers
must understand its subject matter as revealed in its form and function,
and we must experience what it communicates about the relevant values
of the artist and society.

In this lesson we learn that the architect is bound by four basic,
interrelated necessities. And if architecture is to be artistically
meaningful, it must satisfy these necessities. The first of these is the
technical or structural requirement of the building; the second is the
function or use for which it is intended; the third is its spatial

relationship; and the fourth is content. Form adjusts and adapts to these four necessities if it is successful.

Structural requirement is the most obvious necessity, to be sure, simply because the building must *stand,* and to achieve this end, the architect must know his or her materials and their potentialities. Furthermore, the building must stand in such a way that it reveals its function or use. Does this require us to say, then, that form follows function? No, for there is no general agreement on this point, but on the other hand, the architect does not use form to *disguise* function.

The building must also be constructed in such a way that it fits its spatial context. The way a work of architecture works in space most clearly distinguishes architecture from the arts of painting and sculpture. (Note that the textbook faults Frank Lloyd Wright's famed Solomon R. Guggenheim Museum for poor use of its spatial context, although it meets the other three necessities.)

Through content the architect must communicate something significant about him- or herself and society that we might otherwise not perceive. Architecture that so communicates stands as a rich historical record of its time.

In the television program for this lesson we will study form and meaning through the highly expressive works of the colorful Spanish genius, Antoni Gaudi (1852–1926). If we have not before seen architecture created with lines that are not predominantly geometric and straight, we may experience a feeling of "future shock" on first viewing Gaudi's creations. Gaudi believed in the rightness and fitness of natural forms and organic structures, yet he had strong feeling for the Gothic and an affinity for the curving, sinuous lines of the Art Nouveau, a movement that gained great prominence in Europe in the late nineteenth century. He had a deep, abiding love for the Catholic Church, and he was convinced that architecture is a noble art. We see these values expressed boldly throughout those portions of his work that are shown in the television program.

Asked to design a "workers' colony" and garden, Gaudi turned a barren Barcelona hillside into a fantasy setting that is an exploration of natural shapes conceived with fluidity and curving of line. We observe that in its preference for bright colors, the Park Güell approaches the modern, though it was completed in 1914. The Palacio Güell and the Casa Vicens, palatial dwellings created by Gaudi, manage to combine the Spanish-Moorish artistic-cultural forces of the region with the architect's strong feeling for natural and organic forms. We see the tiered curves of the Casa Mila flow like a flamenco dance.

In the Casa Battlo, Gaudi avoids rectangular geometry, creates overtones of the organic, and manages to express a religious intent—all at the same time. He creates space in which forms and details relate to each other in free-flowing rhythm, and he attempts to erase separation between interior and exterior. Its columns are expressive of human bones, its structure has a skeletal aspect, and its colors are organic, changing with the light. There is religious feeling in the symbolic shape (a dragon's back?) and strong curvature of the roof.

Especially his great devotion to the Catholic Church, but also his strong feeling for the organic and the Gothic, are all expressed in the design of a great church, which Gaudi planned for ten years but never built. The Temple of the Sagrada Familia (Temple of the Holy Family) was to have been paid for by votive offerings, and Gaudi's purpose in building it was to "expiate the sins of a materialistic age." Only the crypt of the church was built.

Gaudi's vision combined modern Gothic with twisted forms of shin and thigh bones and tilted columns arched outward like human bones to replace conventional braces and buttresses. The dramatic verticality of the church's Gothic heights were to be transformed by lofty space. Gaudi's Gothic spires pointed not only to the sky, but also to forces of the past and to the ideas of the future.

The television program concludes with the comment: "He [Gaudi] was not an antiquarian nor a mere devotee of Art Nouveau, but a poet who brought together technology and faith in a positive vision full of compassionate strength and humanity, which makes him a great pioneer of modern architecture."

LEARNING OBJECTIVES

ON COMPLETING YOUR STUDY OF THIS LESSON, YOU SHOULD BE ABLE TO:

1. Describe the architect's relationship to society and its values, according to the statements made in the text by Abell and Panofsky.

2. List the four "necessities" textbook authors Martin and Jacobus claim architecture must meet if it is to be artistically meaningful.

3. Understand the functional aspect of architecture.

4. Appreciate the ways in which architecture can be revelatory of the past.

5. Name some of the most notable works of Antoni Gaudi.

6. List three important influences upon his life that can be seen in Gaudi's work.

7. Identify unique characteristics of two of Gaudi's works.

ASSIGNMENTS

BEFORE VIEWING THE PROGRAM:

Read the "Overview" and familiarize yourself with the "Learning Objectives" for this lesson.

Consult a dictionary or an encyclopedia to acquaint yourself with these terms:

> Art Nouveau
> Gothic

In the textbook, Chapter 6, "Architecture":
- •Read pages 164–176 ("The Architect," "Technical Requirements of Architecture," "Functional Requirements of Architecture," "Spatial Requirements of Architecture," and "Revelatory Requirements of Architecture").

Look over the "Aids for Study" for this lesson.

VIEW THE TELEVISION PROGRAM *Architecture: Meaning in a Poet's Vision.*

AFTER VIEWING THE PROGRAM:

Review what you have learned, using the "Aids for Study" again.

Evaluate your learning with the "Review Quiz," then check your answers with the "Answer Key" at the back of this study guide.

In accordance with your own interests or your instructor's assignment, complete selected "Additional Activities."

AIDS FOR STUDY

1. What was a basic technical requirement for the construction of the Parthenon? Do the features listed in the perception key "Parthenon and Chartres" (on pages 165–167) relate to technical requirements or to other considerations?

2. Did you have difficulty determining or at least approximating the functions of the buildings in Figures 6–11 and 6–12? Does the written description of the Guggenheim Museum suggest details to you that are in harmony with the purposes of an art museum? In what way did the building, in the opinion of the textbook authors, fail to meet one important requirement?

3. Are "spatial requirements" of architecture simply technical or artistic or both?

4. What is meant by "revelatory requirements"? Does it seem to you that the textbook authors feel the architect must reveal society's values, rather than his or her own, or is this an oversimplification? What values are revealed, do you think, by the Union Carbide Building, or by Le Corbusier?

5. Early in the program, we see the Shrine of the Black Virgin. Which influence on Gaudi's life was mentioned here? How are his religious beliefs reflected in the subject matter of later works?

6. The Palacio Güell was a townhouse designed and built by Gaudi for his patron. Recall at least one unconventional example of its design.

7. The Casa Battlo is described as having both organic feeling and religious symbolism. Recall details of this building that seem to

make reference to skeletal structures. Where is religious symbolism seen?

8. The Park Güell is described as a "fairy-tale setting." In what way did Gaudi employ architecture to create a fantasy? Recall in particular the entry and forecourt, the imaginatively shaped columns. Which types of pillars are examples of Gaudi's "exploring new forms of structure guided by examples provided by nature"?

9. How important to Gaudi was his project for the Temple of the Sagrada Familia (Temple of the Holy Family)? In referring to the crypt of this work that was completed, the narrator comments that "the crypt can give only an incomplete idea of Gaudi's intentions for a building in which he hoped to merge all the elements—wall, column, arch—in one rhythmic space continuum." To which style of architecture do two of these elements belong, according to your reading assignment? What are other elements of the Gothic style?

10. What elements of Gothic style did Gaudi emphasize? Which one did he eliminate? To him, the Gothic was the superlative style, yet he improved it by finding new solutions to problems that had faced former architects. What were these solutions?

11. Try to describe Gaudi's relationship to his society and its values in terms of the statements made by Abell and Panofsky.

12. Do you think Gaudi's unconventional work meets the four basic "necessities" described by the textbook as being essential to architecture that is art? Why? Can you think of an example from the television program that alludes to a technical requirement that Gaudi solves? Do the Park Güell, the Casa Güell, the Casa Vicens, and the Temple of the Holy Family reveal anything about function or values?

REVIEW QUIZ

Select the one best answer or briefly fill in the answer.

1. The stress placed upon a column in the beam-and-lintel construction of the Parthenon is a
    a. technical requirement.
    b. functional requirement.
    c. space requirement.
    d. revelatory requirement.

2. The functional requirement of architecture is that
    a. a building provides sufficient space to allow persons to perform the functions required.
    b. all materials must function together to withstand the stresses on it.
    c. the form of the building should reveal its purpose or function.
    d. the form of the building should reflect the values of the architect and his society.

3. Which of the following is a "revelatory requirement" of architecture as described in the textbook?
    a. Sufficient lighting and ventilation should be provided in a building.
    b. A structure such as the Union Carbide Building should reflect the nature of commercial enterprise.
    c. The Guggenheim museum should not perfectly harmonize with the surrounding buildings.
    d. The towers of the church in the Temple of the Holy Family are so constructed as to remain stable.

4. Of the influences on Gaudi's life, which one had the greatest impact on his selection of subject matter, particularly his final works? *Catholicism*

5. Which of the influences on Gaudi's life is reflected in his use of free, curving lines?

Art Noveau

6. Which architectural style of the past had the greatest influence on Gaudi's work?

Gothic

7. The Park Güell included such features as
   a. Medieval towers.
   b. treelike pillars.
   c. dragon-shaped roof.
   d. dignified, squared corners.

8. The Park Güell was designed to include
   a. living quarters for workers.
   b. theaters.
   c. shops.
   d. all of the above.

9. Briefly list the four requirements a work of architecture must meet if it is to have artistic meaningfulness.

technical/structural
function
spatial relationship
Content

10. Textbook authors Martin and Jacobus feel that architecture must interpret essential values of a society because
    a. it is the most important art.
    b. architects must be engineers, psychologists, and sociologists as well.
    c. it is public.
    d. it has more potential for meaning.

ADDITIONAL ACTIVITIES

1. Gaudi was referred to in this program as "a poet" and "poetic." Discuss some similarities between architecture and poetry. Perhaps you might try a comparison using the requirements set forth in the reading assignment. Or you might use the poem *Ars Poetica* (in Lesson 17) as a frame of reference.

2. Read the section "Sculpture and Architecture Compared" in Chapter 5 of the textbook (pages 101–104). Discuss the point where one art merges into the other, or where you would place a line of demarcation between the two. Consider, in particular, the exterior views of Gaudi's crypt, and the criticism made of the houses of Mies van der Rohe (see the perception key "Farnsworth Residence and the Palazzo Farnese," page 192) that they "were made to be looked at rather than lived in."

3. Each culture and epoch inherits and then develops values unique to it. The textbook suggests that buildings, in particular, reflect the values of the past. In another unit, it was suggested that the elements and form of a drama remained notable only while it still spoke to the values of the succeeding ages. Is this true with architecture, or do notable structures, like Chartres for instance, draw our sustained interest because we share for a moment the older values? Discuss this question, using examples of older architecture if possible.

LESSON 29

ARCHITECTURE

THE SHEPHERD OF SPACE

In this unit we have considered some elements that are basic to architecture as art. We have considered the orientation of architectural structures to earth and sky and learned of necessities that must be present if architecture is to have artistic meaning. We have been shown examples of architecture in America and in the Old World, and we have looked closely at the works of a bold architect whose culminating work drew upon the past but, even as it did so, powerfully foreshadowed the future of modern architecture. For the most part, we have been viewing completed structures, with the exception of Gaudi's Temple of the Holy Family, which he designed but never built.

In this last lesson of the unit we will share the thoughts of noted architect Gio Ponti on the genesis (or insight) of the architect and the process of his art. In a way, this is akin to learning from Ingmar Bergman how a film director nurtures an emotional tone into a complete work, or listening to Henry Moore's words about how a sculpture is inspired.

In short, Ponti's ideas are much like a restatement of the genesis of any art, yet some speak uniquely to architecture. And he gives us special insight into the importance of content, rather than the design of form or the selection of subject matter.

Ponti distinguishes between "builders and architects" and "buildings and architecture." A work of architecture is a work of art, he says, and an architect is an artist. "Buildings and builders are something else, something very respectable, but something else." Furthermore, for Ponti, an artist is a realist who transposes dreams into reality and reveals himself by his imagination.

Ponti describes for us what he calls the "genesis" of an architect: He begins by imagining his entire creation—including walls, spaces, earth, and sky; then he "animates" his imagined creation by picturing living persons in every room, hall, portico, stairwell, and foyer of his structure. The architect also "hears" the noises of human life and work in his interiors. But before he can transpose his dream into reality, he must learn well the craft of the artisans (a "manual genesis"); he must learn to love his trade; and he must develop a sensuous conception of his work. He will not be daunted by limited means. He will paint and inspire landscapes. He will "interpret" those who will use or live in his structure, and his structure will be used by those persons happily.

And now the architect must finally commit himself to the values of obligation and work. For Ponti, the right of an architectural work to *be* is in its beauty, not its function. A work of architecture *assumes* beauty as a function, yet—paradoxically—it will function entirely only if it is beautiful.

In harmony with Ponti's emphasis upon beginnings, and in concluding this unit, we are asked to consider the question of the role of architecture in city planning. As noted in the textbook, no use of space today is more critical than it is in the city, and the issue of space and architecture is especially relevant to city planning. Our attention is called to New Haven's "monstrous" downtown parking garage, a monument to the automobile that overshadows all that is lovely in the central city, including the campus of Yale University.

To prevent or correct such ruination of cities, should we relegate the automobile to the fringe areas, decentralize downtown areas and divide them according to functions such as offices, restaurants, shops, and theaters—leaving open space and opportunity to be sensitive to the structures and spaces that may be located here? Should we keep the central cities and establish outlying rural villages? Or has the flight to the suburbs already forestalled this latter solution?

We are left with questions, not solutions.

But in conclusion, our textbook reminds us that "architects are the shepherds of space . . . Architects make space a gracious place. Such places, like a home, give us a center from which we can orient ourselves to other places."

ON COMPLETING YOUR STUDY OF THIS LESSON, YOU SHOULD BE ABLE TO:

1. List some of the basic artistic insights (or "geneses") of the architect.
2. Identify which of the insights are unique to architecture as opposed to other arts.
3. Compare Ponti's "genesis of architecture" with the elements of architecture discussed in Lesson 27.
4. Identify some of the problems encountered in city planning.
5. Speculate on an architect's consideration of psychological and emotional values while participating in architecture as art.

BEFORE VIEWING THE PROGRAM:

Read the "Overview" and familiarize yourself with the "Learning Objectives" for this lesson.

Consult a dictionary for formal definition of these terms:

aesthetics
sonorous
stylistic

Review previous lessons in this unit to refresh your understanding of the concepts of:

architecture
function
revelation
space

Look over the "Aids for Study" for this lesson.

VIEW THE TELEVISION PROGRAM *"Architecture: The Shepherd of Space."*

AFTER VIEWING THE PROGRAM:

In this lesson of the study guide:
   •Read the essay "The Architect, the Artist," by Gio Ponti,
     pages 309–315.

In the textbook, Chapter 6, "Architecture":
   •Read pages 199–204 ("City Planning" and "Summary").

Review what you have learned, using the "Aids for Study" again.

Evaluate your learning with the "Review Quiz," then check your answers with the "Answer Key" at the back of this study guide.

In accordance with your own interests or with your instructor's assignment, complete selected "Additional Activities."

AIDS FOR STUDY

1.   Note how many of the qualities listed by Ponti relate to the human inhabitants of the building. What type of building does Ponti most frequently refer to as an example? Which qualities do not refer directly to the inhabitants?

2.   Do any of the insights of the architect listed by Ponti refer specifically to the *function* of the structure?

3. Which of Ponti's "genesis of architecture" categories seem to relate to technical requirements? Which to functional requirements? Which to revelatory requirements?

4. Which of the insights (geneses) of the architect would apply to at least one other art? Which would apply to sculpture, to music, to drama or film? Which ones seem to apply only to architecture? What is the nature of architecture that such considerations are unique only to it?

5. Does Ponti imply a severe limitation to critical skills? About three-quarters of the way through the article is a paragraph beginning "On the contrary, it so happens that all of us . . . sometimes create something fine but more often something not so fine." He goes on to state that works can only be "schematized" after the fact. Is he "criticizing critics," in this section, or is he pointing out that criticism is separate from the artistic impulse?

6. This essay concludes that function is a fact, not a goal. What requirement beyond function was discussed in the textbook? Is "revelation" related to the concept of beauty implied in this writing? Are there differences, in your view, between the two concepts?

7. Read the last paragraph of the essay again. In what sense may other arts be said to direct human function? In what sense is architecture unique in its capability to direct human motion?

8. We are presented with a dilemma in the form of the New Haven Municipal Garage. If certain assumptions are correct, we are devoting excessive energy and space to the automobile, yet we need the automobile, and we need the parking space. What suggestions can you make that would place the automobile in better perspective in our lives?

9. Do you agree with the critical evaluation of the New Haven Garage as "monstrous prehistoric"?

10. Review again the textbook description (on pages 162–163) of the configurational center, and the lack of that center in such areas as freeways. Assume for a moment that the moments of life that

allow us to be sensitive to space around us, to participate in architecture, other arts, or the natural surroundings, are of great importance. What aspects of modern urban life need to be modified to allow more such time?

REVIEW QUIZ

Select the one best answer.

1. Which one of the following insights, listed by Ponti as essential to the architect/artist, would not be required of the sculptor?
   a. naturalistic genesis
   b. animated genesis
   c. manual genesis
   d. sensuous genesis

2. Ponti wrote that the highest praise for an architect is to
   a. be told his structure reflects its function.
   b. be told a house contributed to happiness.
   c. have the structure considered a part of the landscape, as by a painter.
   d. be in love with his trade.

3. The discussion of "human genesis," "psychological genesis," and "loving genesis" seems to most nearly relate to
   a. technical requirements of architecture.
   b. functional requirements of architecture.
   c. revelatory requirements of architecture.
   d. none of these.

4. In saying "it so happens that all of us . . . sometimes create something fine but more often something not so fine," Ponti is declaring that
   a. not everyone is capable of artistic expression.
   b. most architecture is not beautiful.
   c. art cannot be produced by following certain or constant rules.
   d. one should not put great effort into art.

5. Ponti states that some pieces of architecture have survived long periods because
   a. they served the original function.
   b. they had beauty.
   c. they could take on new functions.
   d. people became stereotyped in viewing architecture.

6. Ponti's use of the term "beauty" is probably most closely related to what the text calls
   a. revelatory requirements of architecture.
   b. sky-oriented architecture.
   c. functional requirements of architecture.
   d. earth-rooted architecture.

7. Ponti states the functionality of architecture is in
   a. its beauty.
   b. its suitability for people's needs.
   c. its direction of human motion.
   d. none of these.

8. The New Haven Garage was selected as an example to illustrate
   a. severely criticized structures.
   b. the dilemma created by the automobile.
   c. the best solution to parking problems.
   d. a poor solution to parking problems.

9. Which of the following patterns was *not* suggested in the text as a solution to city problems?
   a. restrict parking lots to the perimeter of the city.
   b. decentralize the city, with separate areas reserved for factories, offices, residences, and the like.
   c. have residences in rural atmosphere villages in outlying areas.
   d. eliminate private transportation, replacing it entirely with public transportation.

10. City planning is viewed from an architectural perspective because
    a. most of the problems considered in the textbook relate to buildings and structures.
    b. the problems relate to the use of space.
    c. the concern of most city dwellers is primarily with their home.
    d. architectural theory provides ready answers for almost all problems.

ADDITIONAL ACTIVITIES

1. Discuss the life and work of Antoni Gaudi, as presented in the preceding lesson, using the criteria implied by Ponti's "genesis" identifications. Which of these architectural insights does he most strongly reflect in the works you have seen?

2. Select any of the architects mentioned in this unit and evaluate some of their works, commenting particularly upon the apparent consideration for "human, psychological, and loving geneses" that are reflected in them.

3. Select a building you are familiar with—perhaps a school library, an office building, or a factory. Does it seem to you, walking around and through the building, that attention was given to the qualities Ponti suggests? Try to select at least one quality and describe in some detail how the building reflects this architectural insight.

"I prefer the architect to 'provoke' art by means of something else besides rule . . . The architect must hear voices among the walls—women's voices, children's voices, men's voices." By means of epigrams, obiter dicta, fleeting pensées, Gio Ponti (1891–1979) made his vision of the architect's role come alive. In a similar spirit, with quick thrusts, elegant meditations, bold exterior lines, delicate interior detailings, Ponti made his own contributions to architecture, to industry, to architectural journalism, and to the design of churches, houseware, hotels, hospitals, ships, and almost everything else one can create from plans on a drawing board. His magazine Domus was one of the most handsome and influential in the field of architecture. His work and his personality were equally striking in the development of modern Milan and much of the rest of postwar Italy. He had the necessary authority to write a book In Praise of Architecture (from which these pages come), a "book for the lovers of architecture, for those who are enchanted by the civilization of architecture, for those who dream about an architecture that is itself a civilization . . . not a book on architecture but a book for architecture."

THE ARCHITECT, THE ARTIST

Gio Ponti

(I am evoking "the artist." Presumptuous word, obnoxious word when used professionally, as if one were always an artist, as if one could succeed in always being an artist! No, the artist is a man who has a disposition towards art, who has a vocation and sometimes succeeds.)

(We must always start by considering a work of architecture as a work of art and the architect as the artist. Buildings and builders are something else, something very respectable, but something else.) (The real artists are not dreamers, as so many believe; they are terrible realists. They do not transpose reality into a dream but a dream into reality—written, drawn, musical, architectural reality. Do you realize that?)

When building in the country, the architect (the artist) must imagine his walls, his spaces, and the sky (and the changing light, the fog and the multitudinous nights); he must imagine his walls, his spaces, and the waters; his walls, his spaces, and the trees; his walls, his spaces, and the people. The architect, when building in the green world, must proportion walls to trees (trees are proportioned to man.)

(This is the "naturalistic genesis" of architecture. But I add that the architect reveals himself only through his imagination, an imagination independent of everything else.)

The architect (the artist) must imagine for each window, a person at the sill; for each door, a person passing through; for each stair, a person going up or down; for each portico, a person loitering; for each foyer, two people meeting; for each terrace, somebody resting; for each room, somebody living within. (The Italian word for room is *stanza*, a beautiful word; it means "to stay"; somebody staying there; a life.)

(This is the "animated genesis" of architecture. Yet architecture must reveal itself—and we must judge it—by itself, uninhabited, isolated in its own laws.)

When imagining his interiors, the architect (the artist) must hear voices among the walls—women's voices, children's voices, men's voices. He must hear a song lilting from the windows. He must hear shouted names. He must hear whistles. He must hear the noises of human work.

(This is the "sonorous genesis" of architecture. Yet architecture reveals itself by its silences; its eloquence lies in its silence.)

Blessed the ancient architect, who was originally a *muratore* or mason (a beautiful word derived from the Latin *mura*, wall). We architects of today have difficulties in understanding many things and have no feeling for them because we started out as students (what a mistake!). Things live in our intelligence before they do in our senses. For us, *nihil in sensu quod non fuerit in intellectu*, and not as for the ancients, *nihil in intellectu quod non fuerti in sensu*. Our upsidedown Latin is our misfortune, a diminution of our resources, an impoverishment we have in common with engineers. Only the artists among us are saved, because poetry comes to their aid and makes them understand everything.

(What originated from the *muratore* was the "physical genesis" of architecture. Yet architecture goes beyond the senses; it is captured by means of the eyes but for the sake of the spirit.)

The architect of today, the college architect, must learn from all the artisans—from the marble cutter (his polished and smooth surfaces, hammered surfaces, sealed surfaces), from the carpenter, the plasterer, the blacksmith, from all workers and craftsmen. He must learn things made by hand. Nothing, if not first in our hands.

(This is "the manual genesis" of architecture, its living creation. Yet architecture becomes a pure abstract form.)

The architect must also learn from the artisan how to love his trade; how beautiful it is to do something for the sake of doing. Art for art's sake is just that. It does not consist in a form of art without content but in the happiness of doing, doing without minding whether one succeeds or not. One is happy to sing just to be able to sing, and never mind how one sings; what matters is to sing; once in a while one of us will sing well.

(This is the "incantatory genesis" of architecture.)

In order to understand everything about his wonderful trade, the architect (the artist) must have his building in his senses, that is, foresee them (see them first); he must have a tactile presentiment of them through their materials (smooth, rough, cold, and warm). He must test them beforehand with his own prescient eyes under every possible light of the sky (calm, stormy, summer, winter, bright, dull) and under every incidence of the sun (morning, afternoon, and twilight suns).

(This is the "sensuous genesis" of architecture.)

The architect (the artist) must paint. For after all, he must compose landscapes even with his walls. Be it natural or urban, the architect is always constructing a landscape. He should paint for the sake of the appearance (the prospect) and the dimensions of his walls or surfaces; for the sake of their color, and for the sake of their relief (which he must be able to measure and have at his fingertips because of the play of the sun and light, a tactile thing).

(This is the "landscape genesis" of architecture.)

The good work of an architect may inspire a landscape to a painter. Such architecture is not scenography (no painter would make a painting of a set, for as the set is itself painted, his picture would be but a painting painted twice) but a scene of its own and a landscape grounded in life and in nature. A painting is a "test" of the architect's work.

(This is the "scenic genesis" of architecture.)

The architect (the artist) building a house should not look for praise of esthetic, formal, or stylistic values, or of values grounded in taste. These values are soon dated. The highest praise he must aspire to is to be told by the owners of the house, "Sir, in the house you built for us we live (or lived) happily. It is dear to us. It is a happy episode of our life." But for such a compliment the architect must pay more attention to the owners than to esthetics (and only thus will he reach permanent esthetic values, expressed by means of right forms, of forms esthetically beyond discussion, true forms, human forms).

(This is the "human genesis" of architecture.)

The architect (the artist) must interpret the character of the man who lives in the house, of each man in each house; he must build houses to be lived in by men who are alive. *"L'architecture est l'homme,"* they say. They say. But not measured man. The man of Neufert's handbook is the measured man, and Neufert's handbook is not a technical book on architecture. Man is not to be measured; man is a character to be understood.

(This is the "psychological genesis" of architecture.)

(The architect who fails to interpret the life of the inhabitants, transforming it into an expression of civilization and culture, the architect who imposes on them his esthetic feelings only—apart from his presumptuousness—does not build a house but a showcase, an exhibition, and reduces its inhabitants from living human beings to mannequins. They, of course, rebel, and thus come about all those supposed infractions of the presumptuous order of the esthete-architect and his feeling of lese-majeste.)

The architect (the artist) must be curious about men and women so that he may divine their characters; the true architect should fall in love with the owners, men and women, of the house he is going to build or decorate.

(This is the "loving genesis" of architecture. Yet architecture reveals itself without sin.)

The architect (the artist) is not afraid of limited means. The more limited he is, the less free to operate, the better his architecture. Then he works in desperation and performs miracles. He makes up for material difficulties with spiritual values. *Il faut decourager les arts.*

(This is the *nascita povera*, the impoverished birth of the arts. But later on everything is mysteriously rich.)

The architect must despise what is "passing" (stylistic and formal esthetics) and must look for what "remains" in life. Then he will find form (which will be what remains as life passes; a lovely contradiction).

The architect must realize that the permanent values are those of his soul, of his greatness, of his singularity as a man. Art does not consist in "formality" (any form is good, so much so, in fact, that form is continuously changing). Art is a document, a witness of man, of one man, though *one* expression of him. That is why art cannot be repeated, why a copy is not art, why a restoration is not art. That is why a drawing by Andrea del Sarto even if beautiful and perfectly finished has *less value* than an imperfect or unfinished design by Raphael. Because it is the document of a man who is *less great*. That is why works and monuments outside the realm of formally pure values, works like the pyramids and Milan's cathedral, belong to art. Because they are documents of grandeur, unrepeatable heroisms of history, of faith, of men.

They speak.

Art, I repeat, does not lie in the form; it lies in the document of the man. Form is a thing perfect and complete. (Can we imagine an incomplete form? It would not be a form.) Nevertheless form is not indispensable to art, because a mutilated statue (the Victory of Samothrace), an altered painting (the Cimabue in Assisi), a ruin (the "test of ruin" is the great test of architecture because architecture must be able to resist all injuries and express itself even through its remains) inspire us, notwithstanding their mutilation, alteration or ruin, with an artistic emotion, because they are nevertheless *art*.

These works are documents of an artist because they emanate the spirit of the artist who created them, his magnanimity, his thought. A Man speaks.

This measure of art—the measure of Man. (Here the statement "Man is the measure of everything" assumes a different meaning. It becomes the measure of his heroism, of his life, of his authenticity. Academicians are not authentic; technicians are not autobiographical; artists always are and only so. The value of Van Gogh's paintings does not consist only of their formal value, which has been copied by every imitator of Van Gogh with desolate and desolating reverence; their value lies also in his drama and in his autobiography; his paintings are its document. I say to the Van Goghists: "Go and cut your ears!" But we know that even this gesture cannot be repeated.) Every man, I have said, shouts a cry before he dies (I do not mean the moment he dies, but before, during his life). History gathers it, if it is genuine.

The architect (the artist) should doubt esthetic and formal values. He should commit himself to his values of obligation and work. By these means he establishes his own true and valid document, the human document. The architect Muzio once said something very moving, "We have worked for a long time on this project; therefore it is beautiful." (A suggestive way of affirming those values of human obligation that adhere to a work and afterwards radiate beauty.)

This is why medieval cathedrals are beautiful, with their innumerable statues, their infinite sense of obligation and work, their infinite faith, their infinite prayer, and their infinite love (an excess of love; art is something loved excessively; but there are still rejected lovers.) In the Gothic cathedrals this is true even of *the work that cannot be seen*, ornamentation and sculpture (some undercuts, some decorations in the back that nobody can see but that still exist, bestowing supreme artistic worth; an issue of love.)

I realize that if an ass of an architect worked even a hundred years we could never say of his work, "Therefore it is beautiful." But I still believe in this conviction about Beauty; it is the one I like best. What is beautiful must be somehow deserved. It is something God asks of us. The architects who become infatuated with schemes, who believe in predetermined theses and rules, in proportional tracings, graphs, and other miserable tomfooleries move me to laughter and to pity (among them are some real artists, but even these seem unaware of the fact that they are artists only when they disregard their schemes). They subscribe to such theories to get out of hard work, to avoid having to aspire to inspiration, to invoke it, provoke it, and to deliver themselves painfully of it (it is not easy). If their assumptions were correct, everybody would always accomplish perfection, even they. It never happens.

On the contrary, it so happens that all of us (and they too, notwithstanding their procedures) sometimes create something fine but more often something not so fine. Art cannot be made certain or constant. This would be too wonderful! Nobody is more naive about or further removed from art than a calculating man. (It is true—I have found it to be so myself—that works of art can be schematized afterwards, *a posteriori;* we can then have fun rediscovering proportions, curves, inscriptions in circles, spirals, and the like. What cannot be done is to "produce" art by means of *a priori* rules. This would be too easy! Schemes as well as "tradition" and repetition do not exist in art; only history exists, and it does not repeat. And art is history.) Referring to schemes, Corbu says that his *modulor* is only for those who know nothing about proportion *(Le modulor sert seulement a ceux qui ne comprennent rien a la proportion).*

I prefer the architect to "provoke" art by means of something else besides rules. I mean to express this by two paintings I have never painted but that would resemble a votive diptych. One would represent the architect kneeling near his bed, praying like a child, asking for architectural grace, for inspiration. The other would represent the architect asleep, with "ideas" coming to him, through a window open to the sky, along a wire or ray. Along that wire would travel house plans, solutions of volumes, shapes of furniture. This vision is valid, after all. We have our voices, but ideas visit us at night. They are received graces.

The architect (the artist) must take time into consideration, for architecture must age well. New architecture is not yet perfect. Le Corbusier revealed to us the magic of "When the cathedrals were white." This whiteness was the beauty of those prestigious times. But the same cathedrals are now beautiful even if black. Their beauty is that they are *still* beautiful (and maybe even more beautiful).

Every beautiful piece of architecture has survived its original appearance, purpose, and function, and many have served many functions successively. The right of an architectural work to last—and finally, its right to be—lies only in its beauty and not in its function. For it assumes a new function—beauty. Beauty is the most resistant structure and the most resistant material. It opposes the destruction of man, himself the most ferocious ally of time.

The architect (the artist) must not participate in the cult of beautiful materials; nothing is less spiritual and more material than a beautiful material. The fact that the Seagram Building of Mies was made of bronze gave me some doubts about it. Palladio worked with modest materials. A beautiful material is the same for all. Only a few are able to create beauty out of a modest material. Beautiful materials do not exist, anyway. Only the right material exists.

So-called refined people are amateurs. They are not really refined because they always want beautiful, refined materials everywhere. Rough plaster in the right place is the beautiful material for that place. This is real refinement. To replace it with a "noble" material would be vulgar.

The architect (the artist) must consider the functionality of architecture as an implicit fact, never as a goal. Functionality is the goal (and the limitation) of the engineer. A machine functions and is beautiful. Architecture that does nothing but function is not yet beautiful and is not even thoroughly functional. It functions entirely only if it is beautiful. Then it functions forever ("perpetuity," says Palladio). It must function at the artistic level, at the level of enchantment ("*Qu'elle chante,*" says Corbu). It functions even when it no longer functions practically. It functions ultimately as a ruin. It functions poetically. It functions in history, in culture, in magic. This is the ultimate function of architecture—to surpass the function that originated it, to function at the level of art. (The functionality of a machine consists of *its* motion; the functionality of a house, of a room, of a building consists of directing *our* motion.)

EPILOGUE

CONTINUING THE QUEST FOR SELF

OVERVIEW

The purpose of this final lesson is somewhat unusual: Instead of a review of past material, it is a preview of where our study of the arts and the humanities may lead in the coming years. From our studies in this course, we have, it is hoped, developed a sensitivity and alertness to the content of all art forms, not just the ones included in this course. This sensitivity should serve us not only for art forms as they presently exist but also for art forms that the ever-creative and fertile human mind may develop in the future. With such sensitivity, new horizons will constantly appear before us, enabling us to continue the quest for self.

In these lessons, we have also become aware of the unique qualities of each art. The differences in form and approach between film and drama are one example of this uniqueness; yet another example is the fine line that separates sculpture and architecture. Still, in spite of the uniqueness of each, the arts and the humanities, of which the arts are a part, are interrelated. This interrelationship is the topic of the concluding chapter of the textbook, "The Humanities: Their Interrelationships" (pages 441–457). If you have not already done so, you should read this chapter because it synthesizes what we have studied about the arts and the humanities and provides some ideas about future directions for art. The final chapter also highlights how the arts we have studied enhance the three major fields usually included in the humanities: history, philosophy, and theology. In addition to reading Chapter 14, you should, of course, view the final television program in the series.

One goal of this course—in addition to examining the relationship between the arts and humanities—is to explore the relationship between the arts and our emotions, feelings, and values. It would be rare indeed if at least once during this course we did not experience a moment of beauty, a wave of emotion when we perceived and understood clearly what the artist was communicating. Every time we have such an experience—an empathy with the artist—we discover something new about ourselves and are changed, however slightly. Such discoveries and changes are part of our growth as individuals, and growth is a process that should never stop. Only through such experiences can we discover the nature of our relationship to sound, to sensa, to nature, to others.

To aid in your study of this final lesson, we suggest two activities:

First, try to recall an experience in which your perception of one art form was intensified by another art form. One common instance is a film in which the musical background enhances a particular piece of action. You may also have viewed sculpture with music being played simultaneously or heard dramatic readings accompanied by music. Has some of the film you have seen of paintings or sculpture, with its capacity for magnifying and clarifying visual and tactile details, heightened your appreciation and perception of those art forms? Can you relate other examples in which one art enhances another?

Second, relate one or more of your experiences in art participation to one of the humanities or a related field of study that is of special interest to you. You may have encountered a painting, film, or musical work in this course that employed subject matter related to your interests. For instance, if you are interested in European history, did Bach's music or Picasso's *Guernica* lead you to any new insights about the Baroque period or the Spanish Civil War? If your interests are in such social sciences as psychology, sociology, or anthropology, did Shirley Jackson's "The Lottery" provide you with new perceptions about human cultures and group dynamics?

This course is only a beginning in your inquiry and exploration into the diversity and richness of the arts and humanities. Now, it is up to you to use the special skills and perceptive abilities you have acquired in continuing the quest for self.

ANSWER KEY

LESSON 1

1. c (textbook pages 19–20)
2. a (textbook pages 11–12)
3. b (textbook page 2)
4. d (textbook pages 32–35)
5. b (textbook pages 10–14)
6. c (textbook pages 23–25)
7. b (textbook pages 20–25)
8. c (textbook pages 18–19)
9. a (textbook pages 26–28)
10. c (textbook pages 28–29)

LESSON 2

1. c (television program; study guide overview)
2. a (television program)
3. you might list Eisenstein, Kubrick, Bergman, Allen, Coppola, or others you can recall (textbook pages 347, 348, 352, 362, 366; television program)
4. c (textbook page 348)
5. d (textbook page 359)
6. c (textbook page 359)
7. the sizeable investments required for production; film's dependence on modern technology (television program)
8. b (television program)
9. a (television program)
10. d (textbook pages 364–366)

LESSON 3

1. d (television program)
2. a (textbook page 352)
3. a (textbook pages 352–354)
4. c (textbook pages 352–354)
5. a (textbook pages 355–356)
6. b (textbook page 356)
7. b (textbook page 356)
8. b (textbook page 357)
9. b (textbook page 357)
10. b (textbook page 360)

LESSON 4

1. b (study guide, "Style and Medium in the Motion Pictures")
2. c (study guide, "Style and Medium in the Motion Pictures")
3. b (study guide, "Style and Medium in the Motion Pictures")
4. a (study guide, "Style and Medium in the Motion Pictures")
5. d (study guide, "Style and Medium in the Motion Pictures")
6. c (study guide, "Style and Medium in the Motion Pictures")
7. b (study guide, "Style and Medium in the Motion Pictures")
8. c (study guide, "Style and Medium in the Motion Pictures")
9. b (textbook page 351)
10. a (study guide, "Style and Medium in the Motion Pictures")

LESSON 5

1. b (textbook pages 47–49)
2. a (textbook page 48)
3.   descriptive
      interpretive
      evaluative (textbook page 50)
4. d (textbook page 50)
5. a (textbook pages 364–365)
6.   rhythm
      mood
      atmosphere
      tension
      sequences
      tones
      scents (study guide, "Film Has Nothing to Do with Listening")
7. c (study guide, "Film Has Nothing to Do with Listening")
8. a (textbook pages 364–365)
9. b (textbook pages 352–354)
10. a (textbook pages 50–51)

LESSON 6

1. c (study guide overview; television program)
2. a (study guide overview; television program)
3. c (textbook page 246)
4. b (study guide overview; television program)
5. c, h (study guide overview; television program; textbook page 239)
6. b, e (study guide overview; television program; textbook page 249)

7. b (study guide overview; television program)
8. b (textbook pages 242–244)
9. b (textbook pages 249–252)
10. b (textbook page 243; television program)

LESSON 7

1. d (textbook page 244)
2. b (textbook page 244)
3. b (textbook pages 244–245)
4. a (textbook page 245)
5. b (textbook page 246)
6. a (textbook page 246)
7. c (textbook pages 253–255)
8. a (textbook pages 253–255)
9. d (textbook pages 253–255)
10. c (textbook pages 246–248)
11. b (study guide overview; television program)

LESSON 8

1. c (television program)
2. c (television program)
3. a (television program)
4. b (television program)
5. d (television program)
6. a (textbook pages 256–257)
7. c (textbook page 256)
8. b (textbook page 260)
9. b (textbook pages 256–260)
10. b (textbook page 260)

LESSON 9

1. c (textbook page 50)
2. b (textbook page 53)
3. c (textbook page 57)
4. a (textbook page 51)
5. a (textbook page 56)
6. c (textbook pages 53–57)
7. b (textbook pages 53–57)
8. c (study guide, "The Problem Play—A Symposium")
9. a (study guide, "The Problem Play—A Symposium")
10. c (study guide, "The Problem Play—A Symposium")

LESSON 10

1. c (study guide, "A Brief Glossary of Styles and Genres")
2. a (study guide, "A Brief Glossary of Styles and Genres")
3. b (study guide, "A Brief Glossary of Styles and Genres")
4. c (study guide, "A Brief Glossary of Styles and Genres")
5. d (study guide, "A Brief Glossary of Styles and Genres")
6. a (study guide, "A Brief Glossary of Styles and Genres")
7. b (study guide, "A Brief Glossary of Styles and Genres")
8. c (television program; study guide, "A Brief Glossary of Styles and Genres")
9. b (study guide; "A Brief Glossary of Styles and Genres")
10. d (study guide, "A Brief Glossary of Styles and Genres")

LESSON 11

1. d (textbook pages 305, 307)
2. h (textbook page 309)
3. b (textbook page 305)
4. i (textbook pages 311–314)
5. c (textbook page 305)
6. e (textbook page 307)
7. j (textbook page 314)
8. f (textbook page 308)
9. g (textbook page 309)
10. a (textbook pages 279–282)
11. b (textbook page 284)
12. c (textbook pages 273–278)

LESSON 12

1. f (textbook pages 286–287)
2. c (textbook page 291)
3. d (textbook page 287)
4. b (textbook page 288)
5. h (textbook page 289)
6. g (textbook pages 291–292)
7. a (textbook page 291)
8. j (textbook page 291)
9. b (television program)
10. a (television program)
11. b (television program)

LESSON 13

1. d (textbook page 294)
2. c (textbook pages 294–295)
3. b (textbook pages 50–53)
4. a (textbook page 303)
5. d (study guide, "What is Modern Music—and Why Have People Never Liked It, at First?")
6. a (study guide, "What is Modern Music—and Why Have People Never Liked It, at First?")
7. c (study guide, "What is Modern Music—and Why Have People Never Liked It, at First?")
8. b (study guide, "What is Modern Music—and Why Have People Never Liked It, at First?")
9. b (study guide, "What is Modern Music—and Why Have People Never Liked It, at First?")
10. c (textbook page 50; study guide, "What is Modern Music—and Why Have People Never Liked It, at First?")

LESSON 14

1. b (textbook pages 207–209)
2. c (study guide overview; television program)
3. b (study guide overview; television program)
4. d (study guide overview; television program)
5. d (study guide overview; television program)
6. b (study guide overview; television program)
7. a (study guide overview; television program)
8. c (television program)
9. b (television program)
10. a (television program)
11.   any of the following:
       "Dover Beach"
       A Farewell to Arms
       The Great Gatsby
       The Grapes of Wrath
       (television program)

LESSON 15

1. c (study guide overview; television program)
2. a (television program)
3. c (television program)
4. d (textbook pages 220–221)
5. b (textbook page 218)
6. b (television program)
7. a (television program)
8. d (textbook pages 226–228)
9. d (television program; textbook page 220)
10. b (television program)

LESSON 16

1. c (television program)
2. a (television program)
3. c (television program)
4. author exposition (television program)
5. presented from within (textbook pages 213–214)
6. b (television program)
7. c (television program)
8. b (textbook pages 214–215)
9. b (textbook pages 228–232)
10. c (television program)

LESSON 17

1. b (study guide, "How a Poem Is Made")
2. b (study guide, "How a Poem Is Made")
3. b (textbook pages 226–228)
4. d (study guide, "How a Poem Is Made")
5. a (study guide overview for Lesson 15; "Ars Poetica")
6. c (study guide, "Ars Poetica")
7. b (study guide, "Ars Poetica")
8. c (textbook pages 222–223)
9. a (textbook pages 222–223)
10. b (textbook pages 222–223)

LESSON 18

1. b (textbook pages 69–74)
2. c (television program)
3. a (television program)
4. b (television program)
5. d (television program)

6. answers may include: Masaccio, Michelangelo, Leonardo da Vinci, Raphael, Giorgione, Tintoretto (television program)
7. d (television program)
8. answers may include: El Greco, Velásquez, Vandyke, Vermeer, Rembrandt (television program)
9. b (television program)
10. answers may include:
    representational:
    Weber, Stella, Marin, Monet, Gauguin, Cézanne, Degas, Toulouse–Lautrec
    abstract:
    Kandinski, Pollock
    (television program)

LESSON 19

1. d (television program)
2. c (textbook page 75)
3. c (television program)
4. c (television program)
5. a (television program)
6. b (television program)
7. d (textbook page 89)
8. b (television program)
9. a (television program)
10. b (textbook page 73)
11. Cézanne's *Mont Sainte Victoire* (textbook page 73)

LESSON 20

1. a (television program)
2. c (television program)
3. a (television program)
4. c (television program)
5. c (television program)
6. b (television program)
7. d (television program)
8. c (television program)
9. b (television program)
10. b (television program)

LESSON 21

1. d (textbook pages 84–85)
2. a (textbook pages 85–87)
3. d (textbook pages 87–88)
4. b (textbook pages 87–88)
5. b (textbook pages 91–92)
6. d (textbook page 91)
7. c (textbook page 92)
8. d (textbook page 92)
9. a (textbook page 92)
10. b (textbook page 92)

LESSON 22

1. c (study guide overview)
2. b (textbook pages 95–98)
3. life of the pharoahs (study guide overview)
4. beauty of humanity, idealism (study guide overview)
5. realistically (study guide overview)
6. b (study guide overview)
7. c (study guide overview)
8. d (textbook pages 120–126)
9. b (textbook pages 120–126)
10. b, f (television program)
11. a (television program)
12. b (television program)
13. d (television program)

LESSON 23

1. b (textbook pages 100–101)
2. d (textbook pages 108–110)
3. e (study guide overview)
4. a (textbook pages 98–100; study guide overview)
5. c (textbook pages 104–108)
6. e (textbook pages 110–112)
7. a (textbook pages 98–100)
8. c (textbook pages 104–108; study guide overview)
9. painting appeals strictly to the visual sense; sculpture appeals to the tactile sense as well. (textbook pages 97–98)
10. sculpture is designed to be viewed from "outside"; architecture has "living space" within (textbook pages 101–102)
11. b (television program; study guide overview)
12. b (study guide overview)
13. Ghiberti (television program; textbook pages 100–102)
14. Rodin (television program)
15. Michelangelo (textbook pages 110–112)

LESSON 24

1. c (television program)
2. c (televisionprogram)
3. b (television program)
4. a (television program)
5. b (television program)
6. c (television program)
7. c (television program)
8. b (television program)
9. b (textbook pages 127–130)
10. a (textbook pages 127–130)

LESSON 25

1. b (television program)
2. a (study guide, "Notes on Sculpture")
3. d (textbook pages 97–98)
4. d (study guide, "Notes on Sculpture")
5. b (textbook pages 130–135)
6. c (study guide, "Notes on Sculpture")
7. a (study guide, "Notes on Sculpture")
8. b (study guide, "Notes on Sculpture")
9. d (textbook pages 136–137)
10. c (textbook pages 139–142)

LESSON 26

1. a (television program)
2. c (television program)
3. c (television program)
4. b (television program)
5. c (television program)
6. c (television program)
7. b (television program)

8. b (textbook pages 158–160)
9. a (textbook pages 160–162)
10. d (textbook pages 162–164)

LESSON 27

1. c (textbook page 179)
2. a (textbook page 177)
3. c (textbook page 180)
4. a (textbook pages 184–188)
5. b (textbook pages 185–186)
6. b (textbook pages 184–186)
7. b (textbook pages 184–188)
8. c (textbook pages 186–188)
9. a (textbook pages 189–198)
10. b (textbook page 195)

LESSON 28

1. b (textbook pages 165–167)
2. c (textbook page 167)
3. b (textbook pages 168–169)
4.   Catholic religion (or similar answer) (television program)
5.   Art Nouveau (or similar answer) (television program)
6.   Gothic (or similar answer) (television program)
7. b (television program; study guide overview)
8. d (television program; study guide overview)
9.   technical and structural requirements
     function or use
     spatial relationship
     content (textbook pages 167–176)
10. c (textbook page 172)

LESSON 29

1. b (study guide, "The Architect, the Artist")
2. b (study guide, "The Architect, the Artist")
3. b (study guide, "The Architect, the Artist")
4. c (study guide, "The Architect, the Artist")
5. b (study guide, "The Architect, the Artist")
6. a (study guide, "The Architect, the Artist")
7. c (study guide, "The Architect, the Artist")
8. b (textbook pages 199–200)
9. d (textbook page 200)
10. b (textbook page 199)